Youth Justice in Ireland

TOUGH LIVES ROUGH JUSTICE

Ursula Kilkelly
University College, Cork

Foreword by
Fr Peter McVerry, SJ

IRISH ACADEMIC PRESS
DUBLIN • PORTLAND, OR

First published in 2006 by
IRISH ACADEMIC PRESS
44, Northumberland Road, Dublin 4, Ireland

and in the United States of America by
IRISH ACADEMIC PRESS
c/o ISBS, Suite 300, 920 NE 58th Avenue
Portland, Oregon 97213-3644

***Website*: www.iap.ie**

British Library Cataloguing in Publication Data
An entry can be found on request

ISBN 0-7165-2836-3
ISBN 978-0-7165-2836-4 (cloth)
ISBN 0-7165-3348-0
ISBN 978-0-7165-3348-1 (paper)

Library of Congress Cataloging-in-Publication Data
An entry can be found on request

Typeset in 11/13pt Sabon by FiSH Books, Enfield, Middx.
Printed by MPG Books Ltd, Bodmin, Cornwall

This book was written when my little boy Evan was only a few months old. Its completion would have been impossible without the continuing support, patience and understanding of my husband Cathal. I dedicate this book to them.

Contents

Foreword

John is a 14-year-old homeless boy. He leaves his hostel at 9.30 a.m. to go to his training course. He is now, through the Health Service Executive, the responsibility of the Department of Health and Children. At 10.00 am, John is arrested for shoplifting and brought to the Children Court. He is now the responsibility of the Department of Justice, Equality and Law Reform. At 11.00 am, John is remanded in custody to a Children Detention School. He now becomes the responsibility of the Department of Education and Science. In less than two hours, John has been the responsibility of three different government departments, each with different objectives and policies, and sometimes with fundamentally contradictory aims. The lack of co-ordination, and even communication, between departments and the absence of any clear lines of accountability has led to a piecemeal and *ad-hoc* system of addressing the problems of children at risk.

A juvenile justice system is, in my view, hopelessly inappropriate to meeting the needs of children at risk – even if the system were a good one. Any justice system has two objectives: finding a person innocent or guilty of a particular offence, and, if found guilty, imposing an appropriate penalty. The Children Court is perceived by many juveniles as a game of poker: in this game, you first find out how strong is the evidence against you; second, you weigh up the odds as to whether the victim or witnesses will turn up to give evidence; finally, you enquire as to which judge is sitting today. At any stage, you may win the game and you are found 'not guilty' – you then leave the court with the same multiple unmet needs that you arrived with. If you lose the game, then the Court may go into welfare mode and seek a programme that can meet your needs – which in Ireland almost certainly won't exist – but the slow progress through the juvenile justice system has simply delayed the process.

However, it would fly in the face of reality to describe the juvenile justice system in Ireland as anything other than a shambles. Its development, if one can dare use such a word, has been – and continues to be – characterised by both ignorance and apathy.

Virtually no research has been undertaken to find more effective and evidence-based policies. In the absence of such data, policies have been driven by political expediency. A €10-million unit for young offenders was built as a knee-jerk reaction to the tragic death (shortly before a general election) of two Gardaí in a joyriding incident, but, before it was even completed, it was deemed to be no longer necessary and continues to remain idle. It has since been decided to demolish it. The closure of Fort Mitchell prison, where juveniles enjoyed the best education and development services in the prison system, was closed down in order to beat the Prison Officers' Association into submission over its overtime bill. In St. Patrick's Institution, the only remaining detention centre for 16- and 17-year-olds, the workshops, along with one-to-one literacy tuition, were closed to reduce the wages bill, leaving juveniles warehoused in total idleness and boredom – contrary to the United Nations Convention on the Rights of the Child (UNCRC).

The Children Act 2001, the most progressive development in decades in seeking to meet the needs of children who have been in trouble with the law, remains largely unimplemented, five years later, mainly because the non-custodial options, which it requires before a detention option can be considered, require substantial resources which have not been forthcoming. Parts of that Act are now being amended (some actually reversed), even before they have been introduced and tested. The age of criminal responsibility – raised reluctantly in the Children Act 2001 to 12 years of age – is to be reduced to 10, for some serious crimes. Anti-social Behaviour Orders, which can criminalise children for behaviour which is, in itself, non-criminal, are to be introduced – despite the stated desire of the Children Act 2001 to divert children as far as possible from the justice system. The protection of anonymity that most children in trouble with the law now enjoy, as required by the UNCRC, is to be removed at the discretion of the judge. However, on the bright side, the sending of children, some as young as 15, to Mountjoy and other adult prisons, again in contravention of the UNCRC, is to be phased out – but not until 2010!

This is a book that was waiting to be written. No such analysis or overview of the Irish juvenile justice system has been written before. Which is not surprising given the lack of any significant data from which to draw conclusions, and indeed the almost impossible task of comparing or collating data from the many different sources, all of which use different categories. It critically evaluates the Irish juvenile justice system and its treatment of young offenders by reference to international standards, agreed values and best practice. By placing the spotlight so clearly on what is, with some notable exceptions, an embarrassingly defective and incoherent system, and by pointing out what needs to be done to bring it up to international best practice, Ursula Kilkelly has done those young people in our society who are most damaged and most at risk a great service. I found the book a wonderful source of information and analysis and I think it will be essential reading for anyone involved in, or in, the juvenile justice system.

Fr Peter McVerry, SJ
April 2006

Acknowledgements

My friend Donncha O'Connell suggested that I write this book and provided both encouragement and sharp editorial guidance while ensuring that I completed it! Donncha and Mike Milotte are to be congratulated for their initiative in developing the Justice in Controversy series which will, I am sure, make a significant contribution to public knowledge and and debate in Ireland. I am grateful to Lisa Hyde for her valuable assistance in bringing the book to completion and to Fr Peter McVerry, SJ, who is synonymous with justice for young people in Ireland, for writing the Foreword so willingly.

Thanks to Finbarr O'Leary of the Special Residential Services Board, Superintendent Kieran McGann of the Garda Training College, and Kieran O'Dwyer of the Garda Research Unit for information and comments on earlier drafts. I would also like to acknowledge the assistance of my colleagues in the Irish Association for the Study of Delinquency, the Irish Penal Reform Trust and the Irish Youth Justice Alliance.

My students and colleagues on the Criminal Justice LLM Programme at University College, Cork and further afield have contributed greatly to my understanding of issues relating to youth justice, and discussions with many of the professionals involved in the area allowed me to combine theory with practice in writing this book. I am grateful to them all for sharing their knowledge, insights and experiences.

Ursula Kilkelly
Midleton, Co. Cork
April 2006

Introduction: Youth Justice and the Role of International Standards

It is the aim of this book to describe and critically evaluate the Irish youth justice system and its treatment of young offenders. The benchmark against which this analysis is undertaken is, unequivocally, that set by international standards on youth justice. These standards are of varying relevance, significance and usefulness.[1] Their value, however, is in the extent to which they recognise and reflect best practice across jurisdictions, while also representing minimum standards. While sufficiently detailed to provide practical guidance, their generality allows them to be adapted appropriately for each domestic context.

The relevant international standards are discussed at various stages throughout the book. The purpose of this Introduction, therefore, is to consider the status and purpose of the international standards, with reference to using them for auditing purposes as well as to guide the development and implementation of domestic law and policy.

MODELS OF YOUTH JUSTICE

At its simplest, a youth justice system can be described as either 'welfare' or 'justice' in approach. 'Welfare' systems typically focus on the needs rather than the deeds of the child and they respond to a child's offending by attempting to address the underlying causes. Countries which pursue a 'welfare' policy refer offenders to child protection agencies or social services where they are treated alongside non-offending children with similar problems. The well-known Scottish Hearing System is an illustration of this approach, as are European countries like Germany and Sweden which have high ages of criminal responsibility and divert those below this age to the welfare, rather than the criminal justice authorities.[2]

The 'justice' model of youth justice has accountability and personal responsibility as its core values. According to this approach, children, often at a relatively young age, are prosecuted in the courts for the crimes that they commit. The courts impose sanctions in line with normal sentencing principles, although the age and need to rehabilitate the offender may be given particular significance. Emphasis is on due process of law and the application of finite rules. England and Wales, and the United States are typically described as having a 'justice' approach to young offenders.

'Welfare' and 'justice' systems have supporters and critics, and polarised views exist on both sides of the debate. For instance, it is argued that the 'justice' approach, with its focus on individual accountability, is a punitive and harmful way to deal with young offenders, while 'welfare' interventions are seen as a less formal and more lenient approach. While there are frequently historical reasons why states prefer one approach to another, it is also arguable that a pure 'justice' or 'welfare' approach is not sufficiently sophisticated to respond to the range of circumstances in which young people commit crime and the range of measures required to prevent them from re-offending. Moreover, in-between the extremes, neutral observers identify that both 'justice' and 'welfare' approaches have merit. As Doob and Tonry note: 'a criminal law approach need not be particularly punitive, nor a child welfare approach particularly effective'.[3] Others prefer to play down the significant differences between these perspectives noting that, rather than conflicting approaches, 'welfare' and 'justice' may be more accurately defined as 'different techniques for responding to youth crime, which share essentially common aims of crime reduction and behavioural change'.[4] Just as the 'justice' model can be said to be too punitive, the 'welfare' approach may be characterised by informal interventions which lack certainty and finality.[5] But, just as the 'justice' approach can be adapted to take greater account of the needs of individual young offenders (the introduction of restorative justice approaches is an example of this), the 'welfare' model can be developed to ensure greater attention to the child's right to due process.

In many jurisdictions practice is a mixed version of these two perspectives. Ireland has a relatively punitive approach to young offenders – prosecution is the norm for those for whom diversion is neither appropriate nor successful – and thus is closer than many states to the 'justice' approach. At the same time, welfare considerations are not completely absent; the Health Service Executive may be involved where a young offender has unmet needs and the Children Act 2001 also contains a range of community sanctions, designed to ensure that the response to the child's crime meets some constructive objectives. However, the hybrid nature of the Irish youth justice system, which is not wedded exclusively to either 'welfare' or 'justice' ideals, raises the question as to what principles should guide its development and implementation.

INTERNATIONAL STANDARDS

The view advocated by this book is that Ireland should develop and implement its law and policy on youth justice in line with international standards. Preferring neither a 'welfare' nor a 'justice' approach, the international rules on youth justice recognise a core set of values, which reflects wide consensus as to what works in this area, based on the principles of human rights. These standards are contained in a wide variety of international instruments, comprising binding international law and recommended best practice. In the former category are the United Nations Convention on the Rights of the Child (CRC) and the European Convention on Human Rights (ECHR). In the latter are the Beijing Rules, the Riyadh Guidelines and the Rules for the Protection of Juveniles deprived of their Liberty.[6]

The UN Convention on the Rights of the Child

The CRC was adopted by the United Nations in 1989 and ratified by Ireland in 1992. Although not incorporated into domestic law, the CRC is binding international law, which imposes legal obligations on the State. In addition to its status as a binding treaty of international law, the almost universal acceptance of the CRC gives its principles and provisions a moral force, strengthening the duty to implement its standards at domestic level.

The CRC contains three guiding principles which are relevant to all children (art 2) including those in conflict with the law:[7] they require non-discrimination in their enjoyment of rights; that the child's best interests be a primary consideration in all matters (art 3); and that the child's voice is heard and taken into account in all decision-making concerning the child (art 12). With regard to youth justice, the CRC provides that children in conflict with the law have the right to be treated 'in a manner consistent with the promotion of the child's sense of dignity and worth, which reinforces the child's respect for the human rights and fundamental freedoms of others and which takes into account the child's age and the desirability of promoting the child's reintegration and the child's assuming a constructive role in society'. It recognises that children should be detained only as a measure of last resort and for the shortest appropriate period of time, and prohibits the imprisonment of children for life. In addition to recognising the traditional right to due process, the CRC provides that children have the right to have charges explained to them in language they understand and the right to have their privacy respected at all stages of their proceedings. The CRC requires states to establish an age of criminal responsibility below which children will be presumed not to have the capacity to infringe the criminal law, and provides that they must develop measures for dealing with children without resorting to judicial proceedings, provided that human rights and safeguards are fully respected. The CRC requires that a variety of dispositions – including care, probation, guidance, foster care, educational and vocational training – are available to ensure that children are dealt with in a manner appropriate to their well-being and proportionate both to their circumstances and the offence.

The implementation of the CRC is monitored by the Committee on the Rights of the Child, which considered Ireland's first report on implementation in 1998.[8] At this time, the Committee was particularly critical of the Government's failure to implement the CRC in the area of youth justice and detention, and recommended that it

> take all available measures to ensure the prompt enactment of the Children Bill 1996 (as it then was) especially in relation to the administration of the juvenile justice system, with due regard to the principles and provisions of the Convention, and other international standards such as the Beijing Rules, the Riyadh Guidelines and the UN Rules for the Protection of Juveniles Deprived of their Liberty.[9]

Ireland's composite second and third report to the Committee was submitted in 2005 and is due to be considered in Geneva in September 2006. While notable achievements – the appointment of an Ombudsman for Children and the National Children's Strategy for instance – will be welcomed, the continuing failure to implement the Children Act 2001 in full and the introduction of Anti-Social Behaviour Orders, which are inconsistent with many CRC provisions, will undoubtedly feature among the Committee's concerns. The continuing failure to take measures to give the CRC effect in domestic law is also likely to raise concern.

The European Convention on Human Rights

Ireland is also a party to the European Convention on Human Rights (ECHR) 1953. Although the ECHR makes no explicit reference to children's rights, the case-law of the European Court of Human Rights has highlighted the relevance of the ECHR to children in conflict with the law. However, unlike the CRC, the ECHR has been given further effect in Irish law. The ECHR Act 2003 requires the courts to take the Convention and its case-law into account in relevant cases and also provides that public bodies (including, for example, An Garda Síochána, the Probation and Welfare Service and the Courts Service) must act in a manner compliant with the Convention. The Act also provides for a remedy for the breach of an ECHR right when this does not occur.[10]

The case-law of the European Court of Human Rights is of particular relevance to youth justice and detention in Ireland.

According to the Court's judgments in *T v. UK and V v. UK* in which it found that the trial of the two boys who murdered toddler James Bulger was unfair, the Court ruled that when children are on trial, measures must be taken to ensure that they enjoy the right to understand and participate in the criminal process.[11] The Court has also made it clear that children have the right to liberty and can only be detained within the terms of the Convention. In a case against Ireland in 2002, the Court held that non-offending children can only be detained in conditions which provide for their educational supervision, broadly interpreted as education and/or therapeutic care. In *DG v. Ireland*, Ireland was found to have breached this latter requirement by detaining in St Patrick's Institution a child who had not committed a criminal offence and for whom no educational supervision was available.[12]

International Rules and Guidelines

The remaining documents that comprise international standards on youth justice are non-binding rules adopted, principally, by the General Assembly of the United Nations consisting of:

- the UN Standard Minimum Rules for the Administration of Juvenile Justice, 1985 (the Beijing Rules);
- the UN Rules for the Protection of Juveniles deprived of their Liberty, 1990; and
- the UN Guidelines for the Prevention of Juvenile Delinquency (the Riyadh Guidelines), 1990.

While these rules have no binding force *per se*, they have the authority of a resolution of the General Assembly and reference to them in the Preamble of the CRC confirms their importance in interpreting the CRC's provisions on youth justice.[13]

The Rules recognise, in varying detail, the rights to which children and young people in conflict with the law are entitled. Between them, they prioritise early intervention and prevention and emphasise the need to provide opportunities, including education, to all children along with support for the child's family and community. They reflect that for most children, offending is of a transient nature, and recommend, accordingly, that responses to it should avoid intervening formally in the child's life and labelling the child in a negative way. All the documents recognise the negative effects on children of involvement with the criminal justice system and highlight the need to divert children away from it altogether or, when this is unavoidable, to take measures to protect them from its most harmful effects. A core theme throughout the Rules is that any intervention in the child's life must seek to protect his/her well-being, rights and development, and must treat the best interests of the child as a significant consideration. They make clear that specialisation and training are crucial to the maintenance of high standards in the youth justice system, and that modern systems of data collection and evidence-based review and reform are necessary to ensure that the system can respond to the ever-changing nature of youth crime and the needs of society. The Rules recommend the adoption of an integrated, multi-agency approach to youth justice in order to facilitate co-ordinated initiatives and effective communication between all bodies in the area. The importance of discretion is recognised, as is the need to place checks on the exercise of power by those with a decision-making role. Complaints mechanisms must be made available to all children in conflict with the law, who must be given appropriate information and opportunity to be involved in decisions about their care and treatment. Maximising the potential of any intervention – diversion, prosecution or detention – to ensure that the child goes on to play a constructive role in society is a further theme, and the rights of children and young people are paramount throughout.

The Value of International Standards

International standards and rules have a number of important features. First, with respect to the treaties, the CRC and the ECHR constitute binding international law and place obligations on the state to fully comply with their principles and provisions. Regardless of whether Ireland is required to give these instruments the force of national law, transforming them into law and policy is nonetheless an important and effective way to implement their provisions in full. It also safeguards against international embarrassment in the event of being found in breach. The fact that the Government has chosen to give further effect to the ECHR by passing the ECHR Act 2003 strengthens the case for incorporating the CRC into domestic law also. While this could be undertaken on a statutory or sub-constitutional basis, the proposed amendment of the Constitution to give express recognition to children's rights provides the opportunity to incorporate at least the general principles of the CRC at constitutional level. This approach would not only enhance Ireland's reputation among the international community, it would also represent a commitment to promoting and protecting the rights of children and young people by ensuring the implementation of the principles and provisions of the CRC in all areas.

Beyond their legal standing, all international instruments set out above reflect minimum standards and best practice across many jurisdictions. Drafted with ample flexibility and discretion to allow their application, with adaptation, to the unique domestic context, they provide a positive, rights-based framework within which the needs of children in conflict with the law can be addressed. Collectively, they provide useful guidance and advice which has the potential to inform the development of law, policy and practice in the area of youth justice and can also be used to implement law and policy in line with Ireland's international obligations. The standards also act as a benchmark against which the treatment of children in conflict with the law can be measured. As an auditing tool, these instruments, taken alone or together, can be used to evaluate the extent to which domestic law, policy and practice in the area of youth justice complies with international norms.

While not without their shortcomings – they do not recommend any particular age of criminal responsibility, for example – the standards represent collective wisdom and experience on youth justice. Their underlying rights-basis highlights the principles that must govern the youth justice system and guide how children within it should be treated. Whether using the standards to audit law, policy and practice or implementing them as part of a process of reform, their rights-framework has the potential to challenge traditional mind-sets and practices. This can be a valuable process whereby the diverse range of individuals, groups and statutory agencies working in the system reach a common shared position on the values to inform everybody's work. It also provides a touchstone for young people themselves, around whom the system should revolve.

Applying International Standards

For these reasons, the framework of international standards was chosen here to evaluate the Irish youth justice system. The chapters which follow thus aim to subject each element of the system to discussion and analysis in the light of international standards.

Chapter One presents a picture of young offenders highlighting their common characteristics and the nature of their offending. The importance of accurate, up-to-date and comprehensive data collection is emphasised in light of the need to adopt an evidence-based approach to youth justice informed by international standards. Chapter Two presents a critical analysis of the Children Act 2001 discussing its background, implementation, shortcomings and recent revision. This analysis takes place against the backdrop of Ireland's international commitments and considers whether the system is moving further away from the enlightened approach that the Children Act represents. Chapter Three looks at the issue of directing young people from the criminal justice system and, while celebrating its success, considers critically whether the Garda Diversion Programme meets the requirements of international law. Chapter Four looks at the relationship between An Garda Síochána and young people, focusing on the treatment of young people in police custody, their attitudes towards one another and complaints mechanisms. Chapter Five evaluates the trial of children in both the Children Court and the Circuit and Central Criminal Courts in light of international guidance on the trial process. It gives particular weight to the duty on the authorities to facilitate the child's involvement in the criminal process and also considers the role of the court in light of youth justice principles. Chapter Six considers the sentencing of children under Irish law and practice and analyses what is required to translate the principle of detention as a last resort from theory into practice. It also asks how compliant are

Anti-Social Behaviour Orders with Ireland's international obligations. Chapter Seven considers places of detention and presents a lengthy and detailed description of the extent to which the experience of detention for children in Ireland meets international requirements. This important chapter looks at the rights of young people who are the most vulnerable in the system. The final chapter brings together the book's themes and conclusions; it makes a number of recommendations for the direction of the youth justice system, which, in 2006, is at another crossroads. It also considers what is necessary to secure the reform and implementation of the system in line with the norms and values of international law.

The book does not set out to produce a comprehensive description or analysis of all the work being done in this area; others have done that important task. Nor does it consider whether enough is being done to prevent offending or at what stage early intervention should take place. It goes without saying that both issues must be vital components of any policy to address the problem of young offending and the problems faced by young offenders, their families and their communities. Others are better placed to conduct such analyses and indeed have been carrying out important work in these areas for years. Moreover, it is important to acknowledge that the State has been making modest progress in these areas, particularly in the area of educational disadvantage, although the areas of early childhood, family support and mental health services are still woefully inadequate. The lack of a fully fledged youth service is obvious but unaddressed in this context.

This book is thus strictly limited in focus to the criminal justice system, or that part of it which purports to administer justice for children. It sets out to audit the law, policy and practice of the youth justice system, as at 30 June 2006, according to international standards.

Notes

1 See generally Fottrell, D., 'Bringing Rights all the way home: some issues of law and policy in international law and juvenile justice', in Pickford, J. (ed.) *Youth Justice: Theory and Practice* (London: Cavendish Publishing, 2000).

2 Buist, M., and Asquith, S., 'Juvenile Crime and Justice in Scotland', in Bala, N., et al. (eds) *Juvenile Justice Systems: An International Comparison of Problems and Solutions* (Toronto: Thompson Educational Publishing, 2002) pp. 107–34.
3 Doob, A.N., and Tonry, M., 'Varieties of Youth Justice', 31 *Crime and Justice* (2004) 1, pp. 1–20.
4 Smith. R., 'Welfare versus Justice – Again!' 5(1) *Youth Justice* (July 2005) 3–16, p. 11.
5 See generally Tanenhaus, D.S., *Juvenile Justice in the Making* (New York, OUP, 2004).
6 See further below.
7 Committee on the Rights of the Child, *General Discussion Day on Juvenile Justice* (13 November 1995), CRC/C/37, available at www.ohchr.org (accessed 16 January 2006).
8 Committee on the Rights of the Child, *Initial Reports of States Parties due in 1994: Ireland* (29 June 1996), CRC/C/11/Add.12, available at www.ohchr.org (accessed 17 January 2006).
9 Concluding Observations of the Committee on the Rights of the Child: Ireland (23 January 1998), CRC/C/15/Add.85, para. 40, available at www.ohchr.org (accessed 17 January 2006).
10 See O'Connell, D., 'The ECHR Act 2003: A Critical Perspective' in Kilkelly, U., (ed.) *The ECHR and Irish Law* (Bristol: Jordan's, 2004), pp. 1–12 and Hogan, G., 'Incorporation of the ECHR: Some issues of Methodology and Process', in the same volume, pp. 13–34.
11 See further Chapter Five below.
12 *DG* v. *Ireland* (2002) 35 EHRR 1153. See further Kilkelly, U., 'D.G. v. Ireland: Protecting the rights of children at risk: a lazy government and unruly courts', 24 *Dublin University Law Journal* (2002) 269–90.
13 Committee on the Rights of the Child, *General Discussion Day on Juvenile Justice*, p. 4.

Chapter One

Young People in Conflict with the Law

INTRODUCTION

Despite a proliferation of reports, Ireland suffers from a dearth of official statistics and empirical research into the characteristics and circumstances of its young offenders. The lack of a single, official system for data collection in this area impedes research and must also make it extremely difficult to plan or make policy. Research in England and Wales and elsewhere has identified the key factors which increase a young person's risk of offending. What data exist here confirm that Ireland's young people have much in common with their neighbours.

The only data available on offending by young people are the records maintained by An Garda Síochána, including the Garda Diversion Programme. There is little information on pathways through the criminal justice system or on re-offending rates among young people.

This chapter aims to paint a picture of Ireland's young offenders, to highlight their typical family circumstances and background. It also considers what we know about the crimes they commit, although the issue of sentencing is dealt with in Chapter Six. The chapter begins by addressing the lack of data in more detail as it is central to understanding young people in conflict with the law and devising appropriate responses to their offending behaviour.

INTERNATIONAL STANDARDS

International standards recognise the importance of maintaining systems of up-to-date, published, aggregated statistical data on all areas of the lives of children and young people. The Committee on the Rights of the Child has highlighted that this is an essential part of implementing the Convention on the Rights of the Child.[1] According to the Beijing Rules, states should collect and analyse relevant data and information to ensure the evaluation and ongoing reform of the youth justice system and, to this end build a regular evaluative research mechanism into the system of youth justice administration.[2] This is vital given that changes in the lifestyles of the young and in the forms and dimensions of juvenile crime can be rapid and drastic, meaning that the societal and justice responses to youth crime quickly become outmoded and inadequate. For this reason, international standards highlight the need to integrate research into the process of developing and implementing policy in youth justice and draw particular attention to the need for regular review and evaluation of existing programmes and measures and for planning within the broader context of overall development objectives. Up-to-date data collection and a constant appraisal of the circumstances and needs of young people are prerequisites to ensuring the appropriateness of responses to youth crime. Independent research in this area should be facilitated, therefore, and involve young people themselves in the process.[3]

AVAILABILITY OF DATA ON YOUNG OFFENDERS AND OFFENDING

The Current Position

Ireland has a particularly poor record in researching and evaluating young offenders and offending behaviour. In 1970, the Kennedy Report noted that there was a considerable lack of research on child care and juvenile justice in Ireland and that meeting the needs of these areas in the future would require 'a continuous programme of research'.[4] This was highlighted also by the Whittaker Report in 1985, which identified the continuing need for 'research, analysis, discussion and deeper understanding' of the issue of juvenile offenders.[5]

Despite these recommendations, there is a continuing gap in the available data on young offenders and offending behaviour in Ireland.[6] The principal problem is that there is no single comprehensive source on young offenders. Ireland still has no central agency with responsibility for collecting and analysing data on young people in conflict with the law and there is no government sponsored programme for researching youth justice and related areas.[7]

There are two principal sources for statistics on offending by young people: the main series of Garda crime statistics and referrals under the Garda Diversion Programme, both published in the Garda Annual Reports. O'Dwyer notes that the former is of limited use regarding young offenders because 'data are not available by individual age for all crimes'.[8] For example, the information on indictable crimes by juveniles is published only in respect to age cohorts up to age 17 while those above that age are included in an older grouping of 17- to 21-year-olds. He notes that 'information is also limited to cases in which convictions were achieved or where the charge was held proved or where an order was made without conviction',[9] and thus is not available on the number of young people involved in the youth justice system, and what happens to them through that process.

Increasing information on young offenders is available from the Probation and Welfare Service, the Courts Service and the Prison Service which are in the process of establishing new data management systems. As Walsh notes, however, 'the manner in which the data is compiled by these agencies imposes major constraints on the scope of what can be learned about juvenile offending and even on the reliability of the conclusions that can be drawn about the incidence of and trends in juvenile offending'.[10]

Thus, even if the available data were up to date and comprehensive, they would not present anything close to a complete picture of young people, their background and family circumstances or their offending behaviour. There is no information on pathways, making it almost impossible to track a young person's journey through the youth justice system, partly because no single agency has this function. Thus, the information must be gleaned from a range of sources and agencies, many with their own system of collecting and storing the data. Further problems arise from the fact that information collected by each state agency in the area is focused primarily on their involvement with the young person, rather than on the individual. For example, the Garda National Juvenile Office database records the decision of the Director as to whether a young person should be prosecuted or admitted to the Diversion Programme. But in cases where prosecution is directed, the database does not record the outcome of the prosecution.[11] In addition to the problems this causes researchers, it highlights the practical difficulties which must be overcome to ensure effective co-operation and exchange of information between agencies.[12]

Research into the circumstances of Irish young offenders is thus an extremely difficult, frustrating and time-consuming process. The most recent study, undertaken by the Irish Association for the Study of Delinquency, took several months to analyse the content of fifty case files from the Dublin Children Court due mainly to the poor state of the court's files, which are paper-based and hand-written, rather than fully computerised. Research of this kind is further frustrated by the fact that court files are organised alphabetically by year of case completion rather than by offender, and so do not provide a full history of a young person's appearance before the Children Court. The court files will generally include charge sheets (a separate charge sheet for every offence) and reports from the Probation and Welfare Service, the Special Residential Services Board, the young person's place of detention, the National Assessment and Remand Unit and/or the Health Service Executive (HSE). The fact that this system is not entirely computerised and contains largely paper-based reports and forms with hand-written entries means that research into these files can only take place on-site. The research process is complicated further by the fact that agencies do not share a unique identifier for each young person in the system (such as their PPS number) and this makes it difficult to confirm whether reports, entries and files relate to the same young person when many young people have similar names or surnames. For example, the young person may be assigned one or more Garda PULSE ID codes; their name may be spelt differently by different agencies, different dates of birth or versions of their name may be used, and the address of the young person may change from entry to entry.[13] Carrying out empirical research of this kind requires the researcher both to analyse the paper files of the Children Court as well as to acquire information from a whole range of other agencies in order to complete the picture.

The National Children's Strategy identified as the second of its three goals that 'Children's lives will be better understood; their lives will benefit from evaluation, research and information on their needs, rights and the effectiveness of services'.[14] Among the objectives to be achieved under this goal are to 'develop an evidence-based approach to decision-making at all levels' and 'to improve the commissioning, production and dissemination of research and information'.[15] Clearly, there is much to be done here to understand better the lives of children in conflict with the law. Nothing specific to this cohort of children has yet been undertaken, however, and a more general commitment to publish a bi-annual 'State of the Nation's Children' Report, made in the Strategy, does not appear to have materialised.[16] Importantly, however, a statistics/research sub-group of the main Children Act 2001 Working Group has been established under the aegis of the National Children's Office (now the Office of the Minister for Children) to identify existing data sources and gaps in the data, and to develop and commission research projects aimed at a more accurate assessment of the impact of new provisions on both the Probation and Welfare Service and HSE services.[17]

The Proposed Reforms

The Youth Justice Review, carried out by the Department of Justice, Equality and Law Reform in 2005, recognised that gaps exist in the data set on youth justice and noted that historical weaknesses and inconsistencies in information gathering inhibit 'the analysis of youth offending and policy development'.[18] It identified as a key feature of other jurisdictions the existence of good statistical data to support evidence-based policy analysis, the development and allocation of resources, and regular evaluation of the youth justice system. In particular, the Review noted that:

> the importance of robust and consistent data on youth offending is recognised as essential in all jurisdictions visited in order to identify and analyse the scale and nature of youth offending. Evaluation of policy and specific interventions with young offenders is also considered essential to assess the effectiveness of policy in addressing its goals and to ensure that specific interventions and programmes are effective in addressing the offending behaviour of individuals. Reliable data is [sic] considered also to be an essential ingredient in the allocation of resources to programmes and projects which are aimed specifically at tackling offending behaviour.[19]

While the Review does not suggest that the proposed youth justice service be given responsibility for the development of effective systems of data collection and analysis, nonetheless it addresses the data deficit in the context of its broader recommendation for leadership in the youth justice system. In particular, it notes that effective leadership and management 'will ensure the development of consistent and comprehensive information about youth offending, will use that robust information base to support evidence-based interventions, policy and practice, will secure value for money outcomes from monitored policy and practice, and will bring a unique focus for the evaluation of spending on youth justice services'.[20]

While this attention to strategic data collection is welcome, it is not clear which agency is to undertake this function. Moreover, the focus on 'value for money' is of concern here. Notwithstanding that accountability for public expenditure is important in state services, there is an inherent danger in seeking to pursue the unattainable goal of economic efficiency in a system that is resource-intensive and which must focus on long-term goals with objectives that go beyond preventing the offending of individual young people. A related problem is the focus on 'outcomes' and the extent to which success of an initiative or intervention is subjected to a purely economic analysis or is measured in the simplistic terms of re-offending.[21] This is particularly problematic given that the Children Act 2001 establishes a number of important interventions, notably conferencing mechanisms and community sanctions, which may be perceived as labour and resource intensive, even though in reality their cost represents a minuscule proportion of the budget for the detention of children or of the long-term cost of allowing children to grow up into marginalised adults. For this reason, the emphasis on economic efficiency must not undermine the long-term focus on ensuring greater standards of treatment for children and young people. It must also ensure higher standards of protection and promotion of their rights in line with our economic wealth as a nation. This is required, *inter alia*, by Article 4 of the Convention on the Rights of the Child (CRC) which does not offer lack of resources as a defence to poor implementation of the CRC but rather requires states to implement the Convention in line with available resources.

While attempts to measure or achieve reduced re-offending are welcome, and falling recidivism rates are a legitimate objective in this context, it is vital that reforms focus not solely on efficiency or meeting targets but on producing a more just, humane and rights-based youth justice system which works for young offenders, their families and their communities in line with best practice and international standards.[22] Political pressure is a significant factor here given the perception that votes are only won with quick fixes. The result of this, as Whyte notes, is that:

> the political stress on 'it's what works that counts' seems often to be applied to complex social difficulties as if good outcomes can be achieved from relatively straightforward interventions. In reality the issue of effectiveness – 'what works' – is a question to be addressed and explored, and not a statement or formula to be applied in any routinised way to individual children and young people.[23]

At the very least, therefore, it is important that any value for money analysis be undertaken on long-term, as well as short- and medium-term bases. Goldson, in highlighting the need for long-term goals that address the social and material disadvantages that beset growing numbers of children and young people, explains that the state has to 'invest in children's futures providing enduring and meaningful opportunities'.[24] Clearly, a short-term economic analysis of such measures would question the affordability of implementing such a programme. As Goldson asks, however, 'can any society which claims to value children, welfare and justice afford not to?'[25] In this regard, it is welcome that apart from the above management-speak, presumably designed to appeal to bureaucrats, the Youth Justice Review recognises that action is being taken across the justice sector to address weaknesses in data collection and expresses an expectation that improved data collection would inform and underpin policy development.[26] It is also recommended here that priority be given to undertaking a series of long- and short-term reviews of the operation of the youth justice system, involving young people themselves, in line with international standards. The centralised collection of data is a vital part of this process.

INTERNATIONAL RESEARCH ON RISK FACTORS

Research in other jurisdictions regarding the factors which place young people at risk of offending shows that young people in conflict with the law share a number of common features and circumstances;[27] although they are not predictors of offending, the prevalence of these factors among offenders highlights their significance as risk factors.[28]

Risk factors can be divided into socio-economic background; family situation; individual factors and educational factors. The single most important influence on a child's development is his/her family and the composition of the family is one aspect of family life that is consistently associated with young people who offend.[29] Research shows that children who live in families with only one parent or in which the family has been disrupted by separation or other change are more likely to display a range of problems, including delinquency, than children living in stable, two-parent families.[30] There is also a significant connection between children placed in foster or residential care and those who end up in the criminal justice system.[31] Within families, however, factors such as the nature of discipline (erratic or inconsistent), the tolerance of behaviour such as drug-taking and the fact that parents or siblings have been involved in the criminal justice system may all predict that a child will come into conflict with the law. School and education are also important influential factors. Children in the youth justice system have often left school early, either because they have dropped out having found school boring or irrelevant, or because their behaviour has resulted in them being suspended or permanently excluded.[32] The influence of a peer group on the behaviour of others is also a very important factor in the educational environment as well as a more general predictor of delinquent or criminal behaviour among young people.

In summary, then, young people at risk of offending often come from families that have experienced breakdown or trauma and who live in disadvantaged, mainly urban areas; they are early school leavers, have low self-esteem, a learning or other disability, and/or alcohol or drug addiction. Many of them have lived out of home or been in care, and have weak attachment to family and strong affiliation with delinquent peers. While many children suffer these difficulties and do not offend, the fact that risk factors tend to converge means that those most likely to offend are those who have experienced multiple disadvantage. Research shows that the greater the number of factors experienced, the greater the incidence of offending.[33]

THE IRISH YOUNG OFFENDER

Background and Family Circumstances

While there has been no single report or enquiry into the youth justice system in Ireland, government studies on the child care system have identified some of the common characteristics of young offenders. The Kennedy Report published in 1970 found that a high percentage of children committed to reformatory and industrial schools suffered from deprivation (such as bereavement, separation or 'illegitimacy') and that a very high proportion were 'generally backward', particularly in the area of education and ability.[34] Digging deeper in its search for explanations for juvenile delinquency,[35] the Committee noted that identifying causes and solutions was a complex matter involving many factors. For example, it referred to the fact that the environment in which children were growing up in the 1970s was different from that experienced by preceding generations of children: parental authority was weakening, the number of parents experiencing parental problems was increasing, the urban environment was providing more and easier targets for delinquent behaviour while increased accessibility to television and other media was helping to shape the outlook and values of young people.[36] The Committee also noted that 'the laws dealing with juveniles, and the enforcement of those laws, were also a factor'.[37] It concluded, however, that the most important causal factor was 'the personality and emotional development of the individual juvenile.'[38]

More recent research demonstrates the importance of social and educational background. In 1997, O'Mahony analysed the circumstances of 108 prisoners in Mountjoy Prison and noted that 37 per cent had lost a parent before the age of 15; 15 per cent had a parent imprisoned; 45 per cent had no substantive work or educational qualifications; 29 per cent were illiterate and 66 per cent were heroin users.[39] In a more recent survey carried out in Wheatfield Place of Detention in west Dublin, the prisoners were found to have very low levels of educational attainment. Of those surveyed, only 16.1 per cent had obtained their Junior Certificate, while only 4.8 per cent had completed the Leaving Certificate.[40]

Returning to O'Mahony's research, while 95 per cent of those interviewed had previous convictions, 31 per cent had received their first conviction before they were 14 and 64 per cent by 17. Seventy-seven per cent had served a sentence in St Patrick's Institution and 13 per cent had spent some time in the State's reformatory or industrial schools. Of those who had served an earlier custodial sentence 7 per cent had first been in custody before the age of 15, and 57 per cent before the age of 18.

More recent research completed for the Juvenile Justice Review Group within the Department of Justice, Equality and Law Reform in 2001 supports these findings. This research analysed the cases of 84 children aged from 10 to 17 years attending the Dublin Children Court. All the children came from relatively large families with an average of 4.6 children, more than twice the national average. Thirty per cent had suffered the loss of one or both parents either permanently or for long periods, and only half of the children had two married parents in the home. Thirty-six per cent of the children lived with the mother alone. On a rough estimate, 80 per cent of the children lived in local authority housing. Only a third of fathers, in families where there were fathers present, were in full-time employment. For over a quarter of the children, parental abuse of alcohol was recorded and for more than one in ten, parental drug abuse. Ten per cent of the children came from homes where there was a record of domestic violence and 17 per cent of them were known to have been victims of physical abuse. Most significantly, 25 per cent of the children had left school before the age of 14, 85 per cent before the age of 16 and 90 per cent were currently out of school. Approximately 30 per cent of young people had at some time been suspended or expelled from school. In a third of cases, the Probation and Welfare Officer had recorded a considered opinion that there was poor or inadequate parental supervision of the child. In almost 40 per cent of cases, another member of the child's family was known to have offended. About half the children were involved in substance abuse of some form, one in three in drug abuse; twenty of these had a serious problem, yet only five had attended a detoxification programme. Forty per cent of the children had had some contact with Health Board psychological services and a further 40 per cent had been in contact with other agencies, such as drug treatment centres and private counselling services.[41]

Pilot research published in 2005 by the Irish Association for the Study of Delinquency (IASD), which analysed 50 files of the Dublin Children Court, confirms these conclusions.[42] Of the 38 young people for whom information was available, 16 lived with both parents, ten lived with their mother only, a further five lived with other relatives mainly grandmothers, five were in HSE care and two were out of home. The relationship between parents was confirmed as having broken down in 14 cases and 26 (out of the 38 young people for whom information on family structure was available) had experienced the absence of one or both parents for significant periods of their childhood. In three cases a parent had died, in five cases one or both parents had served time in prison and in the majority of cases, the father was absent for one reason or another.[43] In 14 cases, a member of the young person's immediate family was reported as having a criminal record.

The IASD research also confirms the severe educational disadvantage suffered by children in conflict with the law in Ireland. Of the 34 young people for whom information was available in this study, nine young people had not completed primary school – three were expelled, two left due to persistent truancy and three had disrupted education because they were in state care. Eight of these nine young people had been sentenced to detention.[44] Of the remaining 25 young people who completed their primary education, 19 did not complete the junior cycle of post-primary school and left education before the age of 16; nine of these were committed to detention. Five young people thus sat their Junior Certificate examination – four of them passed – three left school at this stage while the other two were later expelled.

The IASD research considered in some detail the circumstances of the 18 young people (from the sample of 50) who were sent to detention. All but one had previously spent time in detention and 11 of the group had served a sentence in St Patrick's Institution or elsewhere. Half of these young people had come to the attention of Gardaí before the age of 12. The following factors were also evident in over half of the cases (not all the same cases): negative peer group influence, housing problems, parental substance abuse, other family members with criminal records, absence of one or both parents, while other factors such as physical or sexual abuse, unemployed parents, HSE involvement, history of self-harm and domestic violence were present in a smaller number of cases.[45] All 18 young people sent to detention were reported as misusing alcohol and/or drugs.[46]

Research conducted in 2001 found that two-thirds of the children appearing before the Children Court in Dublin came from a relatively small area of Dublin, characterised by high levels of deprivation.[47] In 2005, the IASD research found that of the 31 young people who were living at home, eight were from Dublin 24 while six were from Dublin 1. The postal districts of Dublin 11, 4 and 7 were also represented in the sample.[48]

Overall, it is clear that the indicators and risk factors that characterise criminal behaviour by young people in other jurisdictions are present in Ireland too: social and educational disadvantage, gender, unsettled family background, negative peer influence and drug and alcohol problems are all prevalent issues in the Irish context.

Offending by Young People

Irish research has highlighted the types of offences that young people commit as theft, criminal damage and drink related offences. Vehicle offences and public order offences are common in large urban areas. While the level of offending by young people has remained stable in the last number of years, an increase was recorded between 2000 and 2002.[49]

According to the Garda figures, there has been little recent change in the type of offences that young people commit. For example, in 1999 the principal offences were larceny (21 per cent), criminal damage (14 per cent), vehicle offences (9 per cent) and public order offences (7 per cent)[50] while these percentages changed little in 2003 or 2004.[51] One trend that has been observed, however, is the increase in the number of drink-related offences from 10 per cent in 1999[52] to 20 per cent in 2003.[53] While this may be due to higher detection rates, the fact that this rate was consistent with that recorded in 2004[54] and with the prevalence of alcohol in other studies of young offending makes it likely that alcohol is increasingly prevalent in the offending of young people. At the same time, children may be more likely to be charged with alcohol-related offences than adults given that it is an offence for a child to drink alcohol. In this regard, it is notable that in 2004, 2,287 charges were laid against children for being drunk in a public place while 1,651 charges were laid with respect to consumption or purchase of alcohol.[55]

According to the IASD research, the 50 young people whose files were analysed faced 551 charges. The ten most commonly occurring charges were theft of property (mostly mobile phones); criminal damage to property; breach of the peace; drunkenness in a public place; assault; robbery of property from a person (mostly mobile phones) failure to appear in court in breach of bail conditions; driving a motor vehicle without the owner's consent; handling stolen property and interfering with a motor vehicle. In line with the Garda figures, theft and robbery offences account for 27 per cent of the charges, followed by public order offences (23 per cent) traffic offences (18 per cent) and criminal damage (10 per cent).

The IASD research also found that young people often accumulated two, three or more charges in one incident.[56] This was a feature of cases observed in another Children Court study where it was noted that certain young people could face numerous charges in respect of a single 24-hour period. This research noted, for example, that:

> while a young person who faces 20 or 30 charges or a long list of previous convictions may have the appearance of a hardened criminal, this may be easily explained in the case of a young person who experiences problems with alcohol or drugs at a particular time in their lives, which commonly combine to give rise to charges of theft and public order, and/or by association with a negative peer group. The latter, for example, may encourage a susceptible or immature young person to get involved in risk-taking behaviour such as car crime, which may then result in them facing a wide range of charges including criminal damage (necessary to steal the car), car theft, dangerous driving and a range of road traffic offences including no licence, no insurance and no tax. Apprehension by a Garda following a night's pursuit in a stolen car may also result in public order charges (if the orders of the Garda are not obeyed) or in some cases a charge of assault (if arrest is violently resisted). In these circumstances, it is not difficult to understand how a young person can, within a relatively short period of time, face a long list of criminal charges.[57]

In fact, the 2004 Garda figures appear to bear this out with relatively high rates of referrals for insurance offences (682), no driving licence (147), threatening behaviour (1,002), failure to comply with a Garda's direction (360) and assault causing bodily harm (431). These contrast with much smaller numbers of more serious offences including drunk driving (55) and sexual assault (58).[58]

Given that only the headline or more serious offence will be recorded for the purposes of Garda statistics, further independent and more comprehensive research is necessary to create a more accurate picture of the crimes committed by young people. Nevertheless, it is clear that the top five offences committed by young people have not changed in the last five years. Drink-related offences, theft, criminal damage, public order and traffic-related offences have all featured consistently.

The ratio of boys to girls in conflict with the law also appears to be relatively constant. With respect to the Garda Diversion Programme, the number of girls involved increased slightly from 17 per cent in 1999 to 23 per cent in 2003. Although this dropped slightly to 21 per cent in 2004, girls still constitute almost one-quarter of children admitted to the Programme.[59] Boys' involvement, on the other hand, decreased from 83 per cent in 1999 to 79 per cent in 2004. This contrasts sharply with the gender profile of those admitted to secure care where almost twice as many girls as boys were admitted to special care between 1996 and 2003.[60] The IASD research found that while eight of the 50 sample Children Court files analysed involved female offenders (16 per cent), only 11 per cent of the total 751 cases prosecuted by the Court during the period covered by the research were girls. The age profile of the sample group was also found to be slightly younger than the age profile of the larger group. Other research has confirmed that over 90 per cent of cases in the Children Court involve boys.[61] The fact that boys represent approximately 80 per cent of cases in the Diversion Programme but almost 90 per cent in the Children Court would suggest either that boys are more likely to commit further offences or, alternatively, are more likely to be prosecuted. Again, further research is required to investigate this.

Information on the age of offenders is available principally from the statistics created by the Garda Diversion Programme. This data shows little or no change in the age profile since 1999. For example, in 1999, 18 per cent were aged 17 years, 23 per cent were aged 16 years, 22 per cent were aged 15, 15 per cent were aged 14 and 22 per cent were under 14 years. With little variation, the figures have remained constant. The 2004 figures, therefore, are that 27 per cent of those involved were aged 17, 25 per cent were aged 16, 19 per cent were aged 15, 12 per cent were aged 14 and 12 per cent were under 14 years.[62]

This may contradict the claim that those coming into conflict with the law are getting younger as it is clear that males aged between 14 and 17 years make up the greatest proportion of known offenders in all the main offence categories.[63] In the IASD research, however, half of the young people had first appeared before the Children Court aged between 12 and 15, while the other half were either 16 or 17 years.[64] This may contradict the Garda figures, although a more wide ranging study is necessary to test this further.

The data from the Diversion Programme also include the times at which criminal activity took place where this is known. While there is little year-on-year variation in the figures, this helps to further understand the nature of young offending in Ireland. Overall, between 1999 and 2003, the majority of the activity (an average of 68 per cent) was reported to occur fairly evenly across the hours from 2 pm to midnight with activity at its highest between 8 pm and 10 pm and at its lowest between 6 am and 8 am. It is possible to conclude that the rate at which offences are being committed drops during school hours – consistent data from 1999 to 2003 show that far less offences were committed before 2 pm with an increase in the rate of offending visible from this time, with a further increase after 4 pm.[65]

In terms of the scale of young offending, according to the Youth Justice Review, the number of recorded offences committed annually by young offenders has remained stable in the last three years at approximately 20,000. More than two-thirds of those are dealt with by means of an informal/formal caution under the Diversion Programme. While young offenders account for about 3.5 per cent of the total population of 10–17-year-olds, they represent less than 20 per cent of the client base of the Probation and Welfare Service. For example, in 2003, 20 per cent of all Probation Orders involved those under 18 years of age.[66] Further data regarding what happens to young people before the Children Court can be found in Chapter Six.

Serious Offences

While the manner in which data have been collected almost completely frustrates the identification of trends in serious or indictable offences committed by young people under 18 years,[67] a number of comments can be made here. The first issue relates to the trend in offences against the person among 14 to 16-year-olds. These count for less than 3 per cent of the total indictable offences for this group and compare with less than 1 per cent for under 14-year-olds. While, after an increase in the late 1980s, these offences almost disappeared in the latter half of the 1990s, since 2000 there is evidence of a significant increase in the numbers. While they dropped to 1 per cent in the second half of the 1990s, they rose to 38 per cent, 26 per cent and 55 per cent respectively for 2001 and 2002.[68] This is clearly an increase of very serious concern and is matched by a similar increase among girls in the same age group for whom offences against the person counted for 11 per cent, 31 per cent and 14 per cent between 2000 and 2002. Accordingly, Walsh notes, offences against the person may be becoming a significant feature among 14–16-year-olds convicted of indictable offences.[69]

At the same time, it is apparent that property offences and larcenies account for the vast majority of indictable offences committed by persons under 21 years between 1976 and 2002. Between them they account for 94 per cent of the total offences committed by this age group. This contrasts with those over 21 years for whom offences against the person are a more common feature. Walsh cautiously identifies property offences, other than larcenies (i.e. vandalism-type offences) as the indictable offence most characteristic of young people under 21 years.[70] Nevertheless, the statistics from the years 2000 to 2002 illustrate 'major upheavals in the patterns in all age and gender groups, apart from the youngest (14 to 16 years)'. The primary factor has been a drop in the share of property offences in the face of significant increases in the numbers of offences against the person, which developments are most pronounced in the oldest age group (17 to 20 years). For this group, offences against the person have effectively overtaken property offences while for others (17- to 20-year-old females and 14- to 16-year-old males) they also feature significantly. Even the 14- to 16-age group for females is affected although, as Walsh cautions, the numbers are still very small.[71] Although reclassification of offences and changes in the practices and patterns of recording indictable offences may be at least partially responsible for these marked changes, it is certainly a trend worthy of more closer analysis when better quality data are available.

PUBLIC PERCEPTIONS OF YOUTH CRIME

Despite the fact that levels of youth crime are relatively stable and the numbers involved relatively small – certainly in serious or persistent offending – public perception is that offending by young people is a serious problem. Over 70 per cent of respondents to the Garda National Survey in 2005 said that juvenile or teenage crime was a problem in their area – 30 per cent of the respondents described it as a 'major problem' while 43 per cent said it was a minor problem.[72] Twenty-four per cent said it was not a problem at all. These figures rose to 77 per cent (major problem) and 20 per cent (minor problem) respectively when respondents were asked the same question about the country as a whole. However, it was a common trend throughout the Survey that people believed that a problem with criminal behaviour was bigger in the country as a whole compared with where they lived. In the survey, a majority of respondents felt that the predominant response to juvenile offending should be treatment rather than punishment. Attitudes would appear to have hardened a little since the 2002 survey in so far as those believing that punishment was the answer rose from 32 per cent to 37 per cent, whereas those who believed in rehabilitation and counselling dropped from 63 per cent to 55 per cent (although the 'don't knows' also increased). Moreover, over 70 per cent felt that the criminal justice system was too lenient on offenders, little changed on the 2002 survey.[73] Regarding the causes of crime, 11 per cent of those questioned cited 'lack of parental control' as the cause, coming third only to drink and drugs (32 per cent) and alcohol alone (18 per cent).[74] The issue of the public perception of youth crime is clearly worthy of more detailed research.

CONCLUSION

The above data highlight the similarities between young offenders in Ireland and elsewhere regarding their socio-economic backgrounds, family circumstances and educational and personal disadvantages. This is important because it allows the lessons of other jurisdictions and international law to be applied here with appropriate adjustments. Nevertheless, the overwhelming conclusion to be drawn in this area is that the statistics and other data available on young people and their offending are wholly inadequate to facilitate the necessary evaluation of current law and policy and to encourage future reform. While some data are presented below with respect to the sentencing process, general data on pathways through the youth and criminal justice systems – particularly on the transition from the youth to the adult system – are missing, along with longitudinal data on the success or otherwise of interventions. The inability to draw meaningful conclusions about the nature of serious offending among young people also poses problems and the fact that the Children Act 2001 deals only with minor offences further isolates this area of the youth justice system from scrutiny.

The commitment made in the National Children's Strategy to understanding better children's lives, together with the recommendations of the Youth Justice Review to improve leadership and management of the system should, if fully implemented, make a significant difference to the quality and quantity of the available data on young people in conflict with the law. This can only aid the process of implementing the Children Act 2001 and, more generally, improve the effectiveness of the youth justice system in line with international standards.

NOTES

1 Committee on the Rights of the Child, *General Measures of Implementation of the Convention on the Rights of the Child*, CRC/GC/2004/5, pp. 11–12, available at www.ohchr.org (accessed 17 January 2006).
2 Rule 30.3 of the UN Standard Minimum Rules for the Administration of Juvenile Justice (the Beijing Rules) adopted by General Assembly resolution 40/33 of 29 November 1985 available at www.ohchr.org (accessed 17 January 2006).
3 Commentary to Rule 30 of the Beijing Rules, *ibid.*

4 *Report of the Committee on Reformatory and Industrial Schools Systems (The Kennedy Report)* (Dublin: The Stationery Office, 1970) Prl 1342 in Walsh, D., *Juvenile Justice* (Dublin: Thomson Round Hall, 2005), p. 471.
5 *The Report of the Committee of Inquiry into the Penal System* (Dublin: Stationery Office, 1985) in Walsh, D., *ibid.*, p. 484.
6 See O'Sullivan, E., 'Juvenile Justice in the Republic of Ireland: Future Priorities' 3/4 *Irish Social Worker* (Autumn/Winter 1996) 14.
7 The National Children's Office has a research programme which covers children as a whole rather than those in conflict with the law as a specific group. However, s. 264 of the Children Act 2001 provides a statutory basis for research into the youth justice system.
8 O'Dwyer, K., 'Juvenile Crime and Justice in Ireland' in Bala, N. et al. (eds), *Juvenile Justice Systems: An International Comparison of Problems and Solutions* (Toronto: Thompson Educational Publishing, 2002) p. 165.
9 *Ibid.*
10 Walsh, D., *Juvenile Justice*, p. 313. See also pp. 313–15.
11 McPhillips, S., *Dublin Children Court: A Pilot Research Project* (Dublin: IASD, 2005), p. 15.
12 See further Chapter Two.
13 McPhillips, S., *Dublin Children Court: A Pilot Research Project*, p. 15.
14 National Children's Office, *The National Children's Strategy: Our Children, Their Lives* (Dublin: Stationery Office: 2000) pp. 37–42.
15 *Ibid.*, p. 40.
16 However, in 2005, the National Children's Office completed a substantial project to develop child well-being indicators which has some relevance in this area. See Hanafin, S. and Brooks, A.M., *Report on the Development of a National Set of Child Well-being Indicators in Ireland* (Dublin: The National Children's Office, 2005). A longitudinal study is also underway.
17 See www.nco.org (accessed 12 January 2006).
18 *Report on the Youth Justice Review* (Dublin: Department of Justice, Equality and Law Reform, 2005) available at www.justice.ie (accessed 4 January 2006) p. 26.
19 *Ibid.*, pp. 26–7.
20 *Ibid.*, pp. 36–7.
21 For a similar concern with respect to the restorative elements of the Garda Diversion Programme see O'Dwyer, K., 'Garda Restorative Justice Programme – Highlights and Insights', paper delivered at a Conference on Youth Justice, Croke Park Dublin, 12–13 September 2005, p. 4.
22 Irish Youth Justice Alliance, *Submission to the Youth Justice Team*, 26 November 2004, available at www.iprt.ie (accessed 15 January 2006).
23 Whyte, B., 'Effectiveness, Research and Youth Justice', 4(1) *Youth Justice* (July 2004) 3–21, p. 3.
24 Goldson, B., 'Children in Trouble: State Responses to Juvenile Crime' in Scraton, P. (ed.), *'Childhood' in 'Crisis'* (London: Routledge, 1997) p. 145.
25 *Ibid.*
26 *Report on the Youth Justice Review*, p. 2.
27 Accessible accounts of the literature in the area are set out in the following

publications: Arthur, R., 'Preventing Youth Crime – The role of the Child Care Act 1991 – Part 1', 9 *Irish Law Times* (2003) 134–55; Centre for Social and Educational Research DIT, *Study of Participants in Garda Special Projects* (Dublin: Department of Justice, Equality and Law Reform, October 2001) pp. 17–40, available at www.justice.ie (accessed 13 January 2006); and National Crime Council, *Tackling the Underlying Causes of Crime: A Partnership Approach* (Dublin: Stationery Office, 2002), pp. 30–2, available at www.gov.ie/crimecouncil (accessed 13 January 2006).

28 The principal studies in this area are Farrington, D., *Understanding and Preventing Youth Crime* (York: Joseph Rowntree Foundation, 1996) and Utting, D., *What Works with Young Offenders in the Community?* (Essex: Barnardos, 2000).

29 Wells, E., and Rankin, J., 'Families and Delinquency: A meta-analysis of the impact of broken homes', 38(1) *Social Problems* (1991), 71–83, cited in Centre for Social and Educational Research, *Study of Participants in Garda Special Projects,* p. 18.

30 Thornberry, T.P., et al., 'Family Disruption and Delinquency', *Juvenile Justice Bulletin* (Office of Juvenile Justice and Delinquency Prevention, US Department of Justice September 1999) available at www.ncjrs.org (accessed 28 November 2005).

31 Include Youth, paper submitted to the UN Committee on the Rights of the Child for its General Day of Discussion on 'Children without Parental Care, 2005, available at www.includeyouth.org (13 January 2006). See also Hanlon, N., and Riley, L., *The Impact of Placement in Special Care Unit Settings on the Wellbeing of Young People and their Families: A Summary Report 2004* (Dublin: Special Residential Services Board, 2004) and Phillips, S., *Dublin Children Court A Pilot Research Project*, pp. 80–1 which found that children in care are over-represented in the Children Court.

32 However, one recent study points to the opposite direction here suggesting that the shock of suspension or exclusion from school prompts parents to address their child's needs and poor behaviour. Hodgson, P., and Webb, D., 'Young People, Crime and Social Exclusion: A Case of Some Surprises', 44(1), *The Howard Journal of Criminal Justice* (2005), 12–28.

33 Graham, J., and Bowling, B., *Young People and Crime: Research Study 145* (London: HMSO, 1995).

34 *The Kennedy Report* in Walsh, D., *Juvenile Justice*, pp. 468–72.

35 Walsh, D., *ibid.*, p. 469.

36 *Ibid.*

37 *Ibid.*

38 *Ibid.*

39 O'Mahony, P., 'Punishing Poverty and Personal Adversity', 7 *Irish Criminal Law Journal* (1997), pp. 152–70.

40 See National Crime Council, *Tackling the Underlying Causes of Crime: A Partnership Approach*, p. 69.

41 O'Mahony, P., 'Contextualising the Children Bill as a response to youth crime', paper delivered at the National Conference of Youthreach Co-

ordinators, Monaghan 12 February 2001, available at www.youthreach.ie (accessed 13 January 2006).

42 McPhillips, S., *Dublin Children Court: A Pilot Research Project.*

43 This is further supported by the conclusions of other research which observed 944 cases in the Children Court and found that both parents attended proceedings in only 10 per cent of cases with fathers alone present in a further 14 per cent. Kilkelly, U., *The Children's Court: A Children's Rights Audit* (Cork, 2005), p. 21.

44 McPhillips, S., *Dublin Children Court: A Pilot Research Project,* pp. 50–8.

45 *Ibid.,* pp. 70–2.

46 *Ibid.*, p. 75.

47 McLoughlin, E., Maunsell, C., and O'Connell, M., *Children in the Irish Juvenile Justice System*, cited (as forthcoming) in Bacik, I., 'The Practice of Sentencing in the Irish Courts' in O'Mahony, P. (ed.), *Criminal Justice in Ireland* (Dublin: IPA, 2002), pp. 363–4. This research undertaken on behalf of the Department of Justice, Equality and Law Reform was never published.

48 McPhillips, S., *Dublin Children Court: A Pilot Research Project*, p. 39.

49 *Report on the Youth Justice Review*, p. 8.

50 An Garda Síochána *Annual Report 1999*, p. 91.

51 The 2004 figures were larceny (18 per cent), criminal damage (10 per cent), vehicle offences (5 per cent) and public order offences (8 per cent). An Garda Síochána *Annual Report 2004*, p. 58. See also An Garda Síochána *Annual Report 2003*, p. 63.

52 *Ibid.*

53 An Garda Síochána, *Annual Report 2003*, p. 63.

54 An Garda Síochána, *Annual Report 2004*, p. 5.

55 *Ibid.*, p. 59. The rate of alcohol-related offences for adults does not appear to be recorded.

56 McPhillips, S., *Dublin Children Court: A Pilot Research Project,* pp. 19–21.

57 Kilkelly, U., *Children's Court: A Children's Rights Audit,* p. 23.

58 An Garda Síochána *Annual Report 2004*, p. 59.

59 *Ibid.*, p. 52.

60 Hanlon, N., and Riley, L., *The Impact of Placement in Special Care Unit Settings on the Wellbeing of Young People and their Families*, pp. 29–30.

61 Kilkelly, U., *The Children's Court: A Children's Rights Audit*, p. 16.

62 An Garda Síochána *Annual Report 2004*, p. 56.

63 Young, P., O'Donnell, I., and Clare, E., *Crime In Ireland: Trends and Patterns, 1950 to 1998*, A Report by the Institute of Criminology, Faculty of Law, University College Dublin for the National Crime Council, (Dublin: Stationery Office, 2001), p. 71.

64 McPhillips, S., *Dublin Children Court: A Pilot Research Project,* pp. 18–9.

65 These figures are unavailable for 2004.

66 *Report on the Youth Justice Review,* pp. 11–12.

67 However, see the forensic analysis undertaken by Professor Dermot Walsh in Walsh, D., *Juvenile Justice,* pp. 316–81.

68 *Ibid.*, p. 374.

69 *Ibid.*, p. 375.
70 *Ibid.*, p. 381.
71 *Ibid.*
72 O'Dwyer, K., Kennedy, P., and Ryan, W., *Garda Public Attitudes Survey 2005* (Templemore Garda Research Unit, 2005) pp. 40–41.
73 *Ibid.*, p. 40
74 *Ibid.*

Chapter Two

The Children Act 2001

INTRODUCTION

The Children Act 2001 contemplates the most comprehensive reform of the Irish youth justice system in one hundred years. It puts in place a modern statutory framework for the treatment of children in conflict with the law and has many new approaches and initiatives designed to target the circumstances of offending children. The Act has been on the political landscape for almost a decade and its full implementation is still several years away. While its potential is far from reached, its reputation has grown into a panacea for the problems of delinquency and youth crime. At the same time, the Act's shortcomings have become clear and the Youth Justice Review and Criminal Justice Act 2006 mean further substantial changes to the Act and the youth justice system as a whole. This chapter aims to look critically at the Act as the foundation of the youth justice system; it examines its origins, outlines its implementation to date and proposed changes, and questions its potential to transform the lives of young people in conflict with the law.

THE ORIGINS AND BACKGROUND OF THE CHILDREN ACT 2001

The Children Act 1908

The Children Act 1908 has provided the primary statutory basis for the treatment of children in conflict with the law in

Ireland for nearly a century. Described as 'an exceptionally liberal and innovative measure for its time',[1] the Act was 'quite an enlightened and flexible piece of legislation'.[2] It reflects a desire to rehabilitate young offenders and recognises that it is inappropriate to expose children and young people to the full power of the criminal justice system. As a result, it makes provision for limits on the nature and length of custodial sentences; places emphasis on non-custodial punishments; puts responsibility on parents for their children's offending; provides summary trial for most offences and protection for the privacy of children and young people in conflict with the law. The Act provides for many of the sanctions which are still in use today. Section 107, in particular, allows a case to be dealt with by placing the offender under the supervision of a probation officer (probation bond), ordering the offender to pay a fine, damages or costs, or declaring the offender to be unruly or depraved so as to enable him to be detained. The 1908 Act also established the system of certification for industrial and reformatory schools.

The Act was amended many times in a piecemeal manner.[3] Despite its apparent inability to keep pace with modern social and legal conditions, the Children Act 1908 is widely accepted to have served Ireland well.

Recommendations for Reform 1970–1980

There has never been an official enquiry into juvenile crime or the juvenile justice system generally in Ireland.[4] Much of the focus has centred on the industrial and reformatory school system, although the recommendations made in this context also concerned the wider issue of juvenile delinquency and addressed its causal factors. Significantly, the Kennedy Report in 1970[5] made a number of pertinent recommendations that are still relevant today. It recommended that the age of criminal responsibility be raised from seven (the position at common law) to twelve years and also commented on the need to bring a case involving a young offender before the court as soon as possible so that he/she could be dealt with while the offence was still fresh in his/her mind. It identified the need to specially constitute the Circuit Courts when hearing appeals from the

Children's Court,[6] to extend the power of the Court to order the presence of both parents of a child in court, and bring all aspects of child care within a composite Children Act, placing it under the remit of the Department of Health.[7]

The theme of governmental responsibility for juvenile crime was also considered by the Henchy Committee in 1974.[8] The principal recommendation of the first interim report of this interdepartmental committee was that:

> [t]here should be established, on a permanent basis, an inter-departmental committee to co-ordinate the activities of children and young persons. Its aim would be to keep the changing needs of the situation under review, to advise on any further provisions ... which it considers from time to time to be necessary or desirable in relation to young persons who have come or are likely to come in conflict with the law...[9]

This committee's second interim report also recommended that a high priority be given to the provision of resources for the treatment of young offenders in the community, including educational facilities, day child psychiatric services and day centres.[10]

However, it was the Report of the Task Force on Child Care Services in 1980 that emerged as the most comprehensive official publication on the subject of care and treatment of children at risk in Ireland.[11] Although it did not recommend raising the age of criminal responsibility,[12] nor was it persuaded by arguments in favour of a 'welfare' approach to juvenile offending, it made a number of significant recommendations regarding the operation of the juvenile justice system and the Children Court,[13] many of which mirror provisions in the Children Act 2001. In particular, it recommended that the adjudication on the child should be informed by the child's welfare and the public interest, that it promote relations between the child and his/her family and that detention be used only 'where there is no acceptable alternative'. To achieve these objectives, it recommended that a wide range of disposal options be made available to the Court. Throughout the Report, great stress was placed on the importance of 'tailoring facilities to cater for the particular needs of different categories of child'.[14]

The Dáil Select Committee on Crime, 1992

Despite the pragmatic nature of these recommendations, further political inertia followed. Ten years later, it was a Dáil Report that prompted the Government to finally undertake the task of replacing the 1908 Act. In 1992, the Dáil Select Committee on Crime considered the matter of juvenile crime, its causes and its remedies having decided that it needed 'urgent attention as a social problem'.[15] The Committee received written and oral submissions from a wide group of victims, community groups, public representatives and those working with young offenders. While many expressed a deep unease about juvenile crime, many submissions attached importance to 'trying to break the cycle of offending in a constructive way' by placing critical emphasis on the role of parents, imposing curfews to prevent gangs congregating, or providing constructive leisure and educational activities in the community. The Committee's Report detailed the social background to juvenile crime and recognised the increasing evidence of homelessness among young people, their complex personal and family problems, and increasing rates of truancy, drug problems, unemployment and child abuse. The most substantial part of the Report, however, constituted a 'comprehensive and inter-locking set of recommendations in relation to the development of juvenile justice provision and policy'.[16] It addressed its recommendations not just to those in the criminal justice system but to other government departments, health boards, voluntary bodies and ordinary citizens. The Report took the following approach: first, it identified a number of factors as important considerations in the drafting of legislation and public policy in this area: the vulnerability and welfare of children in trouble with the law; the relevance of adverse social conditions in their lives; the importance of a multi-faceted response to the problem of juvenile crime; the importance of every young person being treated with respect; the desirability of maximising the use of diversion and non-custodial measures; the importance of the efficient operation of the system (in particular the undesirability of long delays between arrest and any final court hearing); the importance of a published policy framework within which all decision-makers in the system can operate; the desirability of key decision-makers having a brief exclusively concerned with children and the importance of the Irish system conforming to international standards and practices.[17]

It pulled together all the objectives central to an effective, rights-based system of youth justice and identified a set of principles, which if implemented, would undoubtedly transform the system of youth justice in Ireland.

In its Report, the Committee made recommendations related to providing a new legal framework for youth justice, the role of parents in relation to young offending, community and custodial dispositions and the role of other sectors outside the formal system. In relation to the legal framework, the Committee concluded that the Children Act 1908 was 'outdated' and 'in need of radical overhaul' and called on the Government to introduce urgently new juvenile justice legislation. Taking into account Ireland's international obligations in the area, the Committee recommended that a substantial number of far-reaching reforms be undertaken, including both the organisation of the juvenile justice system and substantive matters of criminal law. Significantly, the Committee recommended that the new legislation raise the age of criminal responsibility (from 7 years) to 12 and articulate the goals and objectives of the juvenile justice system. A strong recommendation was made for the creation of specialisation within the public bodies which operate in the juvenile justice system – the Department of Justice, An Garda Síochána, the Director of Public Prosecutions and the Probation and Welfare Service. The Report specifically recommended that special juvenile courts be established and that judges receive appropriate training. Diversionary mechanisms were recommended to be placed on a statutory basis and new statutory duties were recommended to require a range of public authorities to put in place support measures to prevent delinquency and co-operate with the juvenile justice authorities.

From a structural point of view, the Committee recommended that juvenile crime prevention committees be established in each Garda division, which should also contain a specialist Juvenile Bureau. Court facilities and procedures were recommended to be improved and both non-custodial and custodial dispositions were recommended to be rationalised along with the introduction of mandatory regulations for all residential and custodial centres for young offenders to ensure that the rights of all young people detained there are respected. The Committee also recommended that structures be developed to maximise the involvement of volunteers in the juvenile justice system, that the Minister for Justice publish an annual report on the operation of the juvenile justice system and fund research into all aspects of the system. It was recommended that a commitment be made to meet Ireland's international obligations under the Convention on the Rights of the Child (CRC) and other UN instruments on juvenile justice.[18]

The Committee went further in recommending that a number of substantial reforms be undertaken via new legislation. Recognising that parenting is a challenging and complex role, the Committee endorsed the use of family and parental supports recommending that structures for parental counselling and education be put in place across the country by health and education authorities. In addition it supported the 'stick' (rather than the 'carrot') approach of requiring what it described as 'laggard' parents to attend the Garda Station and the Court with their child, and imposing fines on parents for the offences committed by their children, although it recognised clear problems of enforcement in this context.[19]

The Committee recommended the need to establish a range of sanctions for juvenile crime on a continuum of intervention ranging from light (involving no prosecution) to heavy (detention) by putting in place a wide range of dispositions including cautions, victim–offender mediation, conditional discharge, a range of probation orders involving supervision, a voluntary residential placement, mentoring, challenging sporting and educational activities, community service orders and fines. With regard to the use of custodial placements at the extreme end of this scale, the Committee recognised the 'serious difficulties' that existed in relation to 'present residential/ custodial provision for young people in trouble'.[20] It found that they were expensive, involved unacceptably high levels of recidivism and did not involve appropriate placements, adequate regional distribution or sufficient places for girls.[21] The Committee went on to note that the use of secure facilities should be kept to an absolute minimum because they are not only extremely expensive and of questionable efficacy, but also because custody in itself fails to generate within the young person the motivation, self-discipline and know-how necessary to stay out of trouble. For this reason, it recommended that a range of facilities be developed to provide for those young people for whom a non-custodial sanction is not suitable. Among the measures proposed were many approaches which have enjoyed success in other jurisdictions including local community-based residential units, family placement schemes (akin to fostering), probation hostels, regional schools with a strong emphasis on outdoor pursuits, a training ship and, as a last resort, secure units. In this latter respect, it stressed that the authorities must employ only specialised and trained staff in such units and must apply very rigorous controls to ensure that each place is put to optimal use at all times and is used only by young people who absolutely require a secure place. It also recommended that a small number of residential treatment facilities be put in place to accommodate what it described as psychiatrically disturbed young offenders.

The final section of the Committee's recommendations focused on the contribution of other sectors to juvenile justice provision. In this regard, it highlighted the responsibilities and functions of such bodies in the area of crime prevention as follows: local authorities were encouraged to take more seriously their role in planning, the provision of recreational facilities and maintaining street lighting; health boards were urged to make effective provision for homeless children and children at risk, to consider establishing adolescent teams with representatives of the Probation and Welfare Service, youth services and the education system and to manage fostering schemes for children in trouble with the law. Further recommendations were made with regard to commerce and industry, the role of schools, particularly with regard to the reduction of truancy, expanding youth projects and the early identification of children at risk, and the importance in schools of civil and social education, physical education, and drug and alcohol education.

The Committee's conclusions and recommendations are set out in some detail here because they reflected and still reflect established consensus on how children in conflict with the law should be treated and how a progressive youth justice system should be structured and run: emphasis on positive early intervention, family support and education for those at risk of offending, a highly efficient and specialised youth justice system for those who offend, and a wide range of community and custodial sanctions for young people convicted of offences. The Committee made all the recommendations necessary to formulate a strategic plan for the drafting of new legislation designed to tackle the problem effectively. The fact that few of these principles – with the exception of detention as a last resort and the maximising of diversion – were included in the Children Act 2001 suggests that the appalling state of the current system is attributable not to those who have had the opportunity to propose reform, but to those who have chosen to ignore their recommendations. This, while some of the issues raised were taken into account during the drafting of the new legislation, many were not. The result is that despite its recommendations the problems identified so succinctly in the Report in 1992 remain the dominant and serious concerns of 2006. Indeed, the Committee's Report shares a large degree of similarity with the conclusions of the recent Youth Justice Review[22] and with the guidance of international standards.

The Impetus for Reform

Overall, it is clear that while a number of reports have made significant recommendations for change to the both the welfare and juvenile justice systems in Ireland since the late 1960s[23] they have been generally ignored by successive governments. While others have reflected on the numerous reasons for this failure to introduce much needed change,[24] the lack of political will can be identified as the principal reason for inaction. Youth justice is not a vote-winner; the numbers involved are relatively small and the children themselves have no political power. As to why change happened when it did, some argue that Ireland's international commitments under the CRC and the pressure brought to bear by the Committee on the Rights of the Child was influential.[25] While it is true that the compatibility of the Children Act 1908 with these standards was a cause for concern, the impetus for change is likely to be far more mundane, i.e. that the need to reform the legislation, which had been amended several times, was outmoded and complicated to work with, could no longer be avoided.[26] As Walsh explains: 'the need for reform was not seriously questioned. The only argument was over what shape the reforms should take and how and when they should be introduced.'[27]

The Children Bill 1996

Although the publication of the Dáil Select Committee Report in 1992 gave strong impetus to reform, it was 1996 before the new Children Bill was published. According to the Dáil Debates, the primary objective of the Bill was to update and streamline the legislation governing the whole area of juvenile crime, and the role of the courts and young offender centres in dealing with such crime.[28] In line with the recommendations of the Dáil Select Committee, the Bill was designed to update the Children Act 1908, comply with the CRC and put in place a statutory framework within which a modern juvenile justice system could be developed.[29] However, the dissolution of the Dáil in 1997 lead to the lapse of the Bill. While the further delay caused was regrettable, it was also advantageous insofar as it allowed the legislation to be subjected to further review.

The Children Bill 1999

The Children Bill was introduced into the Dáil in a radically altered state in 1999. While much of the Dáil debate appeared to concern the party political matter of to what extent the current Bill, prepared by the Government, differed from the former version, prepared by the Opposition, several opportunities were taken by John O'Donoghue, TD, Minister for Justice, Equality and Law Reform, to proudly reiterate the Bill's many distinguishing features. Describing it as 'one of the most important and far reaching Bills to have been brought before the House in many years', the Minister described it as a 'blueprint for a new system of juvenile justice which will charter the course of that system for many years to come'. Referring to it as 'balanced, comprehensive, innovative and imaginative', its provisions were, he stated, 'distillation of the accumulated wisdom and the best practice world-wide in the area of juvenile justice'. Like a proud father, the Minister modestly told the Dáil that he had produced an 'enlightened, enduring and forward thinking Bill' which will 'affect the lives of many thousands of children and their parents ... for the better'.[30] None of the questions or criticisms put to the Minister by the Opposition managed to dilute his overwhelming sense of satisfaction with the Bill he was presenting to the House or the content of the Bill itself.

THE CHILDREN ACT 2001: AN OVERVIEW

The Children Bill 1999 became law as the Children Act 2001 when it was signed by the President on 8 July 2001. Whether it lives up to the high praise heaped on it by its proud author is considered below and elsewhere in this book. In this section, however, it is proposed to outline the main features of the Act giving an indication, five years after its enactment, of the extent to which it has been implemented.[31] A further section below outlines some of the ninety-three amendments to the Act undertaken by the Criminal Justice Act 2006 and considers their likely impact.

The Act is said to put in place a modern statutory framework for the juvenile justice system[32] and in so doing it both repackages and replaces the provisions of the Children Act 1908 giving them a twenty-first-century make-over. Significantly, and consistent with the CRC, the Act defines the child as a person under the age of 18 years (s. 3) bringing all those who commit minor offences under that age within the juvenile justice system.[33] This is not insignificant as 'children', 'youthful offenders' and 'juvenile offenders' were all terms used to identify the different treatment those under 18 received under the criminal law. Although the choice of 'child' to describe those under 18 years is in line with the CRC, the term 'young people' would more accurately have described those between the ages of 12 and 18 to which the Act applies. It would also be more in line with practice in other jurisdictions.

More importantly, however, section 52 of the Act raises the age of criminal responsibility from 7 to 12 years meaning that children under that age will no longer be deemed to have the capacity to commit a criminal offence. Part 5 of the Act also places the common law presumption of *doli incapax* on a statutory basis with the effect that children between 12 and 14 years are presumed to be incapable of committing an offence because they did not know that what they were doing was wrong: this is a rebuttable presumption. This effectively raises to 14 the age at which a child can be tried for an offence and it is an important safeguard for those not mature enough to have the capacity to commit a criminal act. Finally, it makes provision for children under 12 who commit what would otherwise be a criminal act to be taken to their parents or to the Health Services Executive (HSE) if the apprehending Garda has reasonable grounds to believe that the child is not receiving adequate care or attention. Part 5 of the Act, containing these provisions, has not been commenced and is being substantially amended by the Criminal Justice Act 2006.[34]

For children over the age of criminal responsibility who commit an offence, diversion from prosecution via the Garda Diversion Programme is a possibility.[35] Where such a child admits responsibility for the crime committed and agrees to be cautioned, he/she may be admitted to the Programme and receive an informal or formal (or restorative if the victim is present) caution. The Juvenile Liaison Officer (JLO) may also decide to convene a family conference – inviting the child, his family, any victims of the child's offending and others involved in the child's life, such as a teacher, community worker or social worker – to draw up an action plan to prevent the child from re-offending. Part 4 of the Act, which places the Diversion Programme on a statutory footing, was commenced on 1 May 2002.[36]

Should the child reoffend or be refused or not considered for admission to the Garda Diversion Programme, he/she will be prosecuted and brought before the District Court, sitting as the Children Court.[37] Beforehand, he/she can be questioned at a Garda station but only within the strict terms of Part 6 of the Act, which sets out the child's right to be treated with respect, to have his/her parent present at questioning and to consult a solicitor. These provisions were commenced on 1 May 2002.[38]

Should the child appear before the Children Court, which must sit at a different time or place to the ordinary District Court, the child's parents are required to attend the proceedings, which must be held in private in order to protect the child's identity. At this stage of the process, the Act offers a wide range of approaches and sanctions designed to address if not also punish a child's offending behaviour. Section 77 is a key provision which aims to bridge the gap between the 'justice' and 'welfare' systems for children before the Children Court found to be in need or at risk. In such circumstances, the Court can divert the child to the attention of the HSE which is then required to undertake a family welfare conference with a view to deciding the best course of action to be taken to address the child's needs. This may include taking action under the Child Care Act 1991.[39] Section 77 has not yet been commenced.

Alternatively, where the child accepts responsibility for his/her behaviour, he/she may be directed to the attention of the Probation and Welfare Service for the purposes of a family conference – similar to that under the Garda Programme – designed to devise an action plan to prevent the child from re-offending. The action plan is subject to the supervision of the Court, which, depending on the child's compliance with its terms, can dismiss the charge or resume the proceedings against the child at any stage. The provisions relating to the Probation-led family conference were commenced on 23 September 2004.[40]

If the Court finds the child guilty of an offence it may order a Probation and Welfare Report or a Victim Impact Report to assist it in choosing the most appropriate sanction for the child. Moreover, Part 9 of the Act makes provision for a wide range of sanctions including an order for fines, costs or compensation; an order imposed on parents, such as a parental supervision order or an order that a parent be bound over; a community sanction, such as a probation order, a day centre order, an order restricting movement or an order requiring supervision by a suitable person or mentor, and an order placing a child in detention or combining detention with supervision in the community. When choosing between these available sanctions, the Children Court may take into account as mitigating factors the child's age and level of maturity and it must ensure that the measure interferes as little as possible with the child's education, training or employment; takes the form most likely to maintain and promote the development of the child; takes the least restrictive form appropriate in the circumstances and respects the principle of detention as a last resort. Few of these sanctions have been enacted with the exception of the order for costs, compensation and damages and the restriction on movement order, which were commenced on 1 May 2002.[41]

The Act prohibits the detention of a child in prison and provides, instead, that children under 16 years shall be detained in a Children Detention School (the industrial and reformatory schools) under the auspices of the Department of Education and Science, while those over 16 years must be detained in a Children Detention Centre under the auspices of the Department of Justice, Equality and Law Reform. These provisions, set out in Part 10 of the Act, have not been commenced.[42]

Although it principally legislates for existing practice in many areas, the Act also has many positive, new and innovative features. Principal among them are the three different types of conference – family welfare conferences run by the HSE under Part 2, family conferences run by the Gardaí under the Diversion Programme under Part 4, and family conferences ordered by the Children Court and run by the Probation and Welfare Service under Part 8. Based on the family conference model introduced into the youth justice system in New Zealand in 1989,[43] the core objective of the conference under the Children Act is to provide professional support to families in crisis in order to help them meet the needs of their child. The models run by the Gardaí and the Probation and Welfare Service also have a restorative function and are designed to resolve conflict between the child and his/her victim or society as a whole. While fears had been expressed that a child would be 'over-conferenced' (or alternatively end up a very skilful negotiator!) by virtue of being subjected to three different forms of conference, it is not envisaged that children will be subjected to all three conferences in practice, rather it is expected that the most suitable diversionary route will be chosen to meet the particular needs of each young person.[44] Nevertheless, where the Act is fully operational, it is not unlikely that a child who has had a family conference under the Garda Diversion Programme will have another organised by the Probation and Welfare Service by order of the Children Court. Care will have to be taken to ensure that lessons are learned from one conference to the other and that work is not duplicated unnecessarily in this area.

The other significant contribution of the Act is in the area of diversion from detention. Apart from recognising the principle of detention as a last resort, the Act puts it into practice – including as a mandatory sentencing principle to guide the courts – by providing for a broad range of community-based sanctions. These non-custodial alternatives to detention – which include residential placements, provision for attendance at day centres and vocational and training programmes, mentoring schemes and parental sanctions – are widely recognised to hold the key to preventing young people from re-offending.[45]

Despite these positive features, for the most part the Act simply updates and consolidates existing legislation governing the treatment of children in conflict with the law. While that is an important task, the legislation does not in itself overhaul or radically reform the youth justice system for twenty-first century Ireland. In contrast, proposals for change made pursuant to the Youth Justice Review, carried out by the Department of Justice, Equality and Law Reform in 2005, have this potential particularly in so far as they aim to put in place the infrastructure to co-ordinate implementation of the Act, which the Act itself failed to address. This is discussed below.

PROMISES AND POTENTIAL

The Act was broadly welcomed by those working with and for children in conflict with the law. At the time of its introduction, it was described as 'highly significant',[46] applauded for its 'daring and for its commitment to innovation'[47] and the Act's positive features and comprehensive nature were stressed.[48] Its attempt to reform the complex and difficult area of youth justice has been described as 'ambitious'.[49] The National Crime Council has referred to its potential to have 'a long-term beneficial impact on the development of enlightened strategies for a more inclusive response to crime and its causes'.[50]

Some commentators have been more sceptical of the Act's claims to be a 'radical departure from past practices'[51] and highlighted aspects of its content as a reiteration of standards contained elsewhere[52] or a repackaging and representation of current provision.[53] While others have recognised that the Act includes 'some significant opportunities for developing child-centred approaches and supports for those working with young people in difficulty', they have noted how these 'innovations are juxtaposed with proposals which appear to focus on placing blame and exacting retribution'.[54]

In general, the legislation was warmly welcomed although many expressed caution that co-ordination, funding and resources would be key to its ultimate success.[55] A commonly held view in this regard is that 'the success of the Act in truly reforming this area depends largely on putting the necessary resources in place to achieve its effective implementation. Training is also vital given the new challenges which implementation of the Act poses.'[56] According to the Special Residential Services Board, one of the agencies set up under the legislation, 'significant additional resources are required to implement the Act, particularly by the juvenile justice system, for the provision of facilities, a wide range of care and support services and for the implementation of community sanctions'.[57] The Children's Rights Alliance has noted that support for early intervention is also essential to the Act's implementation:

> Public investments in community and statutory services offering prevention, early intervention and diversion must be made if the Act is to be fully and successfully implemented. Its effective functioning will also require the full staffing of the social work and child care services which are currently experiencing severe shortages of workers.[58]

O'Sullivan expressed the view that the legislation (he was referring to the then Children Bill 1996) would not be sufficient in itself to reduce youth crime, rather there would have to be a holistic, integrated and comprehensive response to juvenile crime at a local and departmental level.[59] Others stressed the need for back-up services to enable the Probation-led parts of the Act to be effective.[60] The need for a genuine multi-agency approach was also seen as key to the Act's successful implementation.[61]

Whatever support was evident for the signing of the Act on 8 July 2001, the delay in commencing its various sections has since called into question the Government's commitment to the legislation. Repeated calls for its full and urgent implementation are made by non-governmental bodies, statutory agencies and those in Opposition. In 2003, the National Crime Council recommended strongly that the Act be 'fully implemented within a set time frame'.[62] The Irish Youth Justice Alliance, a coalition of solicitors, non-governmental bodies, academics and community organisations working in the area has also consistently called on the Government to implement and fully resource the Act. In 2005, submissions to the Project Team on the Irish Youth Justice System set up in the Department of Justice, Equality of Law Reform stressed the need to urgently implement and resource all parts of the legislation. As the Report on the Youth Justice Review explains: 'Many contributors were of the view that the provisions in the Children Act 2001 provide a sound legal basis for a modern youth justice system and stated that what was now required was the full implementation of the Act combined with the necessary resources to effectively support its implementation.'[63] The Irish Youth Justice Alliance, for example, has stressed the need for the Act's full and immediate implementation and called for a detailed plan and deadline to guide this process to be published without delay.[64]

Feature, news and opinion pieces in the newspapers, as well as in the letters pages, have also highlighted the urgent need to implement and fully resource the legislation. For example, Owen Keenan, then Chief Executive of Barnardos, wrote in February 2004 that 'slow implementation' and 'the failure by Government to resource it (the Act) adequately has meant that children continue to end up in crisis before the Children's Court'. In contrast, he noted how 'the astute and properly resourced implementation of the Children Act 2001 would open up a range of services to support children in trouble'.[65]

So, despite the recognised potential of the Act, and the considerable concensus that exists around the need to implement and resource it, a lack of urgency about its implementation appears to dominate political thinking. As Seymour highlights: 'the slow pace at which the Act is being implemented ... gives further credence to the view that juvenile justice is not a high priority on the political landscape'.[66]

COMMENCEMENT OF THE CHILDREN ACT 2001

Co-ordinating and Resourcing Implementation

The complexity and length of the Children Act 2001, combined with the spread of responsibility for its provisions across three government departments, meant that its implementation would always be a difficult task. The inter-dependent nature of its provisions complicated that process because it required all three government departments to act together. Accordingly, it was decided to implement the Act on a gradual basis.[67] After the Act was passed, responsibility for its implementation was given to Brian Lenihan, TD, Minister for State with special responsibility for Children who is supported in this role, with particular regard to the cross-cutting areas of the legislation, by the National Children's Office.[68] Given the Act's spread across three government departments, this was an important and prudent move. The junior minister's absence at the cabinet table and his lack of an independent budget frustrated this process however. In this way, the Government's decision in December 2005 to establish the Office of the Minister for Children, incorporating the National Children's Office, is a significant move which should improve co-ordination and implementation of the Children Act 2001.[69]

Despite the obvious challenges involved in the Act's implementation, there does not appear to have been a plan for bringing its provisions into force, no ring-fenced budget set aside for this purpose and there is currently no indication or commitment to a deadline when the Act will be fully operational.[70] Early estimates suggested that most of the Act would be in force by the end of 2003,[71] but the reality is reflected by the admission by Brian Lenihan, TD, that the Act is unlikely to be fully operational until 2008, the 100th anniversary of the Children Act 1908.[72] Given the rate of progress to date, this estimate, given in 2003, may not be met.

At the time of its introduction into the Dáil, the Minister for Justice, Equality and Law Reform explained that the most significant resource implications for his Department would arise in implementing the provisions relevant to the Probation and Welfare Service, which he estimated at almost £10 million (€12 million). The Department of Health and Children had received capital funding to enable them to put in place 100 high support and special care residential places by the end of 2001, and the Department of Education and Science was said to have a capital development plan for Children Detention Schools estimated to cost £20 million (€24 million), about half of which was attributed to its responsibilities under the legislation. According to the Minister, 'a co-ordinated plan to implement the Bill [was] well advanced' and plans had already been drawn up in his Department as a matter of urgency to ensure that the necessary number of additional professional and support staff would be in place 'to allow relevant parts of the Bill to come into operation at an early date'.[73]

Commencing the Act

The first Order commencing provisions of the Act was signed by the Minister for Justice, Equality and Law Reform on 1 May 2002.[74] This brought a substantial part of the Act into force – Part 4 placing the Diversion Programme on a statutory basis, Part 6 concerning the treatment of children in Garda custody, Part 7 relating to the Children Court and two of the community sanctions (fines/compensation orders and restriction of movement orders) under Part 9 of the Act. The reality, however, is that the commencement of these provisions had very little effect in operational or practical terms because they represented those parts of the Act that were already in place, or whose commencement required few resources.

On 6 November 2003, the second Commencement Order was signed by Brian Lenihan, TD, bringing Part 11 of the Act into force.[75] Part 11 places the Special Residential Services Board on a statutory footing, although the Board had been established on an interim basis since 2000. The Board has a specific duty to co-ordinate the use of places in Children Detention Schools although it also has a policy and advisory role.[76]

The third Commencement Order was signed, also by Brian Lenihan, TD, on 24 July 2004 bringing into force the provisions in Part 8 of the Act relating to Probation-led family conferencing. These provisions provide an entirely new option for the Children Court in dealing with young offenders, which aims to divert appropriate young people from conviction and sentence. Their effectiveness depends both on adequate awareness in the Children Court of the availability of family conference option, and the development of sufficient confidence among the judiciary that this option will secure an effective and just outcome for the young person and his/her victim. Moreover, the potential of the family conference to have a positive impact is linked not only to providing adequate staffing in the Probation and Welfare Service,[77] but to the availability of the services to which the action plan may direct the young person. The commencement of the family conference, while welcomed, was thus greeted with this concern. As the Irish Youth Justice Alliance noted:

> While there has been a marginal increase in the staffing of the Probation Service and training has taken place to prepare the Service to run family conferencing, no additional resources appear to have been made available to facilitate the full implementation of action plans. For example, if the conference identifies the need for the young person to receive treatment for alcohol or substance abuse, or to undertake a vocational training course, it is not clear what will happen when such a placement is not available due to a lack of resources. In this regard, only the provision of long-term funding for community groups as well as statutory agencies will allow Part 8 of the Act to be effectively implemented.[78]

This highlights the true cost of implementing fully the Children Act 2001 and the extent to which resourcing the infrastructure around the statutory agencies is also vital to its success.

The most recent Commencement Order was signed by the Minister of State at the Department of Health and Children on 30 September 2004; this brought into force significant sections of Parts 2 and 3 of the Act dealing with family welfare conferencing and the making of special care orders.[79]

The four commencement orders together mean that a substantial part of the Act has now been commenced. In particular, the innovative parts of the Act – the three different models of family conference – are now in place to give young people in conflict with the law a chance of early diversion either to the Health Service Executive where he/she has special needs,[80] to An Garda Síochána for a police caution, restorative conference or supervision by a Juvenile Liaison Officer, or the Probation and Welfare Service to draw up a family-oriented action plan to prevent the child from re-offending. While these are welcome developments, no further provisions of the Act have been commenced since September 2004 and key Parts remain unimplemented: Part 5 raising the age of criminal responsibility to 12; Part 10 on detention, and most of Part 9, on the alternatives to detention, remain outstanding. As discussed below, it is proposed to commence Part 5 (with amendments) in 2006. Although it is thought that the provisions in Part 10 concerning Children Detention Schools will be then also commenced, commencement of the remainder of Part 10 is dependent on the building of a detention centre for 16- and 17-year-olds and is thus some years away. Regarding Part 9, although the Minister for Justice suggested that the community sanctions would 'come on stream in mid-2004, subject to the availability of resources'[81] it was several months later in December 2004, that he announced to the Dáil that he had secured funding for thirty new staff at the Probation and Welfare Service to implement those specific provisions of the Act.[82] However, Part 9 is still not in force.

Overall, it is clear that both the delay in commencing the legislation and the piecemeal way in which it is being commenced cause serious concern. Implementation timetables that were made appear to have expired[83] and no further agenda for implementation has been published. This is extremely regrettable, not least given that even when the Act has been commenced in full, it will take some time – at least a decade – before its full impact is felt both by those working with and for young people in this area and, of course, the young people themselves. Moreover, the decision to introduce a wide range of amendments to the legislation in 2006, before it is all fully operational, confirms suspicions as to the level of political commitment to the area. There is also a general criticism to be made here about the extent to which this inaction on the part of the Executive represents an ignoring of the will of the Oireachtas, which so enthusiastically supported the legislation when it was going through the Dáil and the Seanad.

SHORTCOMINGS OF THE ACT

In the absence of its fully resourced implementation, it is difficult to measure the true potential of the Children Act to address offending behaviour, reduce young offending and to improve the lives of young people in conflict with the law.[84] Substantive criticisms of the Act have been relatively rare since its enactment; attention has focussed on its positive features and its potential lest any negativity be used to support political inertia or U-turn on support for the Act. This remains a serious concern given that the Criminal Justice Act 2006 – regarding the age of criminal responsibility, the introduction of Anti-Social Behaviour Orders, amendments to the treatment of children in detention and to the Garda Diversion Programme – threatens to undermine the Act's provisions and principles.[85]

While the amendments are discussed below, the following section questions whether the Children Act 2001 offers a panacea for the present problems of the system,[86] measures the extent to which it is consistent with international principles on youth justice and considers the outstanding areas of the youth justice system that require attention. In this regard, the discussion focuses on three substantive shortcomings of the Act: the lack of a rights framework, children who commit serious crime, and the Act's lack of administrative structures.

Compliance with International Standards: A Rights Approach

The book's Introduction highlights the many and diverse international standards on youth justice against which the Children Act 2001 can be usefully measured. Shannon notes that the Children Act 2001 reflects 'neither a welfare nor a justice model of youth justice. Rather, it reflects a rights-based approach, imported in large from international imperatives'.[87] This statement is only partially true: while international principles are reflected in the Act, it contains little if any express recognition of the rights of young offenders.[88] Absent from the Act, as statements of principle, are the fundamental children's rights provisions prohibiting discrimination between children, requiring that the child's best interests are a primary consideration in all matters concerning the child, and recognising the right of every child to be heard and to participate in relevant decision-making processes set out in articles 2, 3 and 12 of the CRC.[89] Where references to these principles do occur – and they are rare – they are confined to particular areas or decision-making powers within the Act and are not generally applicable. Moreover, they are invariably juxtaposed with consideration for the victim's rights and the interests of society. For example, when deciding to admit a child to the Garda Diversion Programme, the Director must be satisfied that it is in the interests of the child, but also that it would not be inconsistent with the interests of any victim of the child's offending or the interests of society.

Absent from the Act too are clear objectives as to the purpose of the youth justice system. The Act does not contain any commitment to the principles of youth justice or recognise the duties of statutory agencies to exercise their functions in line with these principles. One welcome exception to this is the principle of detention as a last resort, which is expressly recognised in the Act as a mandatory sentencing principle and also effectively implemented by a range of community sanctions.[90] Significantly, too, An Garda Síochána are required to act with due respect for the personal rights of children (s. 55), and the courts must have regard to the principle that children have rights and freedom before the law equal to those enjoyed by adults and, in particular, a right to be heard and to participate in any proceedings of the court that can affect them (s. 96). However, these provisions are confined to their own circumstances and are not broad-based principles designed to apply throughout the system.

Overall, the legislation fails expressly to require respect for the rights of the child in all parts of the youth justice system regardless of which statutory agency or body is involved. Nor does it, in general terms, recognise the rights of young people in conflict with the law to special protection, to age-appropriate treatment, to consideration for his/her welfare, to diversion from the criminal justice system and from detention, and to a proportionate and fair response to his/her offending as required by international standards.[91] As a result, Ireland is undoubtedly falling short of its international obligations. In particular, the Committee on the Rights of the Child has made it clear that effective implementation of the CRC requires the incorporation of its basic principles into legislation in all areas.[92] At the very least, therefore, it is recommended that the CRC's basic principles should be inserted into the Children Act 2001 to ensure that in all cases it is implemented in line with international standards.

Children and Serious Crime

The vast majority of offences committed by children and young people are of a minor nature such as theft and public order. These children are usually eligible for admission to the Garda Diversion Programme or, if prosecuted, they are tried before the specially adapted Children Court which operates *in camera* to protect their identity and is otherwise mindful of their young age and immaturity. When the Children Act is fully implemented, the Children Court will be able to apply a wide range of community sanctions to children convicted of minor offences.

When a young person commits a serious or indictable offence, however, many of these safeguards do not apply. Such young people are highly unlikely to be eligible for admission to the Garda Diversion Programme, they are tried in the public and adult environment of the Circuit or Central Criminal Court, which is not adapted for this purpose[93] and outside of the Children Court they are unlikely to have measures taken in recognition of their age and lack of maturity. To this differential treatment the Criminal Justice Act 2006 has added a much more important factor – a lower age of criminal responsibility – which will mean that children over ten years will be prosecuted if they commit serious crimes of rape, murder or manslaughter whereas only those over twelve will be prosecuted for minor offences.[94]

Overall, it is not clear what consideration has been given to the application of the Children Act and indeed of youth justice principles generally to young people who commit serious crime. Although some jurisdictions exempt children who commit serious crimes from the youth system altogether and try them as adults either on a blanket or a case-by-case basis,[95] other states make no distinction between children on the basis of the crime committed.[96] Irish law does not appear to have given full consideration to either scenario, although it is clear that Parts 7 and 8 of the Children Act (protecting the child's identity from being published or broadcast, keeping the child separate from adults before court proceedings, referring the child to the Probation and Welfare Service for a family conference or to the Health Service Executive for a family welfare conference) do not apply outside the Children Court. Significantly, however, Part 9 of the Act is not limited to the Children Court – thus section 96, which recognises that any court dealing with a child charged with an offence must have regard to the fact that they have rights and freedoms before the law equal to those enjoyed by adults – applies to the Circuit and Central Criminal Courts, as does section 98 setting out the range of probation orders and community sanctions that can be applied when a Court is satisfied of the guilt of a child charged with an offence.[97] The duty on An Garda Síochána under section 55 of the Children Act to respect the rights of children also applies regardless of the nature of offence being investigated.[98] Generally, however, there is a need to give serious consideration to how children who commit serious crimes should be treated with particular reference to adapting the trial process. The Children Act 2001 should be amended accordingly to ensure that all of its principles apply where appropriate to all children.

Lack of Infrastructure

Official reports into aspects of the child care and juvenile justice systems have routinely expressed concern about the issue of accountability for the administration of youth justice and co-ordination between government departments. In 1974, for example, the Henchy Report noted that a 'lack of coordination in the efforts of the wide range of public bodies and agencies' with a role in dealing with the problem of juvenile delinquency compounded the causes of juvenile crime.[99] In 1980, the Task Force on Child Care Services noted that various services for deprived children and children at risk were initiated and developed in a 'piecemeal fashion' and in particular, that the existing allocation of ministerial responsibility for children's services between the Departments of Health, Education and Justice represented an 'unsatisfactory situation from the point of view of effective planning and co-ordination of resources'.[100] In response, it recommended that a new approach was needed requiring the whole range of relevant services to be integrated with family support services and as far as possible, these should be integrated under one government department, namely the Department of Health which would take responsibility for school attendance, the Children Court, residential centres and special schools. The Task Force also recommended that the Department of Health should establish an interdepartmental committee so that close liaison could be maintained between that department and other departments concerned with services for children over which the Department of Health did not exercise direct control. Further recommendations included the establishment of a national children's council to make recommendations on the development of the child-care system and to enhance co-operation between the various bodies and persons engaged in the area.[101]

Although it does not address how to support or facilitate inter-agency co-operation, it is clear that the implementation of the Children Act 2001 depends on it. According to the Minister for State with special responsibility for children, Brian Lenihan, TD:

> Inter-agency co-operation is at the heart of the Act and effective co-ordination and communication are fundamental to its successful implementation. With the co-operation of professionals and agencies involved in delivering services to children at risk and the involvement of children, parents and guardians we can all work to ensure that the most appropriate course of action is taken to meet the needs of each individual child.[102]

Nevertheless, poor co-ordination and communication between

the agencies and governmental departments with responsibility has a detrimental impact on the youth justice system and the children in it. Research into the Children Court concluded, for example, that 'lack of coordination between agencies and poor management of cases causes confusion and delay'.[103] The lack of clarity in government roles in the area has a serious impact on delivery of services within the system as responsibility shared allows children to fall between two stools. According to the Director of Youthreach:

> [t]o a considerable degree, services operate on the basis of hoping that someone else will do the dirty work. This also works in reverse, with those providing services to young people and their families succumbing to mission drift and attempting to resolve all the child's difficulties even though many are outside their compass, for example a Youthreach co-ordinator trying to sort out a housing problem for a participant on the basis that the problem is blocking any prospect of learning. Those who do so usually explain that nobody else is addressing the need and they are generally justified in this view.[104]

Similarly, the National Crime Council has noted that:

> [t]he current allocation of responsibilities between departments and arrangements for inter-departmental co-ordination are unlikely to yield the degree of joint planning and implementation which seems to be required to make a serious and lasting impression on crime. Some new framework will be required, drawing together the various strands of public policy making and also incorporating a wider community view.[105]

The Council also commented on what it described as an 'environment of competition and criticism among agencies'.[106]

The problem of co-ordination was at the heart of contributions to the Youth Justice Review undertaken by the Department of Justice, Equality and Law Reform in 2005.[107] According to the Report:

> [m]any contributors pointed to the fact that while a large number of organisations are involved in delivering youth justice services – the Garda Síochána, Probation and Welfare Service, Prison Service, Health Service Executive – no single agency has the power to co-ordinate service delivery or compel specific action from the agencies. Many contributors regarded the division of responsibility for youth justice across three Government Departments – Justice, Equality and Law Reform, Education and Science and Health and Children – as contributing to an ad hoc approach to addressing the multiple problems of youth offenders.[108]

A further more general conclusion of the Youth Justice Review was that the Irish youth justice system needs leadership to ensure effective management in the implementation of a cross-cutting youth justice policy to underpin an effective and co-ordinated approach to addressing the many aspects of youth offending.[109]

The lack of co-ordination among agencies at local level was also identified as a significant barrier to the effectiveness of the youth justice system in the Youth Justice Review. In particular, the Report found that 'at local level there is a need for Government agencies, in collaboration with the Community/Voluntary Sector, to continue to work together in order to enhance the development of an integrated approach to dealing with young offenders and those at risk of offending'.[110] It recognised that, given the large number of agencies and professionals involved in delivering services within the youth justice system, effective communication and co-ordination at a local level is critical to ensuring cohesion in the State's response to dealing with young offenders, children at risk of offending and their families.

Accordingly, the Review recommended the establishment of a Youth Justice Service to 'bring together services for young offenders under one governance and management structure'. While it noted that this body would sit most comfortably within a care and social services environment, reflecting practice elsewhere, the fact that 'no existing social service structure seems appropriate for the incorporation of a youth care and justice service at this time'[111] persuaded it to recommend placing the body within the Department of Justice, Equality and Law Reform on an interim basis. The objectives of this office, whose position is to be reviewed in five years, are to develop a specific youth justice policy from a single unified perspective; have responsibility for services for young offenders including detention, community sanctions, restorative justice conferencing and diversion projects; and improve the delivery of services through the development of national and local mechanisms to drive change.[112]

The recommendations of the Youth Justice Review in this area, notably the establishment of the Youth Justice Service, have the potential to radically reform the youth justice system including to successfully oversee the implementation and operation of the Children Act 2001. In fact, it is arguable that they have greater potential than the Act itself to reform how youth justice is administered in practice. While the decision in December 2005 to place this Service within the framework of the new Office of the Minister for Children is welcome, it is unfortunate that an independent statutory agency, staffed by those qualified and trained in youth justice standards and approaches, was not considered for this purpose. It is also notable that the reference to its bi-location at the Department of Justice, Equality and Law Reform may give rise to future confusion. In any event, it is vital that the Service make a commitment from the outset to be guided in its work by Ireland's international children's rights obligations and to ensure that all other statutory agencies and bodies in the system operate according to international standards and principles of youth justice.

AMENDMENTS TO THE CHILDREN ACT 2001

Although the Criminal Justice Act 2006 amends the Children Act 2001 in order to implement the recommendations of the Youth Justice Review – including, for example, moving responsibility for detention schools from the Department of Education and Science to the Department of Justice, Equality and Law Reform and reducing the Special Residential Services

Board to an advisory role – other substantive amendments to the Act are also proposed. While these are set out where relevant in the chapters below, two of the principal amendments are considered here.

Age of Criminal Responsibility

Ireland's low age of criminal responsibility has been roundly criticised by national and international bodies,[113] and the recommendation to raise it to 12 was made by many bodies following lengthy deliberation and careful consideration of the issue.[114] Although the Children Bill 1996 proposed to raise the age to 10, it also made provision for raising it eventually to 12 years. This incremental approach was heavily criticised by John O'Donoghue, TD, Minister for Justice, Equality and Law Reform, when introducing the 1999 Bill, which raised the age from 7 to 12, to the Dáil. Indeed, declaring that this was 'an area where we have to make up our minds and act decisively', he declared himself 'proud to be the Minister who has made this decision'.

The relevant part of the 2001 Act has remained uncommenced and ministerial statements made throughout 2005 suggested a tacit, or in the case of the Minister for Justice, Equality and Law Reform, Mr McDowell TD, a quite explicit intention to roll back on this statutory commitment and raise the age to 10 years instead.[115] According to the Minister, the rationale for this decision arose from his discussions with the Minister of State with special responsibility for Children, Brian Lenihan TD. As Mr McDowell explained:

> We believe that the Children Act was unduly optimistic in claiming that no child could commit a criminal offence under the age of 12 years. ... Raising the age from seven to ten years is a reasonable step, but the use of reason comes into play around that time in a child's development. It could seriously scandalise public perceptions of criminal justice if 11 or 12 year old rapists went unpunished, were told their offences were bad behaviour and society did nothing about it, particularly now that 11 year old children are getting pregnant, as we read about during the

summer. We could have a serious collapse of social confidence in our criminal justice system, especially now that children mature younger and are engaged in sexual behaviour, if all sexual activity up to the age of 12 years was, in every circumstance, regarded as being incapable of being criminal.[116]

The proposal to amend Part 5 of the Children Act 2001 was published in January 2006 as part of the Criminal Justice Bill 2004 and contrary to the above statement the age is to be raised to 12 years for all but those charged with serious crimes, for whom the relevant age will be 10 years. According to these amendments, section 52 of the Act, which raises the age at which a child was 'capable of committing an offence', to 12 years, will be repealed and replaced with a new section 52, subsection (1) of which provides that 'no child under 12 years will be charged with an offence'. According to subsection (2), this does not apply to a child charged aged 10 or 11 years who is charged with murder, manslaughter, rape or aggravated sexual assault. Subsection (3) abolishes the principle of *doli incapax*,[117] and subsection (4) provides for referral to the Garda Diversion Programme of a child aged 10 or 11 years who cannot be charged.

The age of criminal responsibility is a complex issue and an important part of the youth justice system. There are both legal and policy reasons for choosing a meaningful age below which children cannot be subjected to the criminal law. In relation to the former, it is arguable that children, particularly young children, do not have the legal capacity to commit a crime, i.e. they do not understand that what they are doing constitutes a serious wrong as opposed to something which is merely bold or naughty. From the policy point of view, it is also important to recognise that for some children any involvement in the youth justice system will have harmful effects that should be avoided. This also recognises that children below a certain age, who are in conflict with the law, deserve the attention of the social or welfare services of the State, and not the crude, punitive instrument of criminal law. Thus, as explained succinctly by the previous Minister for Justice, John O'Donoghue, TD when introducing the Children Bill 1999 into the Dáil, 'That is not to say that children under twelve cannot do wrong, but rather that the invocation of criminal law is not the appropriate response for such young wrongdoers.'[118] This is reflected in the practice of other states where children below the age of criminal responsibility are diverted to the attention of the welfare rather than the criminal justice agencies. Indeed, the same approach is incorporated into the Irish system under Part 5 of the Children Act 2001 which provides that children under the age of criminal responsibility who come to the attention of An Garda Síochána should be brought to the attention of the HSE in certain circumstances. It is simply a matter of the age at which the response should be protective rather than punitive.

The current proposals are to raise the age of criminal responsibility to 10 for serious offences, which will be prosecuted, to raise it to 12 for other offences but to divert those 11- and 12-year-olds who cannot be prosecuted to the Garda Diversion Programme. Thus, children below twelve who come to the attention of An Garda Síochána will either be prosecuted, where their crime is very serious, or admitted to the Garda Diversion Programme. Those over 12 will also either be considered for admission to the Diversion Programme or prosecuted. This will ensure that for serious crimes, Ireland has one of the lowest ages of criminal responsibility in Europe and leaves us is in the company of the US and England and Wales.[119] The potential net-widening effect – where children who have not committed a criminal offence (i.e. cannot be charged) are nonetheless brought to the attention of the Gardaí and thus enter the criminal justice system – is also clear from the other proposals affecting children under 12 years.

Ireland's international obligations are also relevant here. Article 40(3)(a) of the Convention on the Rights of the Child requires that states establish a minimum age below which children shall be presumed not to have the capacity to infringe the criminal law. The removal of the reference to 'capacity' in Section 52 and its replacement with a decision to prosecute is thus directly contrary to this position. According to the Beijing Rules, that age 'shall not be fixed at too low an age level, bearing in mind the facts of emotional, mental and intellectual maturity'.[120] While neither instruments advocate a particular age, the Commentary to the Beijing Rules notes that fixing the age at too low a level risks the issue of responsibility being meaningless. It also advises that there is a 'close relationship' between the notion of responsibility for criminal behaviour and other social rights and responsibilities (such as marital status and civil majority). These principles clearly advocate an age of criminal responsibility at the higher end of the scale and in support of this, the Committee on the Rights of the Child expressed concern at Ireland's low age when considering Ireland's implementation of the CRC in 1998.[121] During its meeting with the Government delegation, the Committee criticised the Government's decision to raise the age to 10 saying it was 'insufficient' given the 'drastic consequences' that children may face when they come into contact with the criminal justice system.[122]

The intention of the Minister for Justice to legislate for an age of criminal responsibility of 10 is contrary both to the prevailing approach in other jurisdictions and to Ireland's international obligations. It is also contrary to the ethos of the Children Act 2001 itself as succinctly observed by the Minister's predecessor John O'Donoghue, TD, who commented in the Dáil that 'as a general rule it seems contradictory to have a piece of legislation whose focus is more on rehabilitation and deterrence than on retribution and then continue to allow possible prosecution of a child who is between the ages of seven and twelve'.[123]

Nevertheless, the current Minister for Justice, Equality and Law Reform is not alone in his view that there are factors other than the welfare of the child that should indicate whether he/she should be prosecuted.[124] This approach allows the circumstances of the individual child to determine whether he/she should be prosecuted, rather than the nature of the crime, consistent with the values of youth justice which require the focus on the offender not the offence. Moreover, regarding the proposal to distinguish between those who commit serious crimes who can be prosecuted at 10 years of age, and those who commit less serious offences, who cannot be prosecuted until age 12, it is worth remembering the view of the Scottish Kilbrandon Report which expressed the view that 'it might be thought that the more serious the offence the more the offender should be subject to procedures which are imbued with welfare considerations'.[125] On this issue, the Scottish Law Commission recognised in 2002 that the age of criminal responsibility expresses important values about the ways in which society should deal with young children who offend. Its recommendation of a fixed age of 12 years (chosen due to the similarity with a child's capacity in civil law) was based mainly on the principle that the criminal process is not a suitable mechanism for dealing with children under that age.[126]

While there is a serious issue as to whether setting the age of criminal responsibility at 10 will continue to be compliant with Article 3 of the European Convention on Human Rights (ECHR),[127] it is also difficult to see from the European Court's judgments how an adult court can be adapted sufficiently to ensure that children as young as 10 receive a fair trial. The cases of *T* v. *UK* and *V* v. *UK*, who were 11 years old during their trial for the murder of toddler James Bulger, thus raise serious questions as to whether the court can be altered sufficiently to ensure that a child so young can participate in and understand the criminal process.[128] The current proposals are problematic for all of these reasons and have been opposed by both the Human Rights Commission and the Ombudsman for Children.[129]

Good Behaviour Contracts and Anti-Social Behaviour Orders

A further layer is to be added to the youth justice system by virtue of the addition of a new Part 12A to the Children Act 2001 dealing with Good Behaviour Contracts (GBCs) and Anti-Social Behaviour Orders (ASBOs) in respect of those between 12 and 18 years.

According to the new section 257A, Anti-Social Behaviour (ASB) is defined as behaviour that caused or was likely to cause harassment; significant or persistent alarm, distress, fear or intimidation or significant or persistent impairment of their use or enjoyment of their property. Where a Garda brings to the attention of the Superintendent that a child has committed such behaviour, and continues to do so despite a 'Behaviour Warning' to desist, the Superintendent may convene a meeting to discuss the behaviour of a child. The meeting is intended to involve the child, his/her parents, the Garda who gave the warning and the Juvenile Liaison Officer if the child is in the

Garda Diversion Programme. If the Superintendent is of the view that the child has committed ASB he shall explain to the child and his/her parents in simple language what the behaviour is and what its effects are. The child and his parents will be asked to acknowledge that the behaviour has occurred and be asked to take measures to stop it. If this happens, a Good Behaviour Contract, lasting no more than six months, is then drawn up and signed by both parents and child. If the child has continued or is in danger of further committing ASB, the Superintendent may reconvene the meeting, consider admitting the child to the Garda Diversion Programme or apply for an ASBO.

ASBOs are to be made by the Children Court under Section 257D in civil proceedings on application by a Garda of at least Superintendent rank. The application must include the extent to which the child has been subjected to other preventive steps and the Court may make an ASBO if it is satisfied that the child is over 12, notwithstanding the application of the above procedures has continued or is likely to continue in an anti-social manner, and the order is necessary in the circumstances. Earlier proposals provided that in deciding whether these requirements are met the court shall have regard to:

(a) the particular circumstance of the person affected, and whether the behaviour would have the same effect on a reasonable person in such circumstances;
(b) the number of occasions on which the behaviour has occurred;
(c) the likelihood of recurrence;
(d) the need for a proportionate response; and
(e) the application of the principle of minimum interference.

However, these were subsequently deleted. The order can be made for up to two years and any child behaving in breach of an ASBO can be arrested without warrant. Breach of an ASBO is criminal offence which may result in a criminal conviction and the application of penal sanctions including detention.

A critical evaluation of ASBOs is undertaken in Chapter Six.[131] However, a number of points fall to be made here. While this model of ASBO has clearly been adapted to fit into the framework of the Children Act 2001 and avoid the problems of the model used in England and Wales, it is unclear what role it is intended to fill given the range of mechanisms already at the disposal of An Garda Síochána and the Courts in this area. In particular, it is difficult to distinguish between the meeting to be convened by the Superintendent to draw up a Good Behaviour Contract and the family conference to be convened under the Garda Diversion Programme, particularly given that it is proposed to expand the Programme to include anti-social behaviour also. In short, this appears to add a further unnecessary layer to the system with the effect of bringing into the criminal justice system at an earlier stage those children whose behaviour is not criminal. The consequences of this vote-winning measure may be a net-widening device of considerable proportions. Application for an ASBO is clearly to be made only when the GBC option has failed or is deemed inappropriate. Given all the procedures to be followed before a Superintendent can apply for such an order, and the factors to be taken into account by the Court before it makes an ASBO, not to mention the resources required to police it, one wonders whether the child will simply be prosecuted instead. Its operation in practice will be the proof of which is the preferred option.

CONCLUSION

O'Sullivan argues that 'considerable efforts will have to be taken to overturn the virtual neglect of the issue of juvenile justice since the foundation of the Irish State'.[130] The passing of the Children Act 2001 marked the beginning of the revolution that is required to undertake this massive task. Despite retrograde amendments to the Act in the Criminal Justice Act 2006, the ongoing implementation of its positive elements is a vital continuation of that process to which the fulfilment of the objectives set by the Youth Justice Review will add much strength if not speed.

Reservations about the level of political commitment to the Act's full implementation and indeed to the whole area of youth justice are inevitable given the many reports that prompted but did not deliver action in this area in the last decades of the twentieth century. The fact that many of the problems identified by the Youth Justice Review were identified by the Task Force on Child Care Services twenty-five years earlier does not give cause for optimism. Focus on infrastructure and leadership at this time is welcome nonetheless, and has the potential to bring about lasting and effective change. The establishment of a Youth Justice Service with a commitment to the principles of youth justice has enormous potential to set high standards to inform the operation of the system. The alleviation of all the other problems identified here could and should flow from this.

NOTES

1 Walsh, D., *Juvenile Justice* (Dublin: Thomson Round Hall, 2005), p. 2.
2 O'Mahony, P., 'Contextualising the Children Bill as a response to Youth Crime', conference paper delivered at the National Conference of Youthreach Co-ordinators, Carrickmacross, Co. Monaghan, 12 February 2001 available at www.youthreach.ie (accessed 6 January 2006).
3 The most important amendments were made by the Children Act 1941, the Children (Amendment) Act 1957 and the Criminal Justice Act 1960. See Walsh, D., *Juvenile Justice*, p. 2.
4 *Ibid.*, p. 465.
5 *Report of the Committee on Reformatory and Industrial Schools Systems* (Dublin: Stationery Office, 1970) Prl 1342 (The Kennedy Report). See further Walsh, D., *ibid.*, pp. 468–72.
6 See further Chapter Five below.
7 Walsh, D., *Juvenile Justice*, p. 471.
8 *First Interim Report of the Interdepartmental Committee on Mentally Ill and Maladjusted Persons* (Dublin: Stationery Office, 974) Prl 4688 in Walsh, D., *ibid.*, pp. 472–4.
9 Para 1.4, cited in Walsh, D., *ibid.*, p. 473.
10 *Second Interim Report of the Interdepartmental Committee on Mentally Ill and Maladjusted Persons, The Provision of Treatment for Juvenile Offenders and Potential Juvenile Offenders* (Dublin: Stationery Office, 1974), Prl 4689 in Walsh, D., *ibid.*, pp. 473–4.
11 Task Force on Child Care Services, *Final Report* (Dublin: Stationery Office, 1980) Prl 9345, in Walsh, D., *ibid.*, pp. 475–81.
12 Some members of the Task Force dissented from this view and recommended that the age be raised to 15 years. Walsh, *ibid.*, p. 478.
13 See further Chapter Five below.
14 Walsh, D., *Juvenile Justice*, p. 478.
15 Dáil Select Committee on Crime, '*Juvenile Crime – its Causes and its Remedies*' (Dublin: Stationery Office, 1992).
16 *Ibid.*, p. 37.

17 *Ibid.*, pp. 38–9.
18 *Ibid.*, p. 50.
19 *Ibid.*, pp. 53–4.
20 *Ibid.*, p. 62.
21 See further Chapter Seven below.
22 *Report on the Youth Justice Review* (Dublin: Department of Justice, Equality and Law Reform, 2005) available at www.justice.ie (accessed 4 January 2006).
23 See, for example, The Kennedy Report and *Report of the Committee to Enquire into the Penal System* (The Whittaker Report) (Dublin: Stationery Office, 1985).
24 See O'Sullivan, E., 'Juvenile Justice in the Republic of Ireland: Future Priorities', 14(3/4) *Irish Social Worker* (Autumn/Winter 1996), pp. 4–7 and O'Dwyer, K., 'Juvenile Crime and Justice in Ireland' in Bala, N. et al. (eds), *Juvenile Justice Systems: An International Comparison of Problems and Solutions,* (Toronto: Thompson Educational Publishing, 2002) pp. 153–88.
25 Seymour, M., 'Juvenile Justice in the Republic of Ireland', Prepared for the Thematic Working Group on Juvenile Justice, European Society of Criminology, available at www.esc-eurocrim.org (accessed 13 October 2005).
26 Quinn, M., 'Youth Crime Prevention' in O'Mahony, P., (ed.), *Criminal Justice in Ireland* (Dublin: IPA, 2002) p. 678.
27 Walsh, D., *Juvenile Justice*, p. 4.
28 *Dáil Debates*, Vol. 460, Col 1436 (23 January 1996) in Walsh, D., *ibid.*, fn 17, p. 5.
29 *Dáil Debates*, Vol. 474, Col 1353-1393 (12 February 1997).
30 *Dáil Debates*, Vol. 517, Col 33-34 (29 March 2000).
31 Only those provisions concerning youth justice matters are concerned here.
32 See generally Walsh, D., *Juvenile Justice*.
33 Those who commit serious offences are treated outside this regime however. See further Chapter Five below.
34 See below.
35 See further Chapter Three.
36 SI No 151 of 2002. Children Act 2001 (Commencement) Order 2002. On the diversion programme see further O'Dwyer, K., 'Juvenile Crime and Justice in Ireland' and Chapter Three below.
37 See further Chapter Five below.
38 SI No 151 of 2002. Children Act 2001 (Commencement) Order 2002. See further Chapter Four below.
39 See further Shannon, G., *Child Law* (Dublin: Thomson Round Hall, 2004) .
40 SI no 468 of 2004. See further Chapter Six below.
41 SI No 151 of 2002. Children Act 2001 (Commencement) Order 2002. See Chapter Six below.
42 See further Chapter Seven on the places of detention for children and

below for the details of the current changes to these provisions of the Act.

43 See Maxwell, G. and Morris, A., 'Juvenile Crime and Justice in New Zealand' in Bala, N. et al. (eds) *Juvenile Justice Systems,* p. 220. Under the New Zealand model, family conferences are used principally to support the court in the sentencing process.

44 Irish Association for the Study of Delinquency, *Children Act 2001 Effective Family Conferencing: the Challenges and Implications for Ireland in the new Legal Environment* Sixth Annual Conference, Dublin, 9 October 2003 (IASD: Dublin, 2004) pp. 23–4.

45 See Breaking Through, *Submission to the Department of Justice, Equality and Law Reform*, November 2004, at www.breakingthrough.ie (accessed 16 January 2006).

46 Murphy, C., 'Key Features of the Children Bill 1999' in *The Children Bill 1999*, papers from a seminar organised by the Children's Legal Centre (unpublished).

47 O'Dea, P., 'Family Conferences in the Children Bill 1999', *ibid.*, p. 17.

48 Raftery, G., 'The Children Bill 1999: Opportunities and Challenges for Practice', *ibid.*, p. 31.

49 Kilkelly, U., The Rights of Children in Conflict with the Law', *Irish Association for the Study of Delinquency Conference 2002 Youth Justice – Human Rights/Needs* (Dublin: IASD, 2002), p. 34

50 National Crime Council, A *Crime Prevention Strategy for Ireland – Tackling the Concerns of Local Communities* (Dublin: The Stationery Office, 2003), p. 55.

51 O'Sullivan, E., 'The Children Bill 1999: Responsibility and Regulation', in *The Children Bill 1999,* p. 9.

52 Ring, M.E., Treatment of Child Suspects in Garda Stations', *ibid.,* p. 21. O'Mahony commented that features of the 1908 Act – 'the possibility of restitution and a form of mentoring and some attempt to mobilise parents to act in a positive way' – were echoed in the new legislation. O'Mahony, P., 'Contextualising the Children Bill as a Response to Youth Crime'.

53 See Walsh, D., *Juvenile Justice*, pp. 5–7.

54 Quinn, M., 'Youth Crime Prevention', p. 679.

55 O'Dea, P., 'Family Conferences in the Children Bill 1999', p. 20 and Raftery, G., 'The Children Bill 1999: Opportunities and Challenges for Practice', p. 32. This claim was still being made in 2005. *Irish Times*, 15 December 2005.

56 Kilkelly, U., 'The Rights of Children in Conflict with the Law', pp. 34–5.

57 Special Residential Services Board, at www.srsb.ie (accessed 6 January 2006).

58 Dooley, R., and Corbett, M., 'Child Care, Juvenile Justice and the Children Act 2001', *Irish Youthwork Scene: A Journal for Youth Workers*, Issue 36 (Dublin: National Youth Federation, 2002).

59 O'Sullivan, E., 'Juvenile Justice in the Republic of Ireland: Future Priorities'.

60 P. O'Dea, 'Family Conferences in the Children Bill 1999'.

61 Kilkelly, U., The Rights of Children in Conflict with the Law', p. 34. See also Kilkelly, U., *The Children's Court: A Children's Rights Audit* (Cork, 2005), p. 91.
62 National Crime Council, A *Crime Prevention Strategy for Ireland*, p. 55.
63 *Youth Justice Review*, p. 30.
64 Submission of the IYJA to the Department of Justice, Equality and Law Reform's Project Team on the Irish Juvenile Justice System, 24 November 2004, available on www.iprt.ie (accessed 14 October 2005).
65 *Irish Times*, 25 February 2004.
66 Seymour, M., 'Juvenile Justice in the Republic of Ireland', p. 20.
67 Lenihan, B., 'Opening Address' in IASD, *Children Act 2001*, p. 8.
68 *Ibid.*
69 The Youth Justice Service is now 'co-located' at this Office, of which Ms Sylda Langford, who chaired the Youth Justice Review, is the newly appointed Director-General. Department of Health and Children, *Press Release*, 13 December 2005 at www.health.ie (14 January 2006). See also *Irish Times*, 14 December 2005.
70 One vague timetable of implementation indicated 2006 as a 'target date' for full implementation. Spillane, F. and Fisher, E., 'The Children Act 2001,' An Overview and Current Position' in IASD, *Children Act 2001*, p. 20.
71 Minister Lenihan suggested in 2003 that eleven of the thirteen Parts of the Act would be commenced by the end of that year. Lenihan, B., 'A new way of dealing with juvenile justice!' Irish Association of Social Workers Seminar, *The Children Act, 2001: Implications for Children's Services for the Future*, 30 April 2003 available at www.nco.ie (12 January 2006).
72 *Sunday Tribune*, 30 November 2003.
73 *Dáil Debates*, Vol. 517, Col. 33–34 (29 March 2000).
74 SI No 151 of 2002 Children Act 2001 (Commencement) Order 2002.
75 SI No 527 of 2003 Children Act 2001 (Part 11) (Commencement) Order 2003.
76 See further Chapter Seven. The SRSB is to lose its co-ordinating role under the reforms proposed in the Criminal Justice Act 2006.
77 In 2004, the Comptroller and Auditor-General found that while funding to the Probation and Welfare has increased in recent years, staffing of the Service is below the level recommended in the First Report of the Expert Group on the PWS in 1998. See Comptroller and Auditor-General, *Report on Value for Money Examination, The Department of Justice, Equality and Law Reform: The Probation and Welfare Service* (Dublin: Stationery Office, 2004), para. 3.31.
78 Submission of the Irish Youth Justice Alliance to the Department of Justice, Equality and Law Reform's Project Team, p. 2.
79 Children Act 2001 (Commencement) (No. 2) Order 2004 (SI No. 548 of 2004). These parts of the Act, which also amend the Child Care Act 1991, are not dealt with here. See further Shannon, G., *Child Law* pp. 398–406.
80 Section 77, the innovative provision which allows the Children Court to divert a child brought before it on a criminal matter to the attention of the Health Service Executive for a family welfare conference has not been commenced however. It is amended by the Criminal Justice Act 2006.

81 Corrigan, J., 'Time to Tackle the Problem of Reoffending Youngsters', *Irish Times*, 31 March 2004.

82 PQ 209, 15 December 2004.

83 For example, the National Children's Office indicated in 2003 that full implementation was envisaged by 2006. See Spillane, F., and Fischer, E., 'The Children Act 2001: Overview and Current Position' in *The Children Act 2001*, p. 20.

84 Seymour, M., 'Juvenile Justice in the Republic of Ireland', pp. 20–1.

85 See *Amendments to Children Act 2001 and Amendments to Criminal Justice (Legal Aid) Act 1962 for inclusion in the Criminal Justice and Children Bill* available at www.justice.ie (16 January 2006). See *Irish Times*, 19 April 2006. See also Criminal Justice Bill 2004, second composite List of Amendments available at www.oireachtas.ie (accessed 16 May 2006). The Act was passed on June 29th 2006.

86 O'Mahony, P., 'Contextualising the Children Bill as a response to Youth Crime'.

87 Shannon, G., *Child Law*, p. 393.

88 Indeed in several areas of the Act (such as the Garda and probation-led conferences), the rights of victims are recognised where the rights of offenders are not.

89 However, section 88 provides that the Children Court must explain its decision for remanding a child in custody in language which the child can understand.

90 Moreover, the Special Residential Services Board has a duty to implement this principle. See further Chapter Seven below.

91 See Introduction above.

92 Committee on the Rights of the Child, *General Measures of Implementation of the Convention on the Rights of the Child*, CRC/GC/2004/5, pp. 11–12, available at www.ohchr.org (accessed 17 January 2006).

93 See further Chapter Five below.

94 See further below.

95 Van Dijk, C., Nuytiens, N., and Eliaerts, C., 'The Referral of Juvenile Offenders to the Adult Court in Belgium: Theory and Practice', 44(2) *The Howard Journal of Criminal Justice* (2005) 151–66 and Horowitz, M.A., 'Kids who kill: a critique of the American Legal System deals with Juveniles who commit Homicide', 63(3) *Law and Contemporary Problems* (Summer 2000), 133–77.

96 For example, in Scandinavian countries all children who commit offences are brought to the attention of social services. See further Doob, A.N., and Tonry, M., 'Varieties of Youth Justice', 31 *Crime and Justice* (2004) 1–20.

97 Section 98 setting out the sanctions that can be imposed on a child found guilty of an offence refers to '*a* court satisfied of the guilt of a child' suggesting that this applies to all courts. This is confirmed by the title given to Part 9 'Powers of *Courts* in relation to Child Offenders'. However, McDermott and Robinson in their note on this provision state that this section 'sets out a non-exhaustive list of the powers of the

Children Court (emphasis added) where it is satisfied of the guilt of a child'. McDermott, P.A., and Robinson, T., *The Children Act 2001* (Dublin: Thomson Round Hall, 2003), pp. 112–13.

98 See further Chapter Four below.

99 *First Interim Report of the Interdepartmental Committee on Mentally Ill and Maladjusted Persons* in Walsh, D., *Juvenile Justice*, p. 473.

100 Task Force on Child Care Services, *Final Report* in Walsh, D., *ibid*, p. 480.

101 Walsh, D., *ibid.*, pp. 480–1.

102 Lenihan, B., 'A New Way of Dealing with Juvenile Justice'.

103 Kilkelly, U., *The Children's Court: A Children's Rights Audit*, p. 90.

104 Stokes, D., *Youthreach Submission to the Department of Justice*, December 2004 available at www.youthreach.ie (16 January 2006).

105 National Crime Council *Tackling the Underlying Causes of Crime: A Partnership Approach*' (Dublin: Stationery Office, 2002), p. 37.

106 *Ibid.*, p. 36.

107 *Youth Justice Review*, 2005.

108 *Ibid.*, p. 31.

109 *Ibid.*, p. 36.

110 *Ibid.*, p. 37.

111 *Ibid.*, p. 43.

112 *Ibid.*, p. 42.

113 Committee on the Rights of the Child, *Concluding Observations: Ireland* (4 February 1998), CRC/C/15. Add 85 available at www.ohchr.org (accessed 15 January 2006).

114 In 1970, the Kennedy Report recommended that the age be raised to 12, the Task Force on Child Care Services were split on the matter and the Dáil Select Committee on Crime also recommended 12 years.

115 The Minister of State with Responsibility for Children, Brian Lenihan TD, was reported as saying that 'The Government will consider raising the age of criminal responsibility from 7 to 10 years as part of a number of reforms to the juvenile justice system due to be announced later this year. *Irish Times*, 16 June 2005. See 'McDowell bids to cut age of criminal responsibility to seven' *Irish Examiner*, 8 September 2005.

116 McDowell, M., *Criminal Justice Bill 2004* Ministerial Presentation to the Joint Committee on Equality, Justice, Defence and Women's Rights, 7 September 2005 available at www.oireachtas.ie (accessed 13 October 2005).

117 As explained above, *doli incapax* is a rebuttable presumption, which was given statutory protection in section 52(2) of the 2001 Act that a child between 12 and 14 years is incapable of committing an offence because he/she did not have the capacity to know that the act or commission concerned was wrong. The new legislation replaces this with a provision giving the DPP the power to proceed with a prosecution against a child under 14 years who has been charged.

118 *Dáil Debates*, Vol. 517, Col. 33–34 (29 March 2000).

119 The age in Canada and the Netherlands is 12, it is 14 in Germany and New Zealand, 15 in Denmark and Sweden, 16 in France and 18 in

Spain. See further Doob, A.N., and Tonry, M., 'Varieties of Youth Justice', p. 6.

120 Rule 4, United Nations Standard Minimum Rules for the Administration of Juvenile Justice (the Beijing Rules) adopted by General Assembly resolution 40/33 of 29 November 1985 available at www.ohchr.org (accessed 18 January 2006).

121 Committee on the Rights of the Child, *Concluding Observations: Ireland*, para. 23.

122 UN Doc CRC/SR437 Summary Record of the 437th Meeting of the Committee on the Rights of the Child: Ireland 03/02/98, para 8.

123 *Dáil Debates*, Vol. 517, Col 33–34 (29 March 2000).

124 Scottish Law Commission, *Report on the Age of Criminal Responsibility*, (Edinburgh: Stationery Office, 2002) pp. 16–17 available at www.scotlawcom.gov.uk (accessed 16 January 2006).

125 Report of the Committee on Children and Young Persons in Scotland, 1964, ('The Kilbrandon Report') Cmnd 2306, p. 26.

126 *Ibid.*, p. 29.

127 This age was not found to breach article 3 of the ECHR in the cases of *T* v *UK* and *V* v *UK*, 16 December 1999. However, five judges dissented from the judgment of the Court on this issue with reference to the relatively higher ages applied by other ECHR states.

128 See further Chapter Five below.

129 See Human Rights Commission 'Observations on Proposals for Amendments to the Criminal Justice Bill 2004 (Youth Justice) 30 March 2006 available at www.ihrc.ie (accessed 10 April 2006) and Ombudsman for Children, 'Advice of the Ombudsman for Children on the proposed changes to the Children Act 2001', April 2006 available at www.oco.ie (accessed 19 April 2006).

130 O'Sullivan, E., 'Ireland' in Mehlbye, J., and Walgrave, L. (eds) *Confronting Youth in Europe – Juvenile Crime and Juvenile Justice* (Copenhagen, AKF, 1998).

131 See also Irish Youth Justice Alliance, 'Recommendations on the Proposal Amendments to the Children Act 2001,' 25 May 2006 available at www.iprt.ie

Chapter Three

Diversion from the Criminal Justice System

INTRODUCTION

Diversion is a key concept within any youth justice system. The term generally refers to efforts to keep young people away from the formal criminal justice system due to the harm, including labelling, that it may cause. The Garda Diversion Programme is the principal means by which children and young people are diverted from the formal criminal justice system in this jurisdiction. The Programme has a long and well established record in diversion which has been consolidated by Part 4 of the Children Act 2001, which placed the scheme on a statutory basis. Other programmes, such as the Garda Youth Projects, which are locally based youth crime prevention schemes, also fulfil this role in a more informal manner.

This Chapter aims to look at these diversionary programmes, to assess their effectiveness and to analyse the extent to which they operate in line with standards of children's rights and youth justice.

INTERNATIONAL STANDARDS

Diversion of children from the formal criminal justice system is mandated by Article 40 (3) of the Convention on the Rights of the Child (CRC), para. b of which provides that whenever appropriate and desirable, states should develop measures for dealing with children in conflict with the law without resorting to judicial proceedings. The Beijing Rules[1] also recognise the importance and value of diverting young people from the formal criminal justice system. Rule 11 recommends that consideration be given, wherever appropriate, to dealing with juvenile offenders without resorting to formal trial by the competent authority. The objective of such diversion, as is explained in the Rules, is to hinder the negative effects and stigma attached to involving children in juvenile justice proceedings.

So, it is widely recognised that diversion is a good thing and an important element of any youth justice system. Nevertheless, international law does not accept diversion unconditionally. In particular, Article 40 of the CRC provides that alternatives to formal proceedings should be used only where human rights and legal safeguards are fully respected. Similarly, Rule 11.2 of the Beijing Rules refers to the fact that those agencies with the discretion to divert young people should do so in accordance with criteria set out in law for that purpose and the Beijing Rules. In other words, the importance of the welfare of the child, the need to promote his/her ability to play a constructive role in society and to only take action that it is proportionate to the offence and to the child's circumstances must apply to diversionary measures as well as to formal interventions.

The Beijing Rules also warn against over-intervention in the lives of young people by recognising that in many cases non-intervention will be the best response.[2] It thus promotes the use of early diversion without referral to alternative social services especially where the offence is of a non-serious nature and where the family, school and others are likely to react in an appropriate and constructive manner.

BACKGROUND TO THE GARDA DIVERSION PROGRAMME

The Garda Diversion Programme, or the Juvenile Liaison Officer (JLO) Scheme as it was known, has been in place since 1963. Initially set up in the Dublin Metropolitan Area, its purpose was to put in place a system for cautioning children who committed offences rather than having them dealt with by way of prosecution. According to the Scheme, the District Officer (Garda Superintendent) referred the child to a JLO, who then visited the child's home and dealt with the matter by way of caution, advice and supervision. Where appropriate, the JLO also provided support to the family. The aim was to prevent further offending and to divert the child away from a possible life of crime. The Scheme was launched nationwide in 1981 and in 1991, the Garda National Juvenile Office was established and given a co-ordinating and monitoring role. The age for admission to the Scheme was also raised from 16 to 18 years.[3]

Despite this expansion, the Scheme had little express political support contrary to the position in England and Wales where diversionary measures were actively promoted during the 1980s and early 1990s.[4] In Ireland, despite its 'great admiration for the excellent work' being done by the JLO Scheme, and its recognition of the desirability to 'maximise the use of diversion', the Dáil Select Committee – whose many recommendations formed the basis for the Children Act 2001 – did not make any specific recommendations as to how this could be achieved.[5]

Nevertheless, the 1980s saw a more than doubling in the annual number of young people cautioned under the JLO Scheme[6] and in the same period, there was a substantial rise (from 44.7 per cent in 1981 to 61.3 per cent in 1990) in the rates of caution as a proportion of all those under 17 convicted or cautioned.[7] This trend has continued apace – in 1999, 7,844 young people were included in the Diversion Programme and in 2004, 12,785 young people were involved.[8] The Programme has thus gone from strength to strength, particularly in recent years. According to the 2004 Garda Síochána Annual Report, the number of young people now deemed to have benefited from inclusion in the Programme since its inception is 160,918.[9] This is an impressive statistic by any standards and explains why the former Minister for Justice, Equality and Law Reform, John O'Donoghue, TD, described the Scheme as 'probably the single most important initiative in dealing with juvenile crime in the 20th century'.[10] It is not surprising, then, that the decision was taken to finally give the Scheme a statutory basis in the Children Act 2001.

THE CHILDREN ACT 2001

The Garda Diversion Programme offers a child who has committed an offence an opportunity to be cautioned *in lieu* of prosecution before the Children Court.[11] The system operates as follows: when a child first comes to the attention of An Garda Síochána he/she is referred to the local Juvenile Liaison Officer, who is a specially trained Garda. If the child fulfils the eligibility criteria for admission to the programme – the child must be over the age of criminal responsibility and under 18 years, he/she must have accepted responsibility for the offence committed and must consent to being cautioned under the programme – the JLO may recommend to the Director of the Programme at the National Juvenile Office that the child be admitted to the Programme. Once admitted, the child will be cautioned formally or informally. Informal cautions, usually for minor or first offences, are administered by the local JLO and this is normally done at the child's home and in the presence of his/her parents. A formal caution, on the other hand, is administered by the local District Officer (although JLOs are increasingly taking over this cautioning role too) and takes place at the Garda station in the presence of the child's parent or guardian. This type of caution may be restorative in nature if the victim of the child's offending behaviour is invited to attend. In such cases, the objective is to 'confront the child with the consequences of his/her offending' ... 'in a low key atmosphere'.[12] When the victim attends, there must be a general discussion among those present about the child's criminal behaviour and the Garda administering the caution may invite the child to apologise and offer some form of compensation to the victim. In this way, the formal caution may operate as a mini-conference where a full conference is neither justified nor required.

Supervision of the child in the community will normally occur following a formal caution, and it generally means that the child will be monitored or mentored in the community by a JLO for a period of twelve months, although this can be varied by the Director. The level of supervision required, which can also be varied by the Director, is decided by the JLO, who must take into account the seriousness of the criminal behaviour, the level of support to and control of the child by his/her parents or guardian, and the likelihood of the child committing further offences.

The Children Act 2001 also introduced a conference into the Diversion Programme, which has been described as a 'major innovation in Irish criminal law'.[13] In respect of a child who is being supervised, the JLO may convene a conference in order to bring together, on a voluntary basis, the child, his/her family and others to establish the reasons for the child's criminal behaviour and discuss how the family can help the child not to re-offend. The JLO is responsible for organising the conference and must both explain the procedures to the child and his/her guardian and ascertain the wishes of the child and the victim with regard to the conference. The JLO also has a particular function to mediate between the child and the victim – JLOs receive special mediation training for this purpose.[14]

One of the principal functions of the conference is to provide a forum within which the child and his/her parents can draw up an action plan with the assistance of others (e.g. the child's teacher, social worker or youth worker) to try to prevent the child from re-offending. The plan may provide for any course of action that would be in the best interests of the child or would make the child more aware of the consequences of his/her criminal behaviour, including requiring the child to make reparation to the victim, participate in sporting or educational activity, stay at home at certain times and away from certain places or people. While there are no sanctions for non-compliance with the action plan, one or more people may monitor the child's compliance with it and the conference may be reconvened to review compliance. The action plan thus takes the form of a contract between the child and those present at the conference and, although it is not legally enforceable, the consent of the parties is required in most circumstances. The seriousness of the plan is reinforced by the requirement that the child must sign the action plan, which is to be written in plain language that he/she can understand.

EXPANSION OF THE PROGRAMME

It may be appropriate at this point to highlight some of the changes to the Diversion Programme and the extension to the diversionary powers of the Gardaí implemented by the Criminal Justice Act 2006.[15] First, it is proposed to extend the Diversion Programme to include 10- and 11-year-old children who, by virtue of raising the age of criminal responsibility cannot be charged with a criminal offence. These children will be required to satisfy the normal criteria for admission to the programme – they must admit responsibility for the criminal offence and consent to be cautioned – despite the fact that they cannot be prosecuted. It will be interesting to see how many of them will choose this route for themselves.

The second proposal is to extend the Diversion Programme to include children who have not committed a criminal offence, but rather have behaved in an anti-social manner.[16] The fact that the legislation proposes also to introduce Anti-Social Behaviour Orders will mean that young people are more likely to accept responsibility for their behaviour and consent to being cautioned than in the previous situation. If they do not, an application can be made for an Anti-Social Behaviour Order, breach of which is a criminal offence.[17] However, the potential net-widening effects of both proposals raises serious concern given that they are likely to draw into the criminal justice system, of which An Garda Síochána are part, children who have not committed a criminal offence. This is notwithstanding that the Programme aims to divert young people from court, prosecution and the criminal process generally and that international standards warn against over-intervention.[18]

The third amendment also purports to deal with anti-social behaviour, although in this instance the mechanism being introduced is called a Good Behaviour Contract. Similar to, yet running in parallel with the Diversion Programme, this process is initiated by a Garda who may give a 'Behaviour Warning', orally or in writing, to a child known or believed to be involved in anti-social behaviour. The child may be required to give his/her name and address for this purpose, and it is a criminal offence to give details that are false or misleading. If the child does not stop behaving in an anti-social manner, a Garda Superintendent may invite the child and his/her parents to a meeting to discuss the behaviour. If the parties acknowledge the behaviour, a Good Behaviour Contract is drawn up to stop it re-occurring. It is signed by the child and his/her parents and supervised by the Superintendent. Where the child does not adhere to the Contract or where this route is not considered appropriate to begin with, the child will be referred to the Garda Diversion Programme or alternatively an application for an Anti-Social Behaviour Order can be made. Given that those who have committed anti-social behaviour can be admitted to the Diversion Programme already, it is difficult to see what added value Good Behaviour Contracts offer here, other than as a preliminary to an Anti-Social Behaviour Order. Their overlap with and relationship to the Diversion Programme may create problems for both young people and An Garda Síochána, although the administrative headache will be for Gardaí alone.

USE OF THE PROGRAMME: THE WORKLOAD OF JLOs

Garda Annual Reports show that the use of the Diversion Programme has increased year on year. However, the number of cautions administered annually has fluctuated in the last decade. Whereas in 1995, 7,541 children were cautioned, this number increased dramatically to 10,539 in 1996 and then dropped again every year in the subsequent four years (to 8,583 in 1997, 7,989 in 1998, 6,430 in 1999[19] and 6,412 in 2000[20]) despite the fact that the numbers of young people involved in the programme increased during this time. No explanation is offered in the Annual Reports for this apparent anomaly in the figures, although it is likely that the heavy workload of individual JLOs (who are responsible for administering cautions but not admission to the Programme) may be the reason. Certainly, the Association for Garda Sergeants and Inspectors (AGSI) expressed this view in its submission to the Department of Justice, Equality and Law Reform's Youth Justice Project Team in December 2004. In particular, AGSI recommended a 'revamp of the Juvenile Liaison Service to reduce paperwork and improve efficiency'.[21]

The Committee established to monitor the effectiveness of the Diversion Programme made reference to the heavy workloads of JLOs in its first report in 2003 and recommended that, in view of the additional time required to hold restorative cautions and family conferences, the 'human resource elements of the implementation of the Act be kept under review'.[22] The Report also set out the number of Garda personnel administering the Programme nationwide from which it is very clear that JLOs are not present in sufficient numbers, particularly in counties with large urban centres. While some areas could be said to have sufficient JLO cover, the continuously increasing workload must make the job of individual JLOs extremely difficult. Moreover, in other areas, there are clearly not enough JLOs to maximise the potential of the Scheme or indeed to ensure its non-discriminatory application at the most basic level. For example, the largest counties appear to have the smallest numbers of Gardaí operating the Programme – for example, County Clare has one Garda, County Mayo has two Gardaí, Counties Galway and Roscommon share four Gardaí, and County Kerry has two Gardaí.[23] Nor is it clear whether individual Gardaí identified in the Report work as JLOs in a full-time capacity.

The merit and importance of the Diversion Programme is widely accepted and political representatives are quick to celebrate its successes when under attack about juvenile crime. Nevertheless, the failure to substantially increase the amount of funding available to the Diversion Programme and to appoint and train greater numbers of JLOs is a more accurate indicator of support for the Diversion Programme.[24] It does not fare well in this respect.

ADMISSION TO THE PROGRAMME

It is clear from the Children Act 2001 that the Director of the Diversion Programme has considerable discretion and power regarding the admission of young people into the Programme and their treatment once they have been admitted. While the Act sets out admission criteria – age when the offence was committed, acceptance of responsibility and consent to being cautioned – these are not necessarily sufficient to ensure admission. Young people can thus request admission to the Programme, but they have no right to be admitted.

The Act specifies that when deciding on admission, the

Director may take into account factors other than the child's eligibility. According to Section 23 of the Act, he must be satisfied that the child's admission to the Programme:

- would be in the best interests of the child;
- would not be inconsistent with the interests of society or any victim of the criminal behaviour, and
- would not be inconsistent with any ministerial regulations concerning types of criminal behaviour to be excluded from the Programme (none of which have been made to date).

However, as McDermott and Robinson explain, 'these criteria may not always point in the same direction. For example, after a high profile offence, society might be clamouring for the child offender to be brought before the courts, but that may very well not be in the best interests of that child'.[25] The same dilemma may arise with regard to taking into account the interests of any victim of the child's offending. However, the Act does not advise the Director as to how he should reconcile conflicting interests when deciding admission, rather leaves it to his discretion to decide who is entitled to be admitted and in what circumstances. For example, with the exception of cases specified by ministerial regulation, the Director has the power to determine that the interests of individual children in being admitted to the Programme are trumped by those of the victim or society as a whole. While this may not be unreasonable in cases of serious crime or where the child in question has already been convicted of offences, confidence in the system as a whole requires transparency in the Director's actions. Indeed, while international standards encourage appropriate discretion at various stages in the youth justice process, they also require 'efforts to be made to ensure sufficient accountability at all stages and levels in the exercise of any such discretion.'[26]

The absence of any check on the exercise of the Director's powers is the real problem here and this is compounded by the fact that he does not publish the grounds for refusing admission to the Programme despite refusing admission to a substantial number of young people every year. In 2003, 17 per cent of the 17,043 referrals to the National Juvenile Office for admission were recommended for prosecution, i.e. were not admitted.[27] The proportion of referrals not admitted rose to 21 per cent in

2004.[28] For children seeking admission to the Programme, and the JLOs making the application on their behalf, there are no precedents or previous decisions to follow. For those seeking to understand and analyse the Programme in operation, this lack of transparency is frustrating. More importantly, transparency is a vital element in maintaining confidence and faith in the system and its absence from the admission procedures means there is little to protect the Programme from the allegations of unequal treatment frequently levelled at diversion schemes.[29]

The lack of a transparent admission process also fuels the suspicion that the success rate of the Diversion Programme is artificially high by virtue of the young people chosen for participation: according to the Garda Síochána in 2002 87.6 per cent of young people involved in the Programme reached their eighteenth birthday without being prosecuted for a criminal offence.[30] Yet, the fact that An Garda Síochána controls admission to the Programme and, to a large extent, the prosecutorial process, raises the question as to whether this figure is unrealistically high. The charge of case selection – that children unlikely to offend are those preferred for admission while those who present with complicated and challenging behaviour are not – also goes unanswered in this context.[31] The fact that children refused admission to the Programme have no right to appeal the Director's decision is also problematic in this regard.

RIGHTS ISSUES IN THE DIVERSION PROGRAMME

Article 40 of the CRC makes it clear that alternative and diversionary approaches should only be pursued where the rights of children are protected. While it might be argued that children would be better off in a diversionary scheme regardless of what rights they must waive, any process which denigrates or sidelines children's due process rights represents not just an alternative to the formal juvenile justice system but an inferior alternative. While some degree of informality may be permitted in the context of diverting young people away from the formal system, the importance of due process rights should not be undermined. These rights are important not just to safeguard the interests of children involved in the diversionary scheme but to enhance their faith in the fairness of its procedures.

The availability of legal representation prior to admission to the Diversion Programme causes concern in this regard. According to Section 23(1)(a) of the Children Act, a child may be admitted to the Programme if he/she accepts responsibility for his/her criminal (and anti-social) behaviour having had a reasonable opportunity to consult with his/her parents and obtained any legal advice sought by or on behalf of him/her. While it is unclear from this wording whether the entitlement to seek legal advice belongs to the child or his/her parents, nonetheless it is submitted that legal advice should be compulsory prior to a child accepting responsibility for criminal behaviour. Keeping the Diversion Programme a lawyer-free zone is clearly consistent with the informality of the process, but concern about the lack of legal support for young people choosing whether to apply to admission to the Programme at all is also legitimate. Indeed, it will become even more important following the amendment to the Programme in the Criminal Justice Act 2006. This will permit the child's acceptance of responsibility and involvement in the Programme to be introduced as evidence in subsequent criminal proceedings and as such will clearly heighten the need for young offenders to make an informed decision, with legal support, prior to admission.[32] While this will be more important in some cases than others – such as where there is a dispute as to the facts, where the police record is not clear, or where certain offences are concerned – making such best practice uniform may be the only way to ensure the system operates equitably across the board. However, the fear of inviting unnecessary bureaucracy is real in a system which relies on informality and in which, for the most part, facts will be uncontested and participation limited to a caution. A compromise might thus be reached by requiring that the JLO ensures that the young person is making an informed decision prior to admission. Where a conference or restorative event is envisaged, however, best practice would appear to require that legal advice is present prior to the young person's agreement to participate.[33]

Related to this issue is the concern that the child must consent to be cautioned in order to be eligible for admission to the Programme. According to Section 23(1), a child's failure to consent to being cautioned or supervised under the Programme may be dispensed with by the Director of the Programme if he is satisfied that it is attributable to undue pressure being brought to bear on the child by any person. As to the circumstances envisaged here, McDermott and Robinson suggest that the aim of this section is to ensure that 'a child is not deprived of the benefits of the Programme by another person who, for their own purposes, wants a child who has admitted responsibility to enter the ordinary court process'.[34] With respect, it is not clear that a parent must be acting in their own interests ('for their own purposes'), as opposed to the child's, to advise a child to withhold their consent here. For example, where a parent believes that the child will be leniently dealt with by the court – for example, he/she may receive the Probation Act and thus avoid a conviction – or that the charge against him/her may not be proven, it may well be in the child's interests to attend the Children Court rather than go through the Diversion Programme. A similar point could be made with respect to children admitted in respect of their anti-social behaviour. This may be the case, particularly, where the child has already learned his/her lesson from the experience and will not benefit from being cautioned or supervised by the a JLO. Indeed, the argument can be made that involvement in the Diversion Programme is wholly inappropriate as such cases do not require a formal response.[35] In such cases, it is difficult to argue that the Director has the power to overrule the lack of consent not least given that a parent's constitutional right to advise and guide his/her child is sacrosanct.[36] Reinforcing this position is the right of everyone to access the courts, and on both grounds, the apparent refusal of a child to enter a Diversion Programme, should, as McDermott and Robinson explain, 'not lightly be set aside'.[37]

THE RESTORATIVE ELEMENT

Introduction

Much has been written about restorative justice and its potential to use the reintegrative shaming approach to change the offending behaviour of young people.[38] The Garda

Programme is one of three areas of the youth justice system into which the Children Act 2001 introduced a restorative element.[39] In other words, the Act provides opportunities for children and the victims of their offending to meet and reconcile in the hope that the child will realise the consequences of his/her actions, offer some reparation to the victim, whose rights will be vindicated in the process. One of these opportunities arises as part of the conference organised by the JLO under the Garda Diversion Programme to which the victim may also be invited.

The restorative justice approaches in the Act are derived mainly from the New Zealand adaptation of the model, which responded to a need to involve communities and community approaches in the treatment of young offenders. The introduction of this model of family group conferencing into the Act has not been without its critics.[40] Moreover, while not all restorative approaches are the same, O'Dwyer explains that 'restorative justice under the Children Act is much more than victim–offender mediation because of the need to focus on prevention. There are two main components in the Garda process: repairing the harm and preventing further offending … Offender accountability is a key objective.'[41]

The application of restorative justice to youth justice is increasingly common – given their susceptibility to change, children make ideal subjects for the restorative approach.[42] However, the young age and vulnerability of the offender also creates problems for the process, given that voluntariness is a very important value in restorative events.[43] O'Dwyer's research into the restorative element of the Garda Diversion Programme notes that 'offenders generally find it difficult to confront those affected by their behaviour and hear first hand about the impact. In several cases it was necessary for chairpersons to probe offenders' stories, sometimes in a challenging way. It would be easy for the experience to become unduly negative for the offender, despite the express wish to separate the deed from the doer, to criticise the offence not the offender'.[44]

This highlights the additional vulnerability of children in the restorative justice approach and the need to apply sensitivity throughout the process so as not to further vilify or marginalise them, particularly in the presence of the victim. It also highlights the potential risks to the rights of young people who participate in the restorative justice. This is discussed further below.

Experience to Date

Despite these risks, initial research into the operation of the Garda family conference appears favourable.[45] In 2001, the Garda Research Unit looked at 147 cases, comprising 134 restorative cautions and 13 Garda conferences, with a view to observing process standards, identifying critical learning points and measuring outcomes.[46] On participant satisfaction, O'Dwyer notes that:

> victims, offenders and offender supporters all expressed very high levels of satisfaction. Some 93–94 per cent gave scores of 4 or 5 on a scale of 1–5 on this measure, where a score of 5 was equivalent to 'very satisfied'. Scores for 'willing to recommend the approach to someone else' and 'glad to have taken part' were equally high.[47]

Completion of agreements was achieved in 89 per cent of cases where agreements included measures such as compensation, work for the community or the victim, donations to charity, returning to school, joining a club, undertaking vocational training, avoiding people or places, changing behaviour, getting counselling, and coming home at certain hours.[48] Apologies or promises not to get into trouble again, while not insignificant, are not included in this figure. This apparent success of the restorative events is consolidated by the research's conclusion that one in five children re-offended with the review period. This is an impressive statistic which highlights that the Programme has a capacity to divert four in five young people from offending. However, the lack of a control study and of other corroborating data relating to the pre-disposition of children to re-offend make it difficult to interpret this figure, as O'Dwyer himself acknowledges. The absence of information relating to case selection (including admission) – would the children have offended/not offended regardless of the Garda intervention or indeed the nature of that intervention – also makes its value difficult to assess. This is true of the rate of success of the Garda Programme as a whole, however, and is not limited to the use of restorative events within that process. Moreover, as O'Dwyer correctly argues, reliance on statistical data to portray the success of restorative events is a crude approach to a complex and multi-faceted process. Using the rate of re-offending as the sole criterion for evaluating success undermines the other achievements of the restorative process – allowing the victim to tell his/her story, compelling the child to consider the consequences of his/her actions and bringing the child's family together with professionals who may be in a position to offer assistance. However, it also makes it more likely that children whose circumstances make them prone to re-offending will not be accepted into the Programme, or deemed suitable for a restorative caution or conference.

According to O'Dwyer, observers of restorative events noted that the 'achievement of key process standards' was generally high. These were defined as respect and fairness on all sides, as well as an adequate opportunity to speak, explain their actions and contribute to any agreement from the offender's perspective and an opportunity to say how the crime affected them and to suggest how the harm might be repaired from the victim's point of view.[49]

More generally, O'Dwyer notes the significant humanising effect of restorative events where both victim and offender see the individual person behind the offence for the first time. Offenders, he found, had not often fully thought through the impact of their crime, whereas victims got an insight into the particular circumstances and needs of offenders. He cogently describes the fact that many events had some 'unexpected element' that helped achieve a satisfactory result or provided a catalyst for unblocking an impasse such as identifying a common experience like a recent bereavement, an offer of a job from the victim, or recognition that the offender's family are caring and concerned about their child's actions.[50]

With this considerable record of success it is to be expected that restorative events are taking place across the country. But they are not. As O'Dwyer notes: 'restorative justice remains a marginal activity in the Irish juvenile justice system'.[51] Once Part 4 of the Act was commenced on 1 May 2002, the new elements of the Diversion Programme, particularly the restorative caution and conference elements, were phased in gradually. While only 29 such events took place in 2002, for example, 118 'restorative events' took place in various locations throughout 2003.[52] A further substantial increase in restorative events was recorded in 2004 when 177 conferences or cautions took place.[53] Despite these increases, the overall numbers are modest compared with the numbers admitted to the Programme as a whole.

Moreover, there remains some disparity in the number of restorative events taking place across the country. While five counties held between 11 and 13 restorative cautions or conferences in 2003, several counties, including Clare, Kerry, Limerick and Dublin North Central and West held none (and only one 2002).[54] While the failure to hold any such events in Clare and Kerry may be explained by the proportionately low number of children admitted to the Programme in these areas – the less children admitted, the less may be suitable for formal caution or conference – the same cannot be said of the Limerick and Dublin areas which had the highest number of young people referred for formal cautions – almost 1,000 referrals respectively. Looking more closely at these figures, it is relevant that in both Dublin North Central and Dublin West, the number of referrals for a formal caution was 23 whereas in Limerick it was 115. Perhaps, a shortage of JLOs is to blame given the labour intensive nature of restorative events?[55] Again, no. Dublin North Central has three Gardaí and one Sergeant, Dublin West has seven Gardaí and one Sergeant working in the Programme. Moreover, Mayo, a large county which has only two Gardaí in the Programme managed to hold eleven events in 2003 out of 63 formal referrals. Workload cannot be the reason here even if it is a problem in Limerick which has only one Garda and one Sergeant in the Programme.

What then is the reason for the failure of the Gardaí in these areas to hold any restorative events – a central part of the Garda Diversion Programme – in either 2002 or 2003, and a modest number in 2004? Such regional variations are not unusual,[56] but centralisation of the decision-making process in the Diversion Programme should be keeping them to a minimum. It is regrettable that the Committee appointed to monitor the effectiveness of the programme had no comment to make about this issue and published these figures without explanation. The lack of transparency is also lamentable: the geographical disparity, which appears to offer participation in restorative events to victims and offenders in some areas but not in others, is a cause for concern.

With regard to case selection, O'Dwyer has warned that the pursuit of numbers should not become a goal in itself and that efforts should be focused where they are most effective. In light of the fact that this is a matter for An Garda Síochána, he has recommended that consideration should be given to the development of an assessment tool for JLOs to assist case selection.[57] This is to be strongly welcomed. Further recommendations regarding transparency are made below.

Rights Issues in the Restorative Process

While clearly positive for those involved, nonetheless the restorative elements of the Diversion Programme pose challenges to the rights of children in theory if not in practice. Some had expressed their concern, during the draft stages of the Children Bill 1999, about the legitimacy and wisdom of having a JLO act as convenor of the family conference under the Garda Programme. The Law Society, for example, expressed anxiety that 'members of the Garda Síochána should not convene or chair family conferences in relation to children' and that an 'independent convenor be provided for'. This, the Law Society, said would overcome 'the practical difficulties which often arise in cases of great distrust between the families concerned and the Gardaí'.[58]

A power imbalance, of which JLOS are undoubtedly aware, naturally exists in any situation where a child or young person sits alone with adults. Further problems arise when this is a restorative justice process. As Haines notes:

> where the offender is a child, in a room full of adults, then this dynamic raises ethical questions about treating children in such a manner, it raises questions about the degree to which such practices implement the provisions of international conventions on the treatment of children, and it raises questions about the likelihood of success

> based on the limited ability of a non-adult to make decisions and take actions in a free and informed manner.[59]

Adults present at restorative cautions or conferences under the Garda Programme can include, for example, the young person's parents (who he/she may not necessarily believe are on his/her side) and members of the police and other statutory bodies with whom the young person may have had negative encounters in the past. A restorative event introduces a victim into this process and while it is not unusual for the victim of a young offender to also be a child, in many cases he/she will be an adult, maybe angry and hoping for revenge. While the aspiration of informality may justify the exclusion of lawyers at such events, consideration should be given to permitting the young person to be accompanied by an independent advocate. The fact that the victim is permitted to be accompanied by a supporter strengthens this claim for equal treatment. Although in practice, offenders are allowed to nominate a support person other than their parent or guardian, it is not clear whether they are encouraged strongly to do so. Moreover, young people may not know or trust another adult sufficiently to carry out this role: in this regard, they should be strongly encouraged either to bring friends or preferably, to choose an appropriate adult from a panel of appropriately trained advocates.

COLONISATION OF DIVERSION

One of the criticisms made of diversionary programmes operated and managed by the police is that they effectively colonise or monopolise the concept of diversion. With respect to the position in England and Wales, Goldson notes that 'the management of the "front end" of the youth justice system is now simply a "matter for the police"...(which) raises a fundamental concern with regard to single-agency colonisation of a critically important stage of the youth justice process'.[60] Others have highlighted the 'desirability of diversionary schemes being administered by someone independent of law-enforcement bodies.'[61]

Whatever about approaches elsewhere, the charge of

colonisation can clearly be made with regard to the role of An Garda Síochána whose members both determine admission to the Diversion Programme and control, in real terms at least, the prosecution process. While schemes with no official involvement are not necessarily better, it is a concern that An Garda Síochána has sole responsibility for the management and administration of the Diversion Programme: the Commissioner retains general control over the Programme, it is managed by an individual member acting as the Director who has substantial powers under the Children Act to decide whether the child is admitted (s. 24), the type of caution to be administered (s. 25), whether to hold a conference (s. 31) and varying the period and level of supervision that the child receives (s. 42). At local level, the administration of the Programme falls under the exclusive remit of the JLO and other Gardaí of senior rank who have functions and duties in respect of cautions, supervision and conferences. In this regard, therefore, members of An Garda Síochána have complete control over the administration and operation of the programme.[42] The latest proposal under the Criminal Justice Bill 2004 to expand the Programme further, especially to include anti-social behaviour, only heighten this concern.

A number of recommendations might be made as a response to the risks posed by this colonisation: the first is to permit the involvement of lay people in the process to ensure it has a multi-agency dimension. While conferences already have this element, the process of determining eligibility to the Programme and suitability for a restorative caution or conference would also benefit from this approach. The second is to ensure that all Gardaí involved in the Programme's administration are specially trained, not just in mediation but in youth justice standards. This is considered further below. The third recommendation, aimed at improving the transparency in the process, is that the Director should be required to publish an annual report regarding the admission process and, in particular, detailing the reasons why young people were refused admission to the Programme. Finally, it is recommended that a meaningful system be put in place to monitor the implementation of the Programme in line with standards of youth justice and equal treatment. This is also considered further below.

TRAINING OF JLOs

According to the Beijing Rules, 'police officers who frequently or exclusively deal with juveniles or who are primarily engaged in the prevention of juvenile crime shall be specially instructed and trained'.[63] Moreover, those exercising discretion at any point in the youth justice system must be specially qualified or trained to exercise it judiciously and in accordance with their functions and mandates.[64] This is reflected in a Policy Statement issued by the Garda Commissioner in 2002, which committed An Garda Síochána to carrying out restorative interventions by properly trained and accredited personnel.[65]

According to the Committee to monitor the Garda Diversion Programme, the training of JLOs requires further examination. In its first report, the Committee reported that training and development for JLOs, the only specialised Gardaí trained to deal with children, includes two weeks general training, three days' training on the principles of restorative justice, ten days mediation training and two days' victim/offender mediation training. Fourteen JLOs were, at the time, receiving mediation training to level two of Mediation Institute Ireland (MII) and three further officers[66] were undertaking a Diploma in the Study of Adolescent Behaviour although these additional qualifications and training were not required.

While the Committee noted in 2003 that it was satisfied with the training being given and noted its constant review by the National Juvenile Office, it recommended that the present level of training be evaluated before a final training programme is decided upon. Indeed, it undertook to consult with the NJO in exploring the feasibility of developing an accredited third level course which could be made available to all JLOs.[67] In 2004, while it reported having examined a proposal on the sourcing of third legal educational qualification for JLOs, no conclusion was reached other than to recommend that the National Juvenile Office continue with its endeavours to secure a suitable third level qualification for JLOs.[68]

EXTERNAL MONITORING OF THE DIVERSION PROGRAMME

The lack of external involvement in the operation of the Programme is clearly a cause for concern both generally and with respect to the rights of specific young people. The establishment under the Children Act of a Committee to monitor the effectiveness of the Diversion Programme is welcome although its inaugural report did not offer much in the way of rigorous analysis of the scheme's effectiveness. For example, the 2003 report – glossy and bilingual – does little other than republish the data from that year's Garda Síochána Annual Report. While its members include lay people, it is unfortunate that its initial work did not look beyond Garda personnel for the substance of its analysis.[69] Its observations are limited to recommendations for research on recidivism, an examination of JLO qualifications and support for reviews already on-going.

The 2004 Report of the Committee is a more substantial document which lays out the Garda statistics in a visual and accessible format. While the presentation is excellent, nonetheless it is difficult to see what level of monitoring of the Programme is being undertaken by the Committee. Indeed, the Garda Research Unit appears to be undertaking much of this role in recent times and the degree to which the Unit has contributed to the understanding and analysis of the operation of the Programme arguably reduces the expectations on the Monitoring Committee. Nevertheless, a more robust scrutiny of the Programme would undoubtedly be welcomed by all those seeking to maximise its potential if not the sceptics who see the scheme as an 'easy way out'. Regardless, the above analysis shows the importance of having an independent body to highlight the Programme's inadequacies as well as its successes.

PRACTICAL PROBLEMS WITH THE PROGRAMME

Under the non-statutory JLO scheme, decision-making as to admission and administration was largely undertaken by individual JLOs operating at local level, although some degree of central approval was required since the establishment of the

National Juvenile Office in 1991. In order to streamline the process and ensure its consistent application, Part 4 of the Children Act 2001 centralised the decision-making process to a much greater degree. Ironically, the fact that each file must now be sent to the National Juvenile Office appears to have complicated proceedings and caused some delay. This is illustrated by the number of cases pending before the Director in 2003,[70] although this was substantially down in 2004.[71]

Further complications are caused by the time-lag that emerges in situations where a child is brought before the Children Court having been arrested and charged, but whose case is then remanded to allow the child's application for admission to the Diversion Programme to be determined. Apart from the delay in determining the child's case, this situation clearly frustrates the objective of the Programme to divert children away from the court system. Yet, this is not an uncommon problem. As Judge O'Donnell of Limerick Children Court explains:

> Recently at Limerick's Children Court, there have been a number of children charged with offences ... brought before the Court having been arrested and charged, rather than by summons. The State have then applied for a remand as the file has been sent to the National Children Office based in Garda HQ to consider whether or not ... the child is to be included in the Diversion Scheme, or whether the case is to proceed in the Children Court.[72]

While it is possible to strike out a charge against a young person belatedly admitted to the Programme, the court appearance obviously negates the objective of the Programme to divert young people away from the criminal justice system. This problem is not limited to the Limerick Children Court. As research into the Children Court noted in 2005, confusion arises not infrequently with regard to the potential involvement of a young person in the Garda Diversion Programme.

> For example, on one occasion, a serious mix up occurred which the judge, the prosecuting Inspector and the

> Solicitor tried to sort out in the presence of the 16 year old boy concerned. It appeared that the young person was diverted to the Garda Programme but an error was made and he was prosecuted instead. No-one appeared to know whether the charge could be removed from the computer system.[73]

In several other cases, predominantly in the Limerick and Cork Children Courts, charges appeared to remain in limbo for long periods as a response from the National Juvenile Office was awaited. In other cases, there appeared to be some confusion as to why a referral had not been made and cases were remanded to allow enquiries to take place.[74]

At the least, communication between An Garda Síochána (including the National Juvenile Office) and the courts needs to be improved and efforts made to explain the operation of the Programme to all personnel in the youth justice system so that the problems highlighted above can be minimised.

ADMISSIBILITY OF EVIDENCE AS TO INVOLVEMENT IN THE PROGRAMME

A central element in any system of diversion is the quid pro quo that it represents – young people accept responsibility for the offence committed and agree to be cautioned while waiving their right to a judicial determination of the charge against them. The bar to prosecution is the incentive required to encourage young people to participate in the scheme which, from their perspective, can be more demanding on them (particularly when supervision, restorative caution or conference is concerned) than a court appearance and a minor sanction such as a small fine. In addition to the bar to proceedings in Section 49 of the Children Act 2001, Section 48 precludes the admissibility of a wide range of evidence relating to the child's involvement in the Programme including any acceptance by the child of responsibility for criminal behaviour, relating to that behaviour, or relating to the child's involvement in the Programme for that behaviour. However, the Criminal Justice Act 2006 amends that provision in a way that has potential to undermine the Diversion Programme itself. In particular, it introduces a new subsection (2) into Section 48 of the Children Act 2001 which will allow the prosecution to put evidence before a court at the sentencing stage regarding that child's involvement in the Diversion Programme.

Contrary to the current position where the Court is not entitled to hear any evidence relating to the child's involvement in the Diversion Programme or any of the offences which gave rise to his/her involvement in the Programme, this amendment will give the prosecution the power to inform the Children Court not only of the child's involvement in the Programme and of the offences giving rise to this involvement but also, importantly, any acceptance by the child of responsibility for that criminal behaviour. Just as McDermott and Robinson expressed surprise at the apparently wide scope of (the original) section 48,[75] so too must the power which the amendment gives to the prosecution to bring matters to the attention of the Children Court be considered sweeping in nature. The amendment is no doubt carefully phrased as the grant of power or discretion to the Prosecution (the Garda Síochána in other words) in respect of cases where children have re-offended following their involvement in the Diversion Programme, rather than the entitlement of the Court to demand such information. Nevertheless it is likely that evidence of this nature will be used in a manner similar to evidence as to previous convictions. The result, ultimately, will be that factors such as evidence of involvement in the Programme, the behaviour which gave rise to such involvement and the young person's accepted responsibility for that behaviour will be taken into account as part of the sentencing process notwithstanding that the child has no conviction in respect of the alleged offences.[76]

The Diversion Programme has had such a long history that the Children Courts are used to working in the absence of the full picture, to the extent that this is what Section 48 means. It is widely accepted that the Programme is the young person's principal shot at diversion and, in that sense, they deserve that it is not taken into account by a subsequent Court. Indeed, the case for making such evidence admissible has not been made out; no research or study has been done to highlight the problems that this situation currently causes. Both the Human Rights Commission and the Ombudsman for Children opposed these changes. Allowing An

Garda Síochána to introduce evidence of previous offences for which the young person accepted responsibility only within the context of fulfilling the criteria for admission to the Diversion Programme is a risky and dangerous business. It will undoubtedly make the Programme a less attractive option for young people and rightly so when they are giving up their right to have their guilt or innocence of such charges determined by a court. More importantly, perhaps, there is a danger that this amendment will have long term implications on the willingness of young people to enter the Programme in the first place. In that sense, rather than freeing up JLOs to deal within the Programme with those responsible for more serious crime,[77] it may well reduce its relevance only to those involved in minor offences. Despite proposals to expand the Programme in other ways as outlined above, the dilution of the Programme in other ways may have begun.

In this context, it is important to note that formalised systems of intervention, such as the statutory Diversion Programme, may involve the sort of consequences for children that they are specifically designed to avoid. Research in Lancashire in the 1980s found that processes of early intervention, however benign, could be linked to spiralling and more intensive interventionist measures which were in turn characterised by increasingly punitive tendencies.[78] More importantly, perhaps, is the link between intervention and up-tariffing, the likelihood that children who have received the opportunity of intervention or diversion at an early stage are treated more harshly when they do re-offend then they would have if they have not been diverted in the first place. According to Haines and Drakeford (commenting on the Lancashire research) 'highly interventionist programmes of treatment often did more harm than good in systems terms because once a young person had tried and failed at treatment then punishment was the inevitable outcome of further criminal justice involvement'.[79] It must be recognised as at least a risk that early intervention, often for very minor offences or even because children are thought to be at risk of offending, has the effect of catapulting children very rapidly into the formal criminal justice system. These fears are even more real in the Irish context with regard to the amendments to the Diversion Programme in the Criminal Justice Act 2006.

MAXIMISING THE POTENTIAL OF GARDA DIVERSION

The issue of case selection and admission to the Programme is central to the success of efforts to divert young people from offending towards something altogether more positive. Deciding who to admit to the Programme, and selecting cases for participation in restorative events, has a direct bearing on the perceived success of the Programme. In particular, at one end of the extreme, admitting only first offenders, who have committed minor offences may maximise the Programme's success rate, and choosing for restorative events only those uncomplicated cases which can be processed quickly will ensure that a similarly successful outcome will be achieved.[80] In this regard, it is interesting that the Minister for Justice, Equality and Law Reform has indicated the suitability of the Programme for more complex and difficult cases. According to Mr McDowell, 'as Garda juvenile liaison officers become more skilled in administering restorative justice, it is planned that they will be able to focus on more complex and high-risk offenders, with a view to further reducing recidivism'.[81]

The significant increase in restorative events necessary to ensure that this happens does not appear to have occurred, two years after the Minister's statement. Nor do the Annual Reports of An Garda Síochána or any other policy documentation show the commitment to applying restorative approaches to more 'complex and high risk offenders'. For this to happen, there must be an increase in the overall appreciation of the value and contribution of restorative events in addressing young offending. Only then, it is submitted, will the significant investment that each restorative event takes be considered worthwhile.

GARDA YOUTH DIVERSION PROJECTS

In addition to the Diversion Programme, An Garda Síochána also operates locally based youth crime prevention schemes previously known as the Garda Special Projects. The first two Special Projects were set up in 1991 following disturbances involving young people and the Gardaí in Ronanstown in November of that year. The Report of the Interdepartmental

Group on Urban Crime and Disorder noted the work of these Projects and recommended their continuance. There are now over sixty-four Youth Diversion Projects in operation under the aegis of the Garda Community Relations Section; they are co-ordinated by the National Juvenile Office.[82] Through a combination of intervention and prevention programmes, Projects aim to prevent crime through community and multi-agency co-operation and to improve the quality of life within the community. They aim to divert young people from criminal or anti-social behaviour, provide suitable activities to facilitate personal development and encourage civic responsibility.[83]

An in-depth evaluation of the effectiveness of the Special Projects was carried out by Trinity College in 2000 and reached a number of positive conclusions about their impact. Bowden and Higgins concluded that the Projects have attracted participation of a significant number of young people and engaged them in worthwhile and beneficial activities, and have been effective in persuading young people to desist from crime and unacceptable behaviour in their areas. According to the authors, however, the influence an individual Project has on young people appears to depend on the nature of the relationship that the young people have with its staff, and the commitment they make to, and the bond they form with, the Project itself. On a more general level, the Projects were found to have developed mechanisms for allowing positive exchanges between individual Gardaí, young people, their families and communities.[84]

Other conclusions of note (in the context of discussions above regarding admission criteria and case selection for the Garda Diversion Programme) related to the way in which referrals were received and dealt with. In particular, Bowden and Higgins noted the lack of a formalised system of referrals to the Projects, and the absence of a common approach for dealing with them as they arrived, with the criteria applied being unclear in many cases. This factor, together with the fact that many Projects did not appear to lay down behaviour change as a pre-requisite condition of participation drew attention to the significant fact that the purpose of the Projects was not at all clear.[85] Moreover, a circular from Garda HQ appeared to complicate rather than simplify matters in this regard. For example, it highlighted the need for Projects to focus on young people who had not offended, but for various reasons were deemed to be at-risk of doing so. The failure to define this category meant that it could be subjected to an extremely broad and unhelpful interpretation, for example to include all young people living in a particular area. Moreover, in light of the danger that the Projects are engaged in net-widening, in particular due to the involvement of children who have needs but who have not offended, the research questioned the Projects' focus on this category of young people. In particular, it was asked how intervention could aim to divert from crime, someone who had not engaged in criminal behaviour. This is also of clear relevance to proposals, discussed above, to expand the Garda Diversion Programme.

The Projects were also found to use different methods of diverting young people from crime, including creating alternative progression or development routes, challenging young people's offending and other unacceptable behaviour through personal development or one-to-one interventions, and providing leisure and recreational activities.[86] Overall, however, Bowden and Higgins found that the Projects focused too much on diverting young people from crime and not enough on their re-direction towards alternative systems such as training, education and employment.

That the Projects examined appeared to achieve so much in the way of successful outcomes (notwithstanding the limits of the research), both with regard to individual participants and meeting broader objectives, seems impressive given the fairly fundamental shortcomings identified in this research. Bowden and Higgins made a number of important conclusions and recommendations as to how the potential of the Projects could be maximised. In particular, they identified the need to build an infrastructure to support the Diversion Projects to fulfil their objectives of youth crime diversion and the prevention of offending, and to develop a set of comprehensive guidelines setting out the aims and scope of youth crime prevention and diversion, the implementation structures required in Project areas, the role of the various agencies involved, and the range of appropriate fundable actions. The guidelines were drafted and published in 2003.[87] In general, they are intended for use as a comprehensive aid to new and existing Garda Youth Diversion Projects and set out in some detail how they should be established, operated, administered and monitored at local level. They specifically reference Ireland's obligations under the Convention on the Rights of the Child and, given that the Children Act 2001 raises the age of criminal responsibility to 12 years, are based on the premise that the age group to be considered for diversion under the Projects is between 12 and 18 years. It is not clear what, if anything, has happened since these positive developments, although there is clearly much potential to be explored in this area.

CONCLUSION

The area of diversion, under both the Diversion Programme and the Youth Diversion Projects, is an overwhelmingly positive element of Garda work. The Diversion Programme, in particular, is one of the most well-managed and coherent parts of the Irish youth justice system and its success rate in preventing re-offending by children and young people is impressive. It is also by far the best researched and analysed area of the system thanks to the detailed and analytical work of the Garda Research Unit, particularly into the restorative elements of the Programme, and the forensic work of Trinity College into the Diversion Projects.

It is not without negative features however. The lack of transparency in the admission figures does not encourage faith in its equal application to all children who meet the admission criteria, and the criteria themselves are also cause for concern. Failure on the part of some Garda districts to fully implement parts of the Programme is also regrettable, as is the failure to expose the whole system to robust external scrutiny.

Concerns are expressed above about the colonisation and monopolisation of diversion by An Garda Síochána and the net-widening effects of intervention. These concerns are considerably heightened in light of the decision to expand the Programme to include children involved in anti-social behaviour and to develop a parallel diversion programme of Good Behaviour Contracts.

With informality as the key to the success to diversion, the more formal and expansive the Programme has become the greater the danger that it diverts young people to another part of the criminal justice system rather than from it altogether. Moreover, it is this lack of multi-agency working that makes it so efficient and so successful. The fact that neither diversion scheme has to integrate with the rest of the juvenile justice or care systems makes it easier to manage and efficient to implement. The irony of that position is clear.

NOTES

1 United Nations (the Beijing Rules) Standard Minimum Rules for the Administration of Juvenile Justice adopted by General Assembly resolution 40/33 of 29 November 1985 available at www.ohchr.org (17 January 2006).

2 *Ibid.*, Commentary to Rule 11. Caution against the net-widening effect of diversion programmes is frequently expressed. See, for example, Cunneen, C., and White, R., *Juvenile Justice: Youth and Crime in Australia* (Melbourne: OUP, 2002), pp. 374–5; Haines, K., 'Referral Orders and Youth Offender Panels: Restorative Approaches and the New Youth Justice' in Goldson, B. (ed.), *The New Youth Justice* (Dorset: Russell House Publishing, 2000), pp. 68–9 and Bala, N., 'The Youth Criminal Justice Act: Diversion, Conferencing, and Extrajudicial Measures for Adolescent Offenders', 40 *Alberta Law Review* 991 (2003), p. 1006.

3 *Report of the Committee appointed to monitor the effectiveness of the Diversion Programme*, 2003, p. 7.

4 See Home Office Circulars (14/1985) and 59/1990 in Goldson, B., 'Wither Diversion? Interventionism and the New Youth Justice' in Goldson, B. (ed.), *The New Youth Justice*, p. 35. In England and Wales in 1993, 90 per cent of boys and 97 per cent of girls were cautioned by the police.

5 Dáil Select Committee on Crime, *Juvenile Crime – its Causes and its Remedies* (Dublin: Stationery Office, 1992), p 55.

6 In England and Wales, the number of young people cautioned between 1985 and 1995 also doubled. See Goldson, B., 'Wither Diversion? Interventionism and the New Youth Justice', p. 36.

7 Dáil Select Committee on Crime *Juvenile Crime – its Causes and its Remedies*, p. 9.

8 An Garda Síochána *Annual Report* 2004, p. 55, available at www.garda.ie (accessed 16 January 2006).

9 Ibid., p 52.

10 *Dáil Debates*, Vol. 517, Col. 33–4 (29 March 2000).

11 Section 49 of the Act provides that a child shall not be prosecuted for the criminal behaviour, or any related behaviour, in respect of which he/she

has been admitted to the Programme.

12 As explained by the Minister for Justice, Equality and Law Reform in his introductory speech at the Second Stage, *Dáil Debates*, Vol. 517, Col. 36 (29 March 2000).

13 McDermott, P.A., and Robinson, T., *Children Act 2001* (Dublin: Thomson Round Hall, 2003), p. 65.

14 JLOs receive ten days generic mediation training to Level 1 accreditation from Mediation Institute Ireland delivered over a four-month period. In addition, fourteen JLOs are reportedly receiving mediation training to MII Level 2. *Report of the Committee appointed to monitor the effectiveness of the Diversion Programme, 2003*, p. 7. See further below.

15 See Criminal Justice Bill 2004, Second composite List of Amendments, 16 May 2006 available at www.oireachtas.ie (accessed 16 May 2006).

16 This is defined under new section 257A(2) of the 2001 Act as behaviour which has caused or was likely to cause to one or more persons harassment; significant or persistent alarm, distress, fear or intimidation, or significant or persistent impairment of their use or enjoyment of their property.

17 See further Chapter Six below.

18 Similar concerns were expressed about the use of the police caution in Northern Ireland which appeared to draw in some very young and petty offenders. See O'Mahony, D., and Doak, J., 'Restorative Justice – Is More Better? The Experience of Police-led Restorative Cautioning Pilots in Northern Ireland', 43(5) *The Howard Journal of Criminal Justice* (December 2004) 484–505, p. 495. See also the Human Rights Commission, Observations for Amendments to the Criminal Justice Bill 2004 (Youth Justice), 30 March 2006, available at www.lhrc.ie (accessed 10 April 2006) pp. 24–5,

19 See An Garda Síochána, *Annual Report* 1999, p. 88.

20 See An Garda Síochána, *Annual Report* 2000, p. 108.

21 AGSI Press Statement, 'State is failing in duty to children', 23 December 2004, available at agsi.ie (accessed 7 November 2005).

22 *Report of the Committee appointed to monitor the effectiveness of the Diversion Programme, 2003*, p. 11.

23 *Report of the Committee appointed to monitor the effectiveness of the Diversion Programme, 2004*, p. 29.

24 Funding allocated to the Programme is determined by the Commissioner. €5.284 million was allocated in 2004. *Report on the Youth Justice Review,* (Dublin: Department of Justice, Equality and Law Reform, 2005), available at www.justice.ie (accessed 4 January 2006) p. 64.

25 McDermott, P.A., and Robinson, T., *The Children Act 2001*, p. 61.

26 Rule 6.2 of the Beijing Rules.

27 An Garda Síochána *Annual Report 2003*, p. 58.

28 An Garda Síochána *Annual Report 2004*, p. 52.

29 Cunneen, C., and White, R., *Juvenile Justice*, p. 375.

30 An Garda Síochána *Annual Report 2002*, p. 106.

31 O'Dwyer also raises this point with regard to case selection for restorative

events noting that the uncomplicated cases are the easiest to resolve in a satisfactory way with little expenditure of resources. O'Dwyer, K., *Restorative Justice Initiatives in the Garda Síochána Evaluation of the Pilot Programme*, Garda Research Unit, Research Report No. 4/01 (Templemore: Garda Research Unit, 2001), p. 6.

32 It is not clear how this provision will work with respect to those admitted by virtue of their anti-social behaviour. It is likely that involvement in the Garda Diversion Programme will be admitted as evidence in an application for an Anti-Social Behaviour Order, the equivalent of prosecution in this context.

33 This is the joint advice of the Australian Law Reform Commission and the Human Rights and Equal Opportunity Commission, cited in Cunneen, C., and White, R., *Juvenile Justice,* pp. 377–8.

34 McDermott, P.A., and Robinson, T., *The Children Act 2001*, p. 60.

35 See Haines, K., 'Referral Orders and Youth Offender Panels', p. 68 and O'Mahony, D., and Doak, J., 'Restorative Justice – Is More Better?'.

36 See Shannon, G., *Child Law* (Dublin: Thomson Round Hall, 2005), pp. 7–9.

37 McDermott, P.A., and Robinson, T., *The Children Act 2001*, p. 60.

38 See O'Mahony, D., and Doak, J., 'Restorative justice – is more better?', and Morris, A. 'Shame, Guilt and Remorse: Experiences from Family Group Conferences in New Zealand', in Weijers, I., and Duff A. (eds), *Punishing Juveniles Principle and Critique* (Oxford: Hart, 2002) pp. 157–78.

39 Restorative justice has many definitions but is broadly accepted to refer to a process which seeks to balance the interests of the parties affected by a crime (the victim and the community) with the need to reintegrate the offender into society. It is not concerned with judging but with restoring social relationships damaged by offending behaviour. See further Commission on Crime Prevention and Social Justice, *Restorative Justice Report of the Secretary General,* 7 January 2002, E/CN.15/1002/5, available at www.ohchr.org (accessed 17 January 2006) pp. 2–3.

40 See Shannon, G., *Child Law*, pp. 421–4. Those who have researched restorative justice in New Zealand, on which international attention has focused since the introduction of family welfare conferences in 1989 have also become sceptical. See Morris, A., 'Youth Justice in New Zealand' 31 *Crime and Justice* (2004), p. 243.

41 O'Dwyer, K., 'Garda Restorative Justice Programme – Highlights and Insights', Paper delivered at a Conference on Youth Justice, Croke Park Dublin, 12–13 September 2005.

42 Commission on Crime Prevention and Social Justice, *Restorative Justice Report of the Secretary General*, pp. 4–5.

43 Walgrave, L., 'Not Punishing Children but Committing them to Restore' in Weijers, I., and Duff, A., (eds), *Punishing Juveniles Principle and Critique*, pp. 93–114.

44 O'Dwyer, K., 'Garda Restorative Justice Programme – Highlights and Insights', p. 4.

45 O'Dwyer, K., *Restorative Justice Initiatives in the Garda Síochána.*

46 The evaluated cases involved 113 victims, 218 offenders and 289 offender supporters. For a variety of reasons, not all could be interviewed. Interviews were completed with fifty-one victims (45.1 per cent), sixty-four offenders (29.4 per cent) and eighty-six offender supporters (29.8 per cent).
47 O'Dwyer, K., 'Garda Restorative Justice Programme – Highlights and Insights', p. 2.
48 O'Dwyer, K., *Restorative Justice Initiatives in the Garda Síochána*, pp. 34–7.
49 These are very important elements of the process. See Cunneen, C., and White, R., *Juvenile Justice*, p. 374.
50 O'Dwyer, K., 'Garda Restorative Justice Programme – Highlights and Insights', pp. 3–4.
51 *Ibid.*, p. 5.
52 An Garda Síochána, *Annual Report 2003*, p. 59.
53 An Garda Síochána, *Annual Report 2004*, p. 54
54 *Report of the Committee appointed to monitor the effectiveness of the Diversion Programme, 2003*, p. 17. In 2004, Clare still had held no conferences, Kerry had held eight and Limerick had held four. The number of conferences in the Dublin region increased overall from twenty-eight to thirty-eight, but while the Western region had eleven conferences, as opposed to none in 2003, almost every other area of Dublin had fewer conferences in 2004 than in 2003. An Garda Síochána, *Annual Report 2004*, p. 54.
55 O'Dwyer's research found that the evaluated cases took an average 11.8 hours between preparation and running of the restorative event, with a range of one to fifty-one hours. He also noted the requirement of further resources at the follow-up stages. O'Dwyer, K., *Restorative Justice Initiatives in the Garda Síochána,* p. 5.
56 See Morris, A., 'Juvenile Justice in New Zealand', p. 262.
57 O'Dwyer, K., Restorative Justice Initiatives in the Garda Sióchána, p. 5.
58 Law Society, *Submissions on the Children Bill 1999*, at www.lawsociety.ie (accessed 2 November 2005).
59 Haines, K., 'Referral Orders and Youth Offender Panels: Restorative Approaches and the New Youth Justice, p. 69.
60 Goldson, B., 'Wither Diversion? Interventionism and the New Youth Justice', p. 37.
61 See the recommendations of the Australian Law Reform Commission and Human Rights and Equal Opportunities Commission in Cunneen, C., and White, R., *Juvenile Justice*, p. 377.
62 The Garda Programme can be contrasted in this regard with the non-statutory schemes such as that operational in Nenagh, Co Tipperary.
63 Rule 12, The Beijing Rules.
64 *Ibid*, Rule 6.3.
65 Policy Statement by the Commissioner of An Garda Síochána, 14 February 2002, in *Report of the Committee appointed to Monitor the Effectiveness of the Diversion Programme*, 2004, p. 30.

66 This rose to five in 2004. *Ibid.*, p. 13.
67 *Report of the Committee appointed to Monitor the effectiveness of the Diversion Programme*, 2003, p. 10.
68 *Report of the Committee appointed to Monitor the effectiveness of the Diversion Programme*, 2004, p. 14.
69 The report explains that it invited presentations from Superintendent Vincent McGuire, Director of the Programme, Inspector Finbarr Murphy, National Juvenile Office and Kieran O'Dwyer, Head of Research in the Garda Research Unit, at p. 9.
70 For example, according to An Garda Síochána *Annual Report 2003*, there were 5,997 referrals pending, p. 58.
71 There were 1,428 cases pending in 2004. An Garda Síochána, *Annual Report 2004*, p. 53.
72 O'Donnell, T., 'The Children Act 2001: A practical analysis from a judicial perspective', Law Society Criminal Law Committee *Seminar for Judges of the District Court*, 3 December 2004, p. 6.
73 Kilkelly, U., *The Children's Court: A Children's Rights Audit* (Cork, 2005) p. 83.
74 *Ibid*, pp. 83–4.
75 McDermott, P. A., and Robinson, T., *The Children Act 2001*, p. 76.
76 As noted above, amendments to the Programme under the Criminal Justice Act raise a similar concern that a child's involvement in the Programme with respect to anti-social behaviour will be admissible in any subsequent civil proceedings for an Anti-Social Behaviour Order.
77 PQ 28296/03.
78 Thorpe et al., *Out of Care* (London: George Allen and Unwin, 1980) in Goldson, B., 'Wither Diversion? Interventionism and the New Youth Justice', p. 43.
79 *Ibid.*
80 In this context, O'Dwyer proposes making a restorative approach mandatory for more serious categories of offence. See O'Dwyer, *Restorative Justice Initiatives in the Garda Síochána*, p. 42.
81 PQ 28296/03.
82 *Garda Youth Diversion Project Guidelines,* 2003, p. 1, available at www.justice.ie (accessed 7 November 2005).
83 Bowden, M., and Higgins, L., *The Impact and Effectiveness of the Garda Special Projects* (2000) available at www.justice.ie (accessed 6 November 2004).
84 *Ibid.,* p. 149.
85 *Ibid*, p. 150.
86 *Ibid*, p. 152.
87 *Garda Youth Diversion Project Guidelines*, available at www.justice.ie (accessed 17 January 2006).

Chapter Four

Young People and An Garda Síochána

INTRODUCTION

While many young people in conflict with the law will come into contact with a variety of different agencies as they pass through the system, the one body with which they must all interact is An Garda Síochána. The police have a central role in the administration of youth justice – they play a key role in the diversion of young people from prosecution, they investigate their involvement in criminal offences, they prosecute them before the Children Court and they have a role in the monitoring and enforcement of community sanctions and bail conditions. Consequently, An Garda Síochána have an influential and important position within the youth justice system and the nature of their interactions with young people are worthy of close examination. The focus of this chapter, therefore, is to consider the extent to which Gardaí carry out their functions in this area in line with international standards.

INTERNATIONAL STANDARDS

International standards concerning the role of the police in the youth justice system highlight the need for specialisation and training within the police. Other relevant standards recognise the rights of young people during investigation and prosecution, two important areas of police activity.

Training and Specialisation

Under Article 42 of the Convention on the Rights of the Child (CRC), the state has a duty to make the principles and provisions of the CRC widely known to both adults and children. Implementation of this and other provisions of the CRC requires, according to the Committee on the Rights of the Child, that those working with children, including the police, must integrate training and capacity-building on children's rights into all professional training codes and educational curricula. This training needs to be systematic and ongoing and be subjected to regular review.[1]

The Beijing Rules also provide that in order to best fulfil their functions, police officers who deal with young people or who are primarily engaged in the prevention of youth crime should be specially instructed and trained.[2] Given that the police are the young person's first point of contact with the youth justice system it is important that they act in an informed and appropriate manner.

Rule 6 of the Beijing Rules highlights the need to use appropriate discretion 'at all stages of proceedings and at the different levels of juvenile justice administration, including investigation, prosecution, adjudication and the follow-up of dispositions'.[3] The Rules stress the need to ensure accountability of any such discretion and the requirement that those who exercise it be 'specially qualified or trained to exercise it judiciously and in accordance with their functions and mandates'. Professional qualifications and expert training are specifically mentioned in this context.[4]

Article 40(3) of the CRC requires that the state develop specialism among authorities and bodies dealing with children accused or convicted of infringing the criminal law. The Beijing Rules, more specifically, recommend that the police should develop specialist units for dealing with young people. Rule 1.6, in particular, recommends that in large cities, special police units should be established to improve and sustain the competence of police personnel, to improve the prevention and control of youth crime and the treatment of young offenders.

Treatment of Young People

The Beijing Rules make specific provision for the rights of young people during the processes of investigation and prosecution. In particular, Rule 10.3 requires that contacts between the police and young offenders be managed in such a way as to respect the legal status of the juvenile, promote his/her well-being and avoid harm to him/her. This is especially important in initial contact between young people and the police, which has the potential to profoundly influence the young person's attitude towards the State and society. Given that the success of any further intervention is largely dependent on such initial contacts, international standards propose that compassion and kind firmness are important in these situations.

TREATMENT OF YOUNG PEOPLE IN GARDA STATIONS

Part 6 of the Children Act 2001 sets out the principles and procedures governing the treatment of children by An Garda Síochána when investigating their suspected criminal behaviour. It places the Treatment of Persons in Custody Regulations as they specifically relate to children on a statutory basis with some changes. This part of the Act was commenced on 1 May 2002.[5]

The Act establishes a general principle that a child suspected of having committed an offence must be treated in a manner appropriate to his/her age and understanding and with respect for his/her rights, dignity, vulnerability and special needs (s. 55). It has been questioned whether the high aspirations referred to here are adhered to in practice[6] and some of these concerns are discussed below.

Accommodation, Questioning and Advocacy

The Children Act 2001 also places more particular duties on An Garda Síochána with respect to the treatment of children in Garda stations. First, it requires that children are kept separate from adults in detention and not held in a Garda cell unless there is no other accommodation available (s. 56). No resources or structures appear to be in place to implement this provision, however, and in the experience of some practitioners, children are placed in cells as a first rather than a last resort. While they are not detained with adults, the fact that cells are frequently arranged in a cluster means that the child is often subjected to the noise, language and other disturbing behaviour emanating from the adults in nearby cells.[7] The recommendation of the Law Society Law Reform Committee that the conditions and procedures for holding children in Garda cells be reviewed in the light of international obligations is reiterated here, along with the necessity to ensure that sufficient facilities are put in place to ensure that children are not held in custody with adults.[8]

Second, where a child is arrested and brought to a Garda station on suspicion of having committed an offence, the child must be informed without delay of the offence in respect of which he/she is being arrested, of his/her right to a solicitor and that his/her parents have been given this information and are being requested to attend the station without delay (s. 57). Importantly, this information must be given to the child in a manner and in language appropriate to the child's age and level of understanding. Similarly, the Garda has a duty to inform a child's parent or guardian that the child is in custody, giving details of the offence in connection with which he/she is being questioned and the child's right to a solicitor. They are also requested to attend the station without delay. This provision is designed to address the previous situation where parents claimed they did not know that their child had been arrested.[9] The converse appears to the problem now in so far as Gardaí frequently find it difficult to contact parents because they are not at home or cannot otherwise be found.[10]

Third, according to section 58, if a Garda is unable to get in touch with the child's parent, guardian or spouse or that person is unwilling or unable to attend the station within a reasonable time, the child must be told of his/her entitlement to nominate an alternative adult (either an adult relative or an adult reasonably named by the child). This alternative adult must then be given information as soon as practicable regarding the fact that the child is in custody, the nature of the offence, the child's right to consult a solicitor and that they are requested to attend the station without delay. There appear to be considerable problems implementing this provision satisfactorily in practice due, principally, to the lack of an appropriate adult scheme or panel. According to Ring, 'experience has shown the most amazing variety of people are called upon to attend as a responsible adult, all of whom in the main are strangers to the child involved, many of whom are members of the public' who are in a position to attend the station.[11] In some areas, peace commissioners are asked to fulfil this role[12] while other examples include a cleaner,[13] who was asked to step into the interview room to be present, and the barman from a next door pub.[14] Given that an interview may have serious implications for a child's future, it is most important that in the absence of a parent or guardian, the person fulfilling this role is independent (including the appearance of independence from An Garda Síochána), aware of his/her role and suitably trained. Instead, the situation appears to be that the persons contacted by Gardaí in such situations have 'no real idea of what their function is or why they are there, consequently, they usually take their lead and advice from the investigating Gardaí'.[15] In this context, there is a clear need to draw up an independent panel of people who could attend Garda stations in such situations and advocate on behalf of the child. Where necessary, members of the panel should receive training to enable them to fulfil this role adequately. Section 70(b) of the Act empowers the Minister for Justice, Equality and Law Reform to make regulations governing the role of any of the adults present at the interview of a child in a Garda station. This provides the ideal mechanism by which to implement these recommendations[16] and such regulations should be drawn up and implemented without delay.

While these duties are set out in unequivocal terms in the legislation, the Act also makes it clear that failure to fulfil these duties will not 'of itself' affect either the lawfulness of the child's detention or the admissibility in evidence of any statement made by the child.[17] According to McDermott and Robinson, 'of itself' is the key phrase here given that there are relevant human rights and constitutional provisions that prevent the application of a blanket immunity of this kind.[18] However, any court considering such an issue would have considerable discretion to examine the surrounding circumstances.

Involvement of the Health Service Executive

An Garda Síochána was given new functions under the Children Act 2001 to liaise with the Health Service Executive (HSE) in respect of children who were in need of care and protection. This occurs in two situations where a Garda has reasonable belief that the child is not receiving adequate care: first with respect to a child under the age of criminal responsibility who comes to its attention (s. 54), and second, in respect of a child who comes to the Garda station on suspicion of having committed an offence (s. 59). In the latter case, this duty is followed by a mandatory duty on the HSE to attend the station within a reasonable time, to use its powers under the Child Care Act 1991 where appropriate, and to be entitled to be present at the questioning of the child. This last provision was important to ensure that a child whose parents did not attend the Garda station was nonetheless represented by an appropriate adult in the form of the representative of the HSE.

A number of issues arise here. First, this situation clearly represents a change in function for members of An Garda Síochána, who are required by the Act to make judgements as to the state of the child's welfare and the capacity of the child's parent or guardian to meet the child's needs. Such assessments demand training insofar as they purport to involve individual Gardaí in a completely new role and because once the judgement is made, mandatory duties follow.[19] A second and important point falls to be made about the likely operation of section 59 and the willingness of Gardaí to involve HSE representatives in what is effectively a policing matter. McDermott and Robinson note that 'there may be cases where the investigating officers are eager to interview a child about an offence and may not always welcome the intervention of the health board (HSE) whose primary function will be the welfare of the child rather than the investigation of the crime'. For section 59 to work properly, therefore, the member in charge will have to show independence from the investigatory process.[20]

In light of these issues, it is perhaps not surprising that section 59 was not commenced with the rest of Part 6 on 1 May 2002. It is of concern, however, that a legislative provision, whose aim is to bring to the attention of social services those children falling under its duty of care under the Child Care Act

1991, remains in limbo. Moreover, the Criminal Justice Act 2006 repeals that paragraph of section 59 entitling the HSE's representative to attend the child's questioning by Gardaí.[21] While this may not prevent the representative from requesting to attend, or indeed being asked to do so in certain circumstances, the repeal of the representative's entitlement to attend removes an important safeguard for children who are otherwise vulnerable in Garda custody.

Detention as a Last Resort?

During its visit to Ireland in 2002, the Committee for the Prevention of Torture, Inhuman and Degrading Treatment or Punishment (CPT) expressed concern about the designation of police cells as places of detention for children. It noted how inappropriate such places are for holding children for an extended period.[22] According to the Government's Response, 'every effort is made to avoid situations where children are held on inappropriate premises due to pressure on places in children detention schools at any given time'.[23] By asserting its right to use police cells for this purpose, the Government is making it clear that its approach in this area is defined by pragmatic considerations rather than concern for the welfare and rights of the child. The Government Response continues: 'In general, a child in these circumstances is subsequently placed in the unit of preference or in an appropriate alternative facility within a twenty-four hour period'.[24] Nevertheless, it is of concern that despite the duty on Gardaí to take into account the child's rights, dignity and vulnerability, there are no child-specific statutory limits on the length of time children and young people can be detained in a Garda cell for this purpose. Nor is there any child-specific limit on the length of time that a child may be held for questioning.[25] The principle of detention as a last resort and for the shortest appropriate period of time, recognised in Article 37 of the CRC, does not appear to be upheld with respect to children detained in Garda stations.[26] This is an obvious gap in the legislation, which should be remedied by including a commitment to limiting the detention of children in Garda stations for questioning or other purposes to the shortest period of time. Efforts should also be made to collate data on the periods that young people spend in Garda custody for questioning and to evaluate the compatibility of these experiences with international standards.[27]

The Darren Goodwin and Brian Rossiter Cases

Concern was expressed above about the extent to which the laudable principles and provisions set out in Part 6 of the Children Act 2001 are adhered to in practice. The cases of Brian Rossiter and Darren Goodwin are particularly worrisome in this regard.

In November 2003, Darren Goodwin was arrested on suspicion of murder and questioned overnight in Portlaoise Garda Station where he eventually confessed to murdering Daragh Conroy, a 14-year-old boy. At Goodwin's trial in the Central Criminal Court in 2004, details emerged of his treatment by Gardaí of which Judge Barry White was especially critical. Judge White first criticised the decision to arrest and question Darren Goodwin in the middle of the night (he was questioned from 3.30 am to 6.35 am, and then again at 8.30 am) telling the court that 'it does not appear to me that there was any urgency that required it [the arrest] on the night in question'. He continued: 'even if it was urgent, I do not consider it appropriate to question the child in his fatigued position'.[28] With respect to the failure to notify the accused and his father of his right to consult a solicitor, Judge White said that the garda in charge at Portlaoise Garda station had 'failed to comply with his statutory obligations' by not doing so. While he concluded that that failure was 'not fatal to the validity of the detention', nevertheless the judge noted that it was perhaps 'indicative of the cavalier attitude of the member-in-charge to a person detained under Section 4'.[29] Judge White also expressed concern about the conduct of the Gardaí during the interviews. According to the judge, 'throughout the second and third interview, the juvenile maintained his attitude that he was not guilty of any offence. That attitude was maintained throughout the fourth interview.' He then went on to criticise Garda detectives and the boy's father – who was present during questioning – for 'raised voices' and 'inappropriate comments' made to the teenager during the fourth interview before concluding that he was 'satisfied that in the course of that interview an endeavour was made to break the will of the juvenile'. Following the fourth interview, the boy was left in the company of his father who subsequently told Gardaí that his son was willing to confess his part in the death of the 14-year-old. 'To say the least', Judge White observed, having viewed the interview tapes, 'there is a reluctance on the part of the juvenile to make any admissions and the admissions are effectively cajoled out of him. Having regard to the atmosphere of the fourth interview, and the demeanour of the juvenile in the fifth interview, I am satisfied that the emanations from him were not the emanations of a free will, I am satisfied they were not freely made.'[30] He went on to note that he was 'satisfied that the juvenile was fatigued' and could be seen yawning several times. He said that the member-in-charge 'did not give any proper consideration as to whether or not it was appropriate to interview the person at that stage'. He also criticised Gardaí for holding the young person in a Garda cell when there were other rooms available, finding this inappropriate with regard to the legislation. Meal arrangements were also found to be unacceptable with Judge White refusing to accept the contention on the part of Gardaí that the accused had been offered breakfast but refused it. The judge also found the extension of the period of detention of the boy was late by one minute and was unlawful. He ruled the five video interviews to be inadmissible as evidence and they were not shown to the jury.

It is not clear what if any action was taken by the Garda Commissioner in response to the judge's criticisms. Given that the interviews were ruled to be inadmissible – a consequence which could, it is submitted, have resulted in the boy's acquittal – it is strongly recommended that steps be taken to ensure that future interviews with children comply fully with Irish legislation and international standards. Gardaí involved in interviewing children and young people should also receive appropriate training.

The case of Brian Rossiter raises concerns of a very different nature. Brian Rossiter was a 14-year-old boy who was arrested in Clonmel on 10 September 2002 with respect to a public order offence. His father allegedly agreed to him being detained overnight in the Garda station in order to give him a 'short sharp shock'. He was found in a coma in a Garda cell the following morning and died four days later on 15 September 2002. While Brian Rossiter had received a black eye in an assault on 8 September, it is not known whether this injury or others received in the intervening period, including while in custody, caused his death.[31] The circumstances of Brian Rossiter's death, including the appropriateness of his detention and the failure to provide him with medical attention, do not appear to have ever been fully investigated.[32]

In 2005, the Minister for Justice, Equality and Law Reform established a statutory enquiry into the matter.[33] Chaired by Hugh Hartnett, SC, the enquiry, set up under the Police Acts, is to determine whether relevant members of An Garda Síochána were in neglect or violation of their duty on 10 and 11 September 2002 during the time of the arrest and death of Brian Rossiter.[34] In particular, the enquiry has been asked to establish whether the circumstances of the boy's death were investigated and all witnesses interviewed.

While the Commissioner explained that he could not comment on the case for legal reasons, in June 2005, An Garda Síochána announced that an in-depth review of Garda practices and procedures with respect to the custody of persons in Garda stations was now to be expanded to specifically address 'the custody of juveniles in Garda Stations including issues relating to medical, legal, welfare and parental involvement'.[35] The necessary amendments to the regulations will be made following this review. Interestingly, this statement from the Commissioner, and the terms of reference published by the Minister for Justice, Equality and Law Reform both refer not to Part 6 of the Children Act 2001, but to the provisions of the Criminal Justice Act, 1984 (Treatment of Persons in Custody Regulations 1987).

The enquiry into the circumstances of Brian Rossiter's death began in September 2005 and although his parents expressed concern about the scope of the terms of reference (they will not necessarily establish what happened to Brian) and the payment of costs for the family's representation, these were resolved and his family agreed to co-operate with the enquiry. While the Chairman decided to conduct the enquiry in private, it is strongly hoped that its report will be made fully public at the earliest opportunity and that all necessary action will be taken to implement its recommendations in full.

RELATIONSHIP BETWEEN YOUNG PEOPLE AND GARDAÍ

International standards highlight the importance of encouraging a positive relationship between the police and young people. Given the police role as 'gatekeepers' to the criminal justice system, the nature of the interaction between young people and the police can have far–reaching consequences.[36] Attitudes are hugely influential in determining outcomes of interventions with young people. As Ring notes, 'if children are to learn by being arrested, detained, diverted or brought before the courts, it is important that they have as much of a positive approach to that as possible'.[37] Despite this, the poor attitudes of young people towards the police are well documented[38] and Ireland is no exception.[39] While many children are dealt with appropriately and with sensitivity and respect by Gardaí, others are not properly treated and are left with a bad opinion of the police and a negative impression of the criminal justice system as a whole.[40] In some cases, young people appearing before the Children Court have complained that they were intimidated, harassed, bullied or ill-treated by members of An Garda Síochána.[41] This raises the need for an effective, age appropriate independent mechanism for the investigation of complaints against Gardaí, which is dealt with below.

Young People's Attitudes Towards An Garda Síochána

Although little research has been carried out into the relationship between young people and An Garda Síochána, the Garda Research Unit carried out a survey among young people about their attitudes towards Gardaí in 2004. Unfortunately, the results are not yet public. In the meantime, useful conclusions can be drawn from research into the impact and effectiveness of the Garda Special Projects conducted by Bowden and Higgins in 2000. As part of this process, the researchers interviewed the young people involved in the Projects about their attitudes towards Gardaí.[42] According to their findings, almost half of the fifty-one young people involved in these Projects indicated that they had generally negative attitudes towards An Garda Síochána; one third were positive and the remainder were either indifferent or gave more nuanced answers. Importantly, the research found that in Projects where Gardaí play a role at programme level, the response of the young people was quite positive towards this involvement. However, in the majority of cases, this did not result in shifts in attitude toward An Garda Síochána as a whole. Generally, the young people drew very clear distinctions between Community Gardaí and regular Garda officers. Moreover, their attitudes appeared to be shaped by other factors, such as their own previous experiences of Gardaí and those of their families and peers. So, although the majority had positive attitudes towards the community Gardaí, this did not translate into positive attitudes towards the force as a whole.

A study of participants in the Garda Special Projects in 2001, designed to develop a profile of risk factors thought to be prevalent in the lives of such young people, also explored the relationship between participants and Gardaí.[43] One hundred and ten young people between the ages of 10 and 17 were asked their opinion on whether Gardaí should be actively involved with the Projects. They were divided in their responses stating, for example, that 'we don't associate with the Gardaí ... if they are involved we don't get involved with the Projects ... we don't like them.'[44] However, other participants felt that it was a good idea to have them involved saying, for example, that '... It stops other young people from causing trouble – we don't get into trouble if they are here – they teach you not to.'[45]

Given the nature of the research, these attitudes may be more typical of young people in conflict with the law than the general population of young people. Measuring the attitudes of the broader population of Irish young people is difficult in the absence of the Garda Attitudes Survey. However, evidence from Northern Ireland, which admittedly has a particular context, may serve to illustrate the nature of the problem here also. In 2004, Hamilton et al. studied young people's views of police accountability.[46] Although confined mainly to the 16 to 24 age range, 56 per cent of young men and 28 per cent of young women reported contact with the police in the previous twelve months. Being stopped and questioned by the police and being moved on were the most frequent reasons for contact and most young people regarded their treatment as harassment, which included 'physical violence, a constant police presence and being watched, confiscation of goods and verbal abuse'. Their experiences of the police were 'predominantly negative' and 24 per cent were 'very dissatisfied' with the police.[47] Disrespectfulness and/or impoliteness' (58 per cent) were the main criticisms. Ellison's research in 2001 supports this finding also, noting that 14- to 17-year-old males are three times more likely to be stopped and searched by a police officer than 18-year-olds. Children from 'socio-economically disadvantaged areas' were also more than twice as likely to have been searched.

Attitudes of Gardaí Towards Young People

While international standards encourage the use of discretion at different stages in the criminal process from diversion to prosecution, research has shown that the use of discretion is moulded by things like the attitude and demeanour of young people in public spaces, their physical and social features and how they interact with the police directly. In other words, police attitudes towards young people can influence the nature of their interaction and have an impact on the way discretion is used.[48]

The Human Rights Audit of An Garda Síochána carried out in June 2004 aimed to identify the extent to which Garda policies and procedures met international standards on human rights.[49] While children's rights were not specifically addressed in this context – see below – results from the focus groups highlighted negative attitudes towards some young people. The (Garda) participants noted, for example, that while terms such as 'gouger' were used with reference to young people, that did not mean that they were treated any differently.[50]

Other research has highlighted the 'inherent police suspicion' of certain groups including young people in social housing.[51] Despite this, 40 per cent of the respondents to the Garda Síochána survey, also completed as part of the Human Rights Audit, rated their own relationship with young people as 'good', with a further 40 per cent rating it as 'okay'.[52] Interestingly, however, respondents' impression of their own relationships were better than their assessments of the service as a whole, suggesting that they were willing to be more open about their perceptions with regard to the organisation than their own personal view.

Improving Relationships Between Young People and Gardaí

There is little doubt that the power imbalance between Gardaí and young people is strong and that Gardaí are firmly in control. The extent to which their role as prosecutor in the Court overlaps with their role in the community is a matter of concern, for operational purposes as well as reasons of principle. Gardaí are required, at once, to be law enforcers, crime investigators and prosecutors, a challenge which does not always allow for the distrust of Gardaí which prevails in many communities.[53]

Measures to improve the relationship between the police and young people must go beyond the adoption of policy and mission statements making commitments to treating young people fairly and with respect. They should involve an integration into police training of the requisite tools with which to understand young people, youth culture and behaviour, and children's rights, and to minimise negative stereotyping of young people from particular areas or backgrounds. There is a particular duty on the police to consider how best to enforce public order laws without infringing the legitimate and lawful use by young people of public places and spaces. An awareness of the right of young people to use such areas is vital in this context. Yet increased powers in relation, for example, to control of anti-social behaviour (generally seen as nuisance behaviour that is less than criminal) mean that this will continue to be a flashpoint in relations between the police and young people in Ireland as elsewhere.[54]

An Garda Síochána are clearly already undertaking work in this area. The Garda Schools Programme, introduced in 1991, introduces primary school children to the work of An Garda Síochána and teaches them how to develop positive attitudes towards them and the work that they do. An initiative in secondary schools has been added to the Programme more recently and is currently being introduced to second level schools throughout the country as part of the syllabus for Social, Personal and Health Education taught at Junior Certificate level.[55]

While schools are an important way to access children and young people in order to foster a positive relationship with the police, there are many young people – those who do not attend regularly or who do not attend at all – who will not be reached via this scheme. It is vital therefore that the outreach work of An Garda Síochána extends to marginalised young people and to this end, consideration should be given to integrating further Garda involvement in community programmes, youth clubs and places of detention.

There is already precedent for such involvement. In addition to their work with individual children as part for the statutory Diversion Programme, Juvenile Liaison Officers carry out important work in the community where they meet and co-operate with parents, teachers, probation officers, social workers, welfare officers and personnel involved in child guidance clinics, public health clinics and the courts. JLOs take an active interest in youth and other clubs operating in the community and give talks to schools and other relevant organisations. This work must be structured, targeted, and carefully monitored to ensure its effectiveness in building positive relationships between Gardaí and young people. Given the resources involved and the importance of their work in the Diversion Programme, JLOs should be supported by other members of An Garda Síochána in this task.

It is instructive in this context to consider the 2005 Policing Strategy to evaluate how genuine the commitment of An Garda Síochána is to building positive relationships with young people. With regard to its second strategic goal (to reduce the incidence of *inter alia* criminal behaviour) the strategy identifies, as action for 2005, the development of divisional initiatives in conjunction with the National Juvenile Office to address juvenile offending.[56] Corresponding performance indicators include: the number of referrals to the National Juvenile Office, informal and formal cautions administered and prosecutions initiated and the number of JLOs who have received training in mediation.

Strategic Goal 5, to increase public confidence in An Garda Síochána, includes a specific action to review the findings of a 2004 national survey of young people's experiences of dealing with Gardaí, victimisation and delinquency (referred to above) and 'take appropriate action'. However, no corresponding performance indicators are listed with regard to addressing the relationship between An Garda Síochána and young people, an issue clearly vital to effective policing in certain areas.

The Human Rights Audit of An Garda Síochána undertaken in 2004 did not specifically consider the extent to which the rights of children and young people may be infringed by the police, directly or indirectly. The fact that the Audit highlights very few issues relating to the rights of children and young people appears to be related to the methodology used. In particular, the Audit was guided *inter alia* by the Council of Europe's document 'Policing in a Democratic Society', which lists other international human rights instruments but surprisingly makes no reference to the Convention on the Rights of the Child or standards on youth justice. The failure to use such indicators appears to have led to a failure to involve children's rights groups in the consultation process. As a result, the Audit does not address the rights of young people and their relationship with Gardaí. The absence of young people from the Audit process is a matter of serious concern for a number of reasons. First, it shows a failure, not just among An Garda Síochána but more widespread, to recognise the importance of the relationship between young people and the police in society. The process, which clearly did not involve children or young people directly, must also be considered flawed in this respect. The consequence of this is that the Garda Human Rights Action Plan for the Implementation of the Garda Human Rights Audit makes no reference to the rights of children and young people. In light of the Audit's aim to suggest ways in which the Council of Europe's auditing guide can be augmented to become a comprehensive tool suited to the needs and future development of An Garda Síochána, it is unfortunate that the opportunity was not taken to re-consider Ireland's international obligations in this context, and to include the areas of children's rights and youth justice in any future benchmarking process. Incorporation of these values into the training which the Audit recommends must also be undertaken as a priority.

TRAINING OF AN GARDA SÍOCHÁNA

International standards are unequivocal about the need to develop specialisation within the police who should undertake appropriate and adequate training on youth justice and children's rights. It is unfortunate, therefore, that existing training was not audited for compliance with these standards during the Human Rights Audit in 2004 for the reasons set out above.

Nevertheless, it is important that student Gardaí receive some training on the Children Act 2001, notably Part 6 on the treatment of child suspects, Part 4 on the Garda Diversion Programme and evidence and court procedure in both Phase I and Phase III of their education. It is welcome that these classes appear to be participatory in nature comprising case studies and group discussion. However, the time allocated to them is short, presumably due to the pressure of the curriculum and may not be adequate to ensure that all Gardaí are equipped with the necessary skills, particularly given the importance of their role in the Children Court.[57] Importantly, however, it is stipulated that student Gardaí shadow Juvenile Liaison Officers for one week to learn best practice in a clinical environment and also undertake communications training. Attention should be given to finding a way to facilitate individual assessment or feedback on this training despite the large numbers.

Overall, however, students do not appear to have sufficient opportunity to consider the application of children's rights and youth justice principles in practice. Nor does there appear to be scope in the current educational curriculum for considering the broader issues around community policing, attitudes to young people and youth culture. It is important that outside agencies such as the ISPCC participate in the delivery of the education during Phase III of the training programme.[58] Consideration should also be given to engaging with community groups, including those involved with the Garda Special Projects, who work with marginalised young people, those at risk of offending as well as those already in the criminal justice system.

On a more general level, there is no specialised youth division within An Garda Síochána although the National Juvenile Office and others involved in the management and delivery of the Garda Diversion Programme have undoubtedly developed a wealth of experience in this area. It is regrettable that this focus has not driven the development of a specialised unit for dealing with children and young people. A youth division within An Garda Síochána would not only develop specific youth-oriented policies, it could also consider the varying issues relating to the use of Garda power, challenges involved in policing young people, including young women, and inform the need for training and continuing professional development in these areas.

INDEPENDENT COMPLAINTS MECHANISM FOR CHILDREN

Formal, independent complaints mechanisms are necessary to act as a check on the exercise of police discretion and to investigate and challenge the abuse or misuse of power in individual cases. International standards make it clear that these must be specially adapted for children in order to be effective, to reflect the fact that the special status of children creates real difficulties for them in pursuing remedies for breaches of their rights. This must include child-friendly information, advice, advocacy and access to independent complaints procedures with necessary legal and other assistance.[59]

The community groups consulted as part of the Human Rights Audit of An Garda Síochána expressed the view that there was no culture of human rights within the force. As one contributor observed 'the Gardaí can manipulate the law. They send a hidden message – "we can lift you at any time". There is no accountability. There is internal corruption. I have seen baton marks on young people. Fear and intimidation are used.'[60] While this may be an extreme view, it is clear from other sources also that young people have complaints regarding their treatment by Gardaí.[61]

The in-house complaints mechanism operated by An Garda Síochána to date clearly did not meet international standards as it was neither independent, effective nor adapted for children and young people. Nor was this situation remedied by the establishment of an Ombudsman for Children insofar as that Office has no remit to receive complaints with regard to the treatment of children by the police or in detention.[62] This means that those who allege that they have been intimidated, harassed or abused by Gardaí have no effective remedy despite the fact that, according to the Ombudsman for Children, 'An Garda Síochána is in contact with some of the more vulnerable children in our society on a daily basis and possesses a wide range of powers in dealing with such children including the power to detain'.[63] Despite this potential for abusive use of power, the Ombudsman for Children is precluded under the legislation from investigating any action taken by An Garda Síochána which would ordinarily fall within her remit.[64]

The decision to establish a Garda Ombudsman Commission under the Garda Síochána Act 2005 is very welcome in this context. While the Commission is independent and has the requisite powers to investigate individual cases, it remains to be seen whether it will develop effective, child-sensitive and age-appropriate procedures to ensure that young people and their representatives can access the complaints mechanisms effectively. These mechanisms are vital to ensure that the rights of children and young people are vindicated in this area. Moreover, it is strongly recommended that information on the Commission and its procedures should be published in language that is appropriate to children's different ages and understanding. Details regarding how to contact the Commission should be given as a matter of right to young people on arrest and to all children who encounter Gardaí in the community and in detention.[65]

It is welcome also that under the Garda Síochána Act 2005 a mandatory investigation will arise on the death of a person in custody or at the alleged hands of a member of An Garda Síochána.[66] This is required both by Ireland's obligations under the International Covenant on Civil and Political Rights[67] and under the European Convention on Human Rights (ECHR).[68] In particular, the ECHR requires that suspicious deaths in custody be investigated in a prompt, independent and effective manner in which the victim's family is fully involved.[69] Moreover, the Court has held that:

> where the events in issue lie wholly, or in large part, within the exclusive knowledge of the authorities, as in the case of persons within their control in custody, strong presumptions of fact will arise in respect of injuries and death occurring during such detention. Indeed, the burden of proof may be regarded as resting on the authorities to provide a satisfactory and convincing explanation.[70]

These principles of international law serve to supplement Irish constitutional protection of the right to life. However, the manner in which the Ombudsman Commission will operate in this area remains to be seen and it will be particularly important whether and to what extent the procedures are adapted in children's cases. It is at least hoped that this new mechanism will help avoid the three year campaign undertaken by Brian Rossiter's parents to have an enquiry established into the circumstances of his detention and his death. Regardless of the outcome of the Hartnett enquiry, there has already been a failure to conduct a reasonably expeditious enquiry into the death of the 14-year-old. It may be some consolation that, under current procedures, this will be avoided in the future.

CONCLUSION

The relationship between young people and Gardaí is a complex one and clearly incorporates, on both sides, all manner of attitudes from one end of the spectrum to the other. While the overall impression of the attitude of young people to Gardaí is unknown, the nature of the relationship appears to vary from community to community and from Garda to Garda. Much will depend on the nature of the young person's interaction with individual Gardaí, with those who benefit from involvement in a Garda Project seeing a more positive side to the Gardaí than those who only encounter them on the street or in the Children Court. Ultimately, however, the duty is on the Gardaí to operationalise the principles of the Children Act and international standards which require them to respect the rights, dignity and vulnerability of young people. If that is secured, there is little doubt that young people's respect of Gardaí will follow.

NOTES

1 Committee on the Rights of the Child, *General Measures of Implementation of the Convention on the Rights of the Child*, CRC/GC/2004/5, available at www.ohchr.org (accessed 17 January 2006).
2 Rule 12.1 UN Standard Minimum Rules for the Administration of Juvenile Justice (the Beijing Rules) adopted by General Assembly

resolution 40/33 29 November 1985, available at www.ohchr.org (17 January 2006).

3 *Ibid.*, Rule 6.1.

4 *Ibid.*, Rule 6.3 and the Commentary to Rule 6. See also Rule 58 of the UN Guidelines for the Prevention of Juvenile Delinquency (the Riyadh Guidelines) adopted by General Assembly resolution 45/112 of 14 December 1990, available at www.ohchr.org (12 January 2006).

5 SI No 151 of 2002. Children Act 2001 (Commencement) Order 2002.

6 Comments made by McCarthy, T., Solicitor, speaker at 'An Outline of the Children Act 2001' a seminar held in the University of Limerick, 11 October 2005.

7 *Ibid.*

8 Law Reform Committee, *Rights-based Child Law: The case for reform – Part 1* (Dublin: Law Society, 2005), p. 93.

9 See Ring, M.E., 'Treatment of Child Suspects in Garda Stations', in *The Children Bill, 1999*, papers from a seminar organised by the Children's Legal Centre (Dublin: Children's Legal Centre, 2000) p. 23.

10 This difficulty is shared elsewhere. See Quinn, K., and Jackson, J., *The detention and questioning of young persons by the police in Northern Ireland* (Belfast: NIO, 2003) p. vii.

11 Ring, M.E., 'Treatment of Child Suspects in Garda Stations', p. 23.

12 McCarthy, T., 'An Outline of the Children Act 2001'.

13 Law Reform Committee, *Rights-based Child Law: The case for reform – Part 1*, p. 94.

14 Ring, M.E., 'Treatment of Child Suspects in Garda Stations', p. 24.

15 Law Society, *Submission on the Children Bill 1999*, p. 2.

16 Law Society Law Reform Committee, *Rights-based Child Law: The case for reform – Part 1*, p. 94.

17 However, it may result in disciplinary proceedings against the Garda in charge. See section 66.

18 McDermott, P.A., and Robinson, T., *The Children Act 2001* (Dublin: Thomson Round Hall, 2003), p. 92.

19 See Ring, M.E., 'Treatment of Child Suspects in Garda Stations', pp. 22–3.

20 McDermott, P.A., and Robinson, T., *The Children Act 2001*, p. 85. See also Walsh, D., *Juvenile Justice* (Dublin: Thomson Round Hall, 2005), pp. 58–9.

21 See Criminal Justice Bill 2004, Second composite List of Amendments, 16 May 2006, available at www.oireachtas.ie (accessed 16 May 2006). The Bill was passed on 29 June 2006.

22 CPT/Inf (2003) 36 Report to the Government of Ireland on the visit to Ireland carried out by the European Committee for the Prevention of Torture and Inhuman or Degrading Treatment or Punishment (CPT) from 20 to 28 May 2002 (Strasbourg: Council of Europe, 2003), p. 41.

23 Government's response to the CPT Report, p. 44.

24 *Ibid.*

25 See also Walsh, D., *Juvenile Justice*, p. 48 for the full legal position.

26 See further Chapter Seven.

27 For an excellent example of the kind of research needed see Quinn, K., and Jackson, J., *The detention and questioning of young persons by the police in Northern Ireland.*
28 *Irish Times*, 30 July 2004.
29 Section 4 of the Criminal Justice Act 1984 makes provision for detention after arrest and in particular provides for the accused to be given reasonable time to rest when in custody between the hours of 12 midnight and 8 am.
30 *Irish Times*, 30 July 2004.
31 Browne, V., 'Tracing the Steps of Brian Rossiter's last Day', *Village Magazine*, 1 July 2005.
32 See Browne, V., 'The making of another cover-up', *Village Magazine,* 17 September, 2005.
33 Browne, V., 'Letter from McDowell to Rossiters' Solicitor', *Village Magazine*, 1 July 2005. See also 'Too Little Very Late' by the same author in the same edition of *Village Magazine.*
34 The full terms of reference for the enquiry were published on the website of the Department of Justice, Equality and Law Reform on 15 September 2005. See www.justice.ie (18 January 2006).
35 An Garda Síochána, Press Release, 'Arrest and Detention of Brian Rossiter at Clonmel Garda Station 10 September 2002, June 2005, available at www.garda.ie (accessed 18 January 2006). The remainder of the press release was to note that the Commissioner could not comment on the case because it was *sub judice* due to proceedings on-going in the courts.
36 Cunneen, C., and White, R., *Juvenile Justice Youth and Crime in Australia* (Sydney, OUP, 2002), p. 239.
37 Ring, M.E, 'Treatment of Child Suspects in Garda stations', p. 25.
38 Cunneen, C., and White, R., *Juvenile Justice,* p. 242 and Kilkelly, U., et al., *Children's Rights in Northern Ireland* (Belfast, NICCY, 2005) pp. 159–60.
39 McCarthy, T., 'An Outline of the Children Act 2001'. See also Ring, M.E., 'Treatment of Child Suspects in Garda stations', p. 25.
40 Ring, M.E., 'Treatment of Child Suspects in Garda stations' p. 25.
41 Kilkelly, U., *The Children's Court: A Children's Rights Audit* (Cork, 2005) p. 85.
42 Bowden, M., and Higgins, L., *The Impact and Success of the Garda Special Projects: Final Report to the Department of Justice, Equality and Law Reform May 2000*, available at www.justice.ie (accessed 6 November 2005), p. 162.
43 Warren, A., *Study of Participants in Garda Special Projects* by the Centre for Social and Educational Research, DIT on behalf of the Department of Justice, Equality and Law Reform (October 2001), available at www.justice.ie (accessed 6 November 2005)
44 *Ibid*, p. 51.
45 *Ibid.*
46 Hamilton, J., Radford, K., and Jarman, N., *Policing, Accountability and Young People* (Belfast: Institute for Conflict Research, 2004).

47 Ellison refers to this as 'adversary contact'. See Ellison, 'Young People and the Royal Ulster Constabulary: A Survey of Inter-Communal Attitudes', 11 *Policing and Society* (2001), 321.
48 Cunneen, C., and White, R., *Juvenile Justice* pp. 242–4.
49 Ionann Management Consultants, *Human Rights Audit of the Garda Síochána,* 2004, available at www.garda.ie (accessed 16 January 2006).
50 *Ibid.,* p. 46.
51 See Chief Superintendent John O'Brien Study of Policing Strategy in the City of Dublin, *ibid.*, fn. 16.
52 *Ibid.*, p. 84.
53 Kilkelly, U., *The Children's Court: A Children's Rights Audit,* pp. 84–5.
54 See further Chapters Two and Six.
55 Details of the Divisional Garda Schools Liaison Inspectors can be found on the Garda Síochána website at www.garda.ie (accessed 18 January 2006).
56 An Garda Síochána Policing Strategy, 2005, p. 6.
57 See the concerns noted following observation of Gardaí in the Children's Court. Kilkelly, U., *The Children's Court: A Children's Rights Audit*, pp. 81–2.
58 I am grateful to Superintendent Kieran McGann, Director of Training and Development at the Garda Training College for this information.
59 Committee on the Rights of the Child, *General Measures of Implementation of the Convention on the Rights of the Child*, pp. 13–4.
60 Ionann Management Consultants, *Human Rights Audit of the Garda Síochána*, p. 53.
61 Kilkelly, U., *The Children's Court: A Children's Rights Audit*, pp. 85–7.
62 Martin, F., 'The Ombudsman For Children: An Analysis Of The Strengths And Weaknesses of The Irish Model', 52(1) *Administration* (Spring 2004) pp. 46–68.
63 Ombudsman for Children *Annual Report 2005* (Dublin: OCO, 2005) p. 25.
64 *Ibid.*
65 See also Law Reform Committee, *Rights-based Child Law: The case for reform – Part 1*, p. 83.
66 Section 91, Garda Síochána Act, 2005.
67 Human Rights Committee, *Concluding Observations of the Human Rights Committee: Ireland*, July 2000 (A/55/40) para 14 available at www.ohchr.org (accessed 18 January 2006).
68 Consistent case-law from the European Convention on Human Rights demands that all cases of suspicious deaths in custody be investigated in an independent and effective way in order to comply with the right to protect life under Article 2 of the Convention.
69 See, for example, *Salman* v *Turkey,* judgment of 26 June 2000, available at www.echr.coe.int (accessed 12 January 2006).
70 *Ibid.*, para. 100.

Chapter Five

Young People Before the Courts

INTRODUCTION

Ireland's youth justice system is based largely on the 'justice' values of individual accountability for criminal conduct. Accordingly, young people who are not diverted from the criminal process under the Diversion Programme are prosecuted and brought before the courts: the Children Court for minor offences and the Circuit and Central Criminal Court for more serious or indictable crimes.[1] Although the Children Act 2001 sets out the range of sanctions that these courts can impose on children, it says little about the environment in which they should be tried or the child-specific rules that should govern the trial process.

Accordingly, the aim of this chapter is to consider whether law and practice in these courts adequately protect the child's right to a fair trial in line with international standards. It also considers the extent to which these courts operate to maximise the opportunity which the interaction with the child provides to address his/her offending behaviour in accordance with best practice in other jurisdictions.

INTERNATIONAL STANDARDS

Convention on the Rights of the Child

The Convention on the Rights of the Child (CRC) sets out the principal values which must guide the trial of children. Article 40(1) provides that children in conflict wlth the law have the right to be treated in a manner consistent with the promotion of their sense of dignity and worth and which reinforces their respect for the rights and freedoms of others. Their treatment must take into account the child's age and the desirability of promoting his/her reintegration and assuming a constructive role in society. Article 40(2) makes more detailed provision for the child's right to due process, including the right to be presumed innocent until proven guilty; to have the matter determined without delay by a competent, independent and impartial tribunal; not to be compelled to give testimony or confess guilt, and to appeal and to an interpreter.

In addition, Article 40(2)(b) recognises specific protections for children, such as:

- the right to be informed promptly and directly of the charges against him/her, if appropriate through his/her parents;
- the right to a fair trial in the presence of his/her parents unless this is not in the child's best interests, taking into account his/her age or situation; and
- the right to have his/her privacy fully respected at all stages of proceedings.[2]

In summary, it is clear that children have rights equal to those enjoyed by adults in the criminal justice system and in addition, they have the right to be treated in a manner which takes into account their age and maturity. They have the right to particularly expeditious proceedings wherein their privacy is protected, and they have the right to be heard and to understand their proceedings, as well as the right to have their best interests and rights taken into account throughout the process.[3]

The European Convention on Human Rights

Although the European Convention on Human Rights (ECHR) makes no specific provision for the rights of children in conflict with the law, the interpretation of its provisions has special significance for the manner in which children are treated by the courts. The ECHR has been given further effect in Irish law through the ECHR Act 2003, meaning that its standards have added value in this jurisdiction.[4]

The ECHR has made a unique contribution to international standards on the child's right to a fair trial. In 1994, the Court held that special arrangements designed to protect young people in the criminal process may be compatible with Article 6 as long as they meet the minimal requirements of an independent and fair trial process.[5] In 1999, in the seminal cases of *T.* v. *UK* and *V.* v *UK*[6] the Court considered the compatibility with the Convention of the trial of two 11-year-old boys in an adult court. The proceedings, which concluded with the boys being convicted of the murder of 2-year-old James Bulger, took place over three weeks in the Crown Court with high levels of media and public interest. Some measures were taken in view of their young age and to promote their understanding of the proceedings, including shortening the hearing times and explaining the procedures to the children in advance. Nevertheless, according to the European Court, 'the formality and ritual of the Crown Court must, at times, have seemed incomprehensible to a child of eleven'.[7] There was also evidence that certain modifications to tlie courtroom – such as the raised dock which was designed to enable them to see what was going on – had the effect of increasing their sense of discomfort during the trial and their sense of exposure to the scrutiny of the press and the public. Considerable psychiatric evidence showed that the boys suffered from post-traumatic stress disorder, making it difficult, if not impossible, for them to instruct their lawyers and follow the trial. In the circumstances, therefore, the Court held that it was insufficient for the purposes of Article 6 that they had been represented by skilled and experienced lawyers given that it was highly unlikely that they would have felt sufficiently uninhibited, in the tense courtroom and in the glare of public scrutiny, to have consulted with them during the trial. Indeed, given their immaturity and disturbed emotional state, the Court considered it unlikely that they were capable of cooperating with their lawyers even outside the courtroom in order to give them information for their defence. These factors, the Court concluded, meant that neither applicant was able to participate effectively in the criminal proceedings against him and both boys were, as a consequence, denied a fair hearing.[8]

While these cases were complex, it is clear that the central issue was the failure to take effective measures to reduce or eliminate both the publicity and the formality of the proceedings in the Crown Court. The relevance of the children's mental state during their trial is not clear;[9] nor is it apparent how significant it is that the Court did not find it incompatible with the ECHR to put them on trial in the first place.[10] What is important, however, is the Court's clear requirement that 'a child charged with an offence [must be] dealt with in a manner which takes full account of his age, level of maturity and intellectual and emotional capacities, and that steps are taken to promote his ability to understand and participate in the proceedings'.[11] This principle requires that in order to receive a fair trial a child must be able to understand and participate in criminal proceedings. According to the Court, a child charged with an offence (not just murder) must be facilitated to understand and participate in his/her trial. The principle has particular relevance to the adult court, but clearly applies regardless of where the child's trial occurs.

In 2004, the Court considered the trial of a child in an adult court in different circumstances. *SC* v. *UK*[12] concerned the trial in the Crown Court of an 11-year-old boy who had a very low intellectual level for his age, meaning that he could not, it was argued, fully comprehend or participate in the trial process or give adequate instructions. According to the Court, the ECHR does not require that a child on trial should understand or indeed be capable of understanding every point of law or evidential detail, not least because given the sophistication of modern legal systems many adults of normal intelligence are unable fully to comprehend all the intricacies and exchanges which take place in the courtroom. However, 'effective participation' in this context 'presupposes that the accused has a broad understanding of the nature of the trial process and of what is at stake for him or her, including the significance of any penalty which may be imposed'.[13]

Thus, the Court said, the defendant should be able to follow what is said by the prosecution witness, explain to his own lawyers his version of events, point out any statements with which he disagrees, and make them aware of any facts which should be put forward in his defence. On the facts, the Court noted that although the applicant was tried in public, steps were taken to ensure that the procedure was as informal as possible and many of the intimidating features of the trial in the *T* and

V. cases were absent. Although the Recorder had the judgment in these cases in mind when exercising his discretion to allow the trial to proceed, the Court noted that two experts who assessed the applicant before the hearing concluded that he had a low intellectual level for his age. One concluded that while he had probably been aware that his actions were wrong, 'his understanding of their consequences may have been adversely affected by his learning difficulties and impaired reasoning skill.'[14] Despite the recommendation that the process be explained carefully to him in a manner commensurate with his learning difficulties, and the efforts to that end by the social worker, the Court noted that the applicant seemed to have little comprehension of the role of the jury in the proceedings or the importance of making a good impression on them. 'Even more strikingly,' the Court said, 'he does not seem to have grasped the fact that he risked a custodial sentence and once sentence had passed and he was taken to the holding cells he appeared confused and expected to go home with his foster father.' In the light of this evidence, the Court found that the applicant had not participated effectively in his trial, in violation of Article 6.[15]

According to the Court, certain duties flow from the decision to deal with a child by way of criminal proceedings, rather than some other form of disposal directed primarily at his best interests and those of the community. In particular, where the child risks not being able to participate due to his young age and limited intellectual capacity, 'it is essential that he be tried in a specialist tribunal which is able to give full consideration to and make proper allowance for the handicaps under which he labours and adapt its procedure accordingly'.[16]

The Court did not see any conflict with this position and the failure on the part of the applicant to argue that he was unfit to plead. It noted, in particular, that it does not follow from a child being fit to plead that he is capable of participating effectively in his trial to the extent required by Article 6. The wide application of this principle is clear.

The right to a fair trial under the ECHR thus requires that steps be taken to ensure the participation and understanding of children in criminal proceedings. According to the Court, this requires that criminal proceedings in which children are involved are adapted to take into account any possible learning, intellectual or developmental difficulty which might hinder the child's effective participation in the process. While no preference is shown for an adult or a youth court, what is clear is that the tribunal in which this hearing takes place must be a 'specialist' one, which is sufficiently flexible to allow the child's circumstances to be fully considered and whose procedures have been modified accordingly. The English High Court has subsequently found the youth court to constitute such a specialised tribunal.[17]

Implementation of T *v.* UK *and* V *v.* UK

Further guidance as to how the trial of children and young people may be brought into line with the requirements of the ECHR may be sought from the Practice Direction concerning the trial of children and young persons in the Crown Court issued by the Lord Chief Justice of England and Wales in February 2000 subsequent to the judgments in *T* v. *UK* and *V* v. *UK*.[18] Reflecting the overriding principle that the trial process should not expose the young defendant to avoidable intimidation, humiliation or distress, the Practice Direction requires that regard be had to the welfare of the young defendant in such cases and that 'all possible steps' should be taken to assist him/her to understand and participate in the proceedings. On a practical level, it requires that, where appropriate, young defendants should visit the courtroom out of hours to familiarise themselves with the surroundings, and that the assistance of the police should be engaged to protect the young person from likely intimidation, vilification or abuse generated by public or media interest. With regard to the trial itself, the Practice Direction specifies that where practicable:

- the trial should be held in a courtroom in which all the participants are on the same or almost the same level;
- a defendant should normally be free to sit with members of his/her family and in a place which permits easy, informal communication with his/her legal representatives and others with whom he/she wants or needs communication;
- the court should explain the course of proceedings to a young defendant in terms he/she can understand, should remind

those representing him/her of their continuing duty to explain each step of the trial to him/her and ensure as far as practicable that the trial is conducted in language which the young defendant can understand;
- the trial should be conducted according to a timetable that takes full account of a young person's inability to concentrate for long periods;
- robes and wigs should not be worn and any person responsible for the security of the young defendant who is in custody should not be in uniform – there should be no recognisable police presence in the courtroom save for good reason;
- the court should be prepared to restrict attendance at the trial to a small number, perhaps limited to those with an immediate and direct interest in the outcome of the trial; and
- facilities for reporting the trial must be provided although restrictions may be imposed to protect the young defendant's rights and interests.

While the Practice Direction gives considerable discretion to the court as to how these rights may be secured to the young defendant, this discretion should be exercised having regard to the principle of what is in the child's best interests.

Trial of Children in Other Jurisdictions

According to the international standards, one of the key issues with the trial of children is to create an environment which guarantees a trial, which is age-appropriate and facilitates their participation and understanding of the process. Related to this, a review of other jurisdictions shows that a new focus on engaging young defendants has become a key feature of the court process.

In 1997, the United Kingdom Government issued a White Paper with a view to reforming the youth justice system, which focused *inter alia* on the Youth Court.[19] The White Paper concluded that 'all too often inadequate attention is given to changing offending behaviour' and, in order to address this, proposed that '[t]he purpose of the youth court must change from simply deciding guilt or innocence and then issuing a sentence'. In most cases, it noted, 'an offence should trigger a wider enquiry into the circumstances and nature of the offending behaviour, leading to action to change that behaviour'.[20] It then went on to identify the need to reform the youth court so that it provides:

> speedier decisions on guilt or innocence, much closer to the date of the offence and with less tolerance of adjournments; a system which is more open, and which commands the confidence of victims and the public; processes which engage young offenders and their parents and focus on the nature of their offending behaviour and how to change it; a stronger emphasis on using sentencing to prevent future offending; and more efficient arrangements for the scheduling and management of cases.[21]

The Home Office subsequently commissioned research of the youth court in operation, focussing in particular on its layout and the engagement of defendants by magistrates.[22] As part of the research, which took place between 1998 and 2000, the courts being observed were encouraged to try things out to find what worked best in particular circumstances. Two conclusions of the research are of particular interest here. The first concerns the need for magistrates to engage defendants. In this regard, the research found that 'direct communication ... was a welcome and viable development, and that on the whole the young offenders themselves responded well to it'.[23] While some magistrates were reportedly apprehensive about making appropriate interventions, the research noted that 'clear guidelines and training' can give magistrates confidence, and that the opportunity to exchange experiences and promote best practice can lead to more effective interventions. Engagement between magistrates and defendants was undoubtedly a popular and successful part of the research.[24] The second conclusion of note relates to the physical layout of the court. The research had encouraged the courts to experiment with different layouts and physical arrangements with most moving to the sharing of a single-level space within the court with young people, sitting together with their parents, occupying a central position. While some had concerns that greater informality would affect the dignity of the court, impact on security and cause everyone sitting in closer proximity to be uncomfortable, most of the participants felt the changes were either 'good' or 'satisfactory'. Overall, it was clear that the layout of the court was an important factor in facilitating engagement.[25]

Subsequently, in 2001, the Judicial Studies Board adopted a Youth Court Bench Book, which was revised in 2005.[26] In addition to being a practice guide for magistrates of the Youth Court, the Book also makes an important contribution to the literature on engaging young defendants in practice, in particular by including a set of pronouncements which encourage the judge/magistrate to use common terminology and to give reasons for his/her decisions. These developments are designed to make the Court more accessible to young people with the effect *inter alia* that his/her greater involvement in the process will cause it to have a great impact on his/her behaviour.

The appearance in New Zealand is that while few young people end up before the Youth Court, nonetheless this body has a number of important differences from the Adult Court. First, the sentencing process is largely in the hands of the family conference, whose findings the judge is expected to endorse. Second, judges are expected to try to involve young people and their parents in the court processes and decisions, and to avoid the use of court orders unless absolutely necessary. Thus, while Morris notes that, generally speaking, the Youth Court is run in much the same way as the Adult Criminal Court except that it is closed to the public, in reality it is a recognisably different forum.[27]

An analysis of the Dutch Youth Court shows that, similarly, 'the proceedings are first and foremost a dialogue between the juvenile judge (magistrate) and the young offender'.[28] While legal jargon and court-specific abbreviations are frequently used, it is typical of judges in the Dutch Youth Court to ask at various points whether what they are saying is clear to the young offender. The Dutch experience is also characterised by a moral dialogue whereby the Court usually undertakes some discussion with the offender about the consequences of his/her wrongdoing and, in most cases, puts questions to him/her that attempt to stimulate feelings of empathy for the victim and reflect on the impact of the offence.

Overall, then, it is clear from international standards and best practice elsewhere that regardless of whether children are tried in an adult or a youth court, every effort must be made to adapt the court physically and procedurally to facilitate the child's understanding and participation. Moreover, in addition to determining guilt or innocence, the judge must undertake to engage directly with the defendant by using age-appropriate language.

THE CHILDREN COURT

Having set out the international standards and best practice in some detail, this chapter will now address how law and practice in the Irish courts meets these standards. This section will consider the Children Court while further below, the trial of children in other courts is discussed.

Background to the Current Position

Under the Children Act 1908 a court of summary jurisdiction was to sit separately as a juvenile court to hear charges against young people up to the age of 17 years.[29] Section 80 of the Courts of Justice Act 1924 made further provision for special Children's Courts in Dublin, Cork, Limerick and Waterford to hear charges against children under 16 years. Despite these provisions, only one of these – the Dublin Metropolitan Children's Court – was formally established and in 1988, that Court moved to a dedicated building in Smithfield, a place with which it has become synonymous. In other circumstances, the Children Court sat (and continues to sit) in the same room as the ordinary District Court, although with evidentially different rules of procedure and jurisdiction.[30]

Little change to these arrangements took place in the years before the Children Act 2001 was passed. Few of the reports into youth crime and justice considered the role of the Children Court in any detail and there was nothing, therefore, to prompt its reform. One exception to this was the Task Force on Child Care Services which, in 1980, recommended the establishment of a Children Court to deal, separately, with prosecutions against children as well as care proceedings.[31] It noted that judges should be encouraged to receive training, that cases should be heard *in camera* and that procedural modifications should be introduced to reduce the formality of proceedings, in particular to enable children and parents to be more positively involved and, without inhibition in the proceedings, to understand and accept their purpose more readily. These recommendations were not implemented, however, and were not reiterated by the report of the Dáil Select Committee which proposed many of the reforms leading to the Children Act 2001.[32]

The Children Act 2001

The failure of various enquiries to address the shortcomings of the court system probably explains why the Children Act 2001 did not undertake any real reform of the Children's Court or its role in the youth justice system. The Act recognises that the Children Court (the possessive form was mysteriously dropped) is a special jurisdiction of the District Court with the purpose of hearing cases against children under 18 years, and requires that it sit at a different time or in a different place from the ordinary courts. In line with the enactment of these provisions on 1 May 2002, special sittings of the District Court take place in Cork and Limerick on a weekly basis and in Galway and Waterford on a monthly basis 'at a different time', whereas the Dublin Children Court sits permanently 'in a different place' from the ordinary courts. As the 2001 Act does little other than reiterate the requirements of the 1924 Act with respect to the sittings of the Children Court,[33] no substantial changes appear to have been made to its operations or procedures at this time or since.

The failure to adapt these courts for children in any substantial way has been the subject of criticism. O'Malley noted in 1994 that 'with a few exceptions, the general squalor of Irish courthouses makes them unsuitable for dealing with any offenders, let alone children'.[34] Moreover, two research projects of varying scope published in 2005 documented multiple problems with the operation and environment of the four Children Courts in Cork, Limerick, Waterford and Dublin and, in general, questioned their ability to administer justice within a reasonable time for children and young people.[35] These problems are discussed further below.

A Missed Opportunity for Reform

The Children Act 2001 fails to make proper provision for the establishment of a youth court system. Moreover, what reform is contained in the Act has not been fully implemented to date. The Act's requirements regarding the organisation of the Court's work attempt to separate the Children Court from the adult criminal justice system and to minimise the negative impact for a young person of an appearance before the Court. These are welcome and important provisions although, taken in isolation, they fall short of prescribing how the Court is to be transformed into an age-appropriate environment in which young people have the right to be heard and to participate in their own criminal proceedings in accordance with international standards. The fact that section 96 of the Children Act, which contains the principles governing the sentencing of young people, recognises this right but does not put in place the measures to make it effective, highlights this inadequacy further. For example, there is no provision made for the physical changes that need to take place in the District Court to facilitate children's participation in the criminal process and communication with their legal representatives and family members. Nor does the Act require as a general principle that legal procedures are explained to young people and age-appropriate language used. It is particularly regrettable that what provisions are contained in the Act do not apply to courts other than the Children Court. Together, this suggests that the Act fails to provide adequately for the child's right to a fair trial as required by international standards.

The Role of the Children Court Judge

In the adversarial criminal justice system, the primary function of the Children Court is to determine each criminal charge against a young person. Accordingly, the role of the judge is to hear details of the charge, consider applications of prosecution and defence parties regarding matters of legal aid and bail, determine the young person's guilt or innocence of the charge and, on conviction, choose the appropriate penalty to be imposed. However, this disguises the truly challenging and complex nature of the role of the Children Court judge. In reality, he/she must identify workable solutions to the range of social, health, educational and psychological problems which young offenders frequently present to the Court. In the absence of an alternative administrative body, the judge co-ordinates the various state agencies involved in the administration of youth justice, and orders enquiries about the availability of places of detention, temporary accommodation, access to assessment, treatment and therapeutic facilities, and vocational and educational programmes. He/she is required to be an efficient administrator, capable of sorting through and managing often dozens of charge sheets, and must be able to absorb quickly the numerous reports and assessments of the young person's situation. On a personal level, the judge may also be expected to act as mediator between the young person and his/her parents and, in the absence of an alternative complaints mechanism, to listen to the grievances of young people about their treatment in detention, by An Garda Síochána or by their solicitor. Responsibility for vindicating the rights and freedoms of young people before the Court also falls to the judge in his/her role as the administrator of justice. The Children Court judge thus has responsibility to ensure that the young person's due process rights are observed, and that they enjoy the right to be treated in a manner which takes into account their age and is consistent with respect for their welfare. In addition, the judge has a duty to vindicate the right of the young person to understand and participate in the proceedings and must also ensure that any sanction imposed is proportionate to the circumstances of the young person and the offence. Vindication of the young person's right to privacy in the criminal process also falls to the judge of the Children Court.

This combination of functions means that the role of the Children Court judge extends beyond the traditional one of determining a criminal charge and upholding the child's constitutional rights.[36] Instead, it demands that the judicial function be combined with that of counsellor, manager and administrator of youth justice: this makes the role not only the most influential and central position in the youth justice system, but also the most challenging. This diverse range of functions of the Children Court judge should be borne in mind when considering the role of the Court in the youth justice process.

Sittings of the Children Court

According to section 71(1)(b) of the Children Act 2001, the Children Court must take place in a different building or room or at a different time or day to other courts. It is thus sufficient under the Act that it fulfil one (and not both) of these criteria and, to this extent, the legislative requirement merely accommodates existing arrangements for the sittings of the Children Court in different districts. In the Dublin Children Court, for example, the Court sits in Smithfield in a different building from the District Court, where it takes place in a specially designed courtroom. This is clearly compliant with section 71 of the Act. The Children Court in Limerick, Cork and Waterford sits in the same venue as the District Court, but at a different time or day. Thus, in Cork, the Children Court sits exclusively every Monday, and Tuesday afternoon is dedicated to the children's list in Limerick. The same principle – different time rather than venue – applies to other districts also with monthly sittings taking place in Galway and Waterford. These arrangements are clearly compliant with section 71.

However, consistency with the requirements of the Children Act is less clear-cut where, as in some towns, the District Court hears cases against children on an ad hoc basis. This occurs, for example, in Tralee, Kilkenny and Thurles. While it may not be practical to create a special environment for one or two cases in such situations, efforts must nonetheless be made to ensure that, despite the physical environment, the Court's process is adapted when hearing cases involving children, especially to enable the child to be involved.

Preventing Contact Between Child and Adult Defendants

Section 71(2) of the Children Act provides that, as far as practicable, sittings of the Children Court must be arranged in such a way that children are not brought into contact with adult defendants or those attending other courts. Compliance with this requirement is guaranteed in the Dublin Children Court where the only court in use in the courthouse hears exclusively children's cases. However, in other District Court buildings, adults and children share the facilities. This is a particular problem in Cork where the two courtrooms face each other, separated only by a small shared waiting area, meaning that separation is not achieved in practice. Neither the letter nor the spirit of the Act is being respected in these circumstances.[37]

The Waiting Areas

While the dilapidated state of many courthouses bemoaned by O'Malley in 1994 has been addressed by the buildings programme of the Courts Service, little attention has been paid to the availability or quality of waiting areas or consultation rooms in some courts. Yet the private nature of the Children Court means that the adequacy of waiting areas in terms of size and facilities is a significant factor in the experience of attending court for both children and their parents.

The quality and standards of the waiting areas for all Children Courts is poor. In Cork and Limerick, conditions are cramped with little indoor seating, and as a result, young people waiting for their cases to be called frequently stand and sit outside the courthouse. In addition to the discomfort involved, these young people risk not hearing their cases being called, which can cause delay.

Notwithstanding that the Dublin Children Court sits in a dedicated building, and only one of two courtrooms is in use, the waiting area is totally inadequate to accommodate all the young people waiting to have their cases called. Many young people thus have no option but to stand in the foyer of the building or to wait on the steps outside. The lack of refreshment facilities and space for children to play means that some families have to spend several hours waiting in very poor conditions. The problem is exacerbated by the length of the list and the sheer numbers of people (defendants, family members, Gardaí and others) involved. While addressing the length of court lists and amending appearance times should reduce the numbers of young people and their families waiting to be called before the Court, the need for satisfactory waitng areas with appropriate facilities must be urgently addressed.[38]

The Child's Right to Participate in and Understand the Process

Engaging the Young Person

International standards make it clear that the child has a right to understand and participate in criminal proceedings against him/her and that the court must facilitate his/her exercise of this right. Best practice in other jurisdictions highlights the extent to which judges are encouraged to engage with offenders and to take a communicative approach to youth justice in order to maximise the potential of the court to change the offending behaviour of the young person.[39]

Observations of the Children Courts in 2003 and 2004 recorded that the extent to which children participated or understood the proceedings varied from court to court,[40] although the general conclusion was that young people struggled to do either. While the physical environment (see below) served to reinforce their distance from the judge and their solicitor, the young person's isolation from the process was derived mainly from the fact that the judge, solicitor and Garda generally failed to address them directly in any manner. Thus, in many cases, the young person was observed straining physically to hear and/or to follow the dialogue between the parties, and appearing visibly confused, anxious and upset at their marginalisation from the process. For other young people, perhaps those who had appeared many times before the Court, their persistent lack of involvement and inability to follow proceedings led to apparent boredom with the process. They were typically observed looking around the courtroom, fixing their hair or biting their nails. Significant numbers of young people appeared motionless, staring straight ahead or at the floor, nervous, frightened and tense, or in some cases utterly lost and emotionless. The inability of young people to follow proceedings was exemplified in the numerous cases where proceedings were concluded without the young person and his/her guardian realising that the case was over. Young people frequently left the courtroom shaking their heads, confused as to what had just happened; in many cases, their only prompt that the case was over was that the next case had been called and another defendant entered the court.

Different types and levels of communication between judges and young people were observed, although the majority of cases involved no communication of any kind. The research observed that, in most cases, the judge did not greet the young person on his/her arrival in court, make eye contact or any form of non-verbal communication with him/her at any stage of the process, or inform him/her of the outcome. Judges frequently referred to the accused indirectly as 'he' or 'she' and tended to look at the young person but address themselves to their solicitor. When a judge did address a young person directly, the intervention was prompted by a request for information, rather than an interest in communicating directly with them. Thus, the judge tended to direct questions, for example, about the young person's age to the solicitor first, only asking the young person directly when the solicitor did not have the information sought. In other cases, the judge refused to hear the young person directly notwithstanding their desire and willingness to be involved. More than one judge was observed telling a young person to be quiet, to put their hand down, or to let their solicitor do the talking on their behalf. The marginalisation of the young person, which results from this approach, was clearly visible throughout this research from the vacant stares of many young defendants. This failure to acknowledge the presence of the young person and to involve them, even to a minimum extent, in the proceedings, served to confirm their isolation from the court process and its irrelevance to them. This was exacerbated by poor acoustics in the courtroom, the physical distance between the parties, and the failure on the part of the solicitor to involve them.[41]

Judicial training is required to raise awareness of their duty to facilitate the involvement of young people in the process and to develop the necessary skills among the judiciary to engage with young people. A forum between judges in the Children Court should also be established to allow them to share experiences in this area. Priority should be given to developing a range of age-appropriate explanations to ensure that young people understand the conditions of their bail or probation bonds, the consequences of breaching them and the reasons for any sanction imposed or adjournment ordered.

The Physical Environment of the Children Court

The Children Act imposes no requirements regarding the type of physical environment in which the Children Court should take place despite the requirement in section 96 that courts must have regard to the child's right to be heard.[42]

Research has observed that the physical environment, layout and structure of the courtroom can have a significant impact on the extent to which young people participate in criminal proceedings against them and on the nature of the court experience more generally.[43] The Children Court currently sits in two distinct settings: a specially adapted courtroom is used in the Dublin Children Court, and the normal District Court building which is used in every other area. In the Dublin court, the small size and single-level of the courtroom facilitates the direct involvement of children in the proceedings. The fact that it has dedicated seating for the young person gives them a formal role in the process and offers them a direct visual line of communication with the prosecutor (the Garda), the judge and their solicitor. Communication between the judge and the young person, and between the solicitor and his/her client is facilitated by their proximity and parents, who sit behind solicitors, can also be easily involved. The size of the courtroom also means that dialogue between all of the court personnel can be heard without difficulty, and everyone is focused on the young person and their case.

The courtrooms in Limerick, Cork and Waterford constitute much more formal and traditional court environments for children's cases. Each court has a raised bench of varying height where the judge sits, with a further row of the bench in front to accommodate the clerk or registrar of the court. Solicitors and the prosecuting Inspector sit in front of this again. This means that in these courts, the judge is physically removed from the young person. In contrast, the solicitor and the prosecutor sit or stand closer to the judge, encouraging and promoting communication between these parties (in preference to the young person). In these courts, the large size of the courtroom and the lack of a dedicated place for the young person to sit or stand mean that they are frequently isolated from the other parties and the process, both physically and otherwise. Unadapted and unaltered, these physical environments are inappropriate settings in which to hold Children Court proceedings.

The impact of the physical environment on the extent to which the young person participates in their proceedings is dramatic. In the large courtrooms, young people are not routinely involved in the process and find participation difficult if not impossible, whereas in Smithfield they have every opportunity to engage with the parties and the process. Learning from the latter experience, measures must be taken to improve the courtroom layout in all courts in order to facilitate the involvement of young people. New courtrooms are not required to address this problem and each court should find its own solution, for instance by identifying seating for the young person and his/her parent or guardian, locating them proximate to the judge, solicitor and prosecuting Inspector in a place that ensures that the proceedings can be heard.

Delay in the Court System

The Dáil Select Committee on Crime recommended that refor of the youth justice system needed to address the long delays between arrest and the final court hearing.[44] This element of the court process did not receive the attention of those who drafted the Children Act 2001, however, and as a result, it continues to be a substantial problem. An analysis of 50 Children Court files from 2004 showed that while half of the young people in the study appeared in court within a month of their first offence, 15 young people appeared in the Court between one and six months after their first offence, while another ten young people did not appear in court until six months after their first offence.[45] Delay is also a serious problem for the young people already in the court system. The same research found that, for many young people, their interaction with the Children Court is a long, drawn-out affair.[46] Notwithstanding that the young people in the study faced a varying number of charges, 20 young people had their cases concluded within six months of their first court appearance, 19 young people were in the system for a year and a further 11 young people had their cases concluded more than one year after their first court appearance. In two cases, the cases took two years from the children's thirteenth to fifteenth birthdays.[47]

Delay in the Children Court system is thus a recognised problem, although there is little to explain precisely why delays occur. The above research noted the reasons for delays were multiple, but included remanding a case for the purpose of ordering a Probation and Welfare Report or an assessment, to secure the attendance of the child or his/her parents, to bring the case before a particular judge or to give the young person one last chance, normally by imposing a Probation Bond.[48] All these reasons were evident also in a more widespread study of the Children Court, which noted that over 80 per cent of court appearances ended in the case being adjourned or remanded for one reason or another.[49] While a streamlining of the process would help to reduce the delays in the system, it is also recommended that judicial consensus be reached on the principles that should inform whether or not to grant an adjournment. In general, judges should be encouraged to scrutinise requests for adjournments very carefully and to balance the basis of the request with the need to deal with the charges against a young person without unnecessary delay. This would ensure that the need to determine a charge without delay takes priority, for example, over the need to adjourn the case to ensure a parent's attendance.[50] The inclusion in the Children Act 2001 of a commitment to proceed expeditiously with charges against young people should also be considered.

Management of the Court List

The Children Act 2001 does not specify how frequently the Children Court must sit, although section 71(4) provides that the Court must sit frequently enough to fulfil its functions. This must require that the Children Court sit often enough to prevent unnecessary delay, particularly given how minimising young people's contact with the system requires that their case be handled expeditiously.

Despite the fact that the Dublin Children Court sits on a permanent basis, the daily list often comprises 50 to 60 cases and puts a considerable strain on the court's resources. This also means that a significant number of young people and their families must wait for several hours for their cases to be heard. The sheer volume of cases to be heard adds pressure and urgency to the proceedings, which has the potential to undermine the quality of the process and the time taken to deal with each case. Despite the best efforts of court personnel, it is not possible to conclude that this court is sitting frequently enough to fulfil its functions adequately.[51]

In addition, the Children Act requires that proceedings be arranged so as to keep the time the accused has to wait to a minimum and also requires that the time on the summons must, as far as practicable, reflect the time the case is likely to be heard. Despite this statutory requirement, research shows that significant delays can be experienced in both Dublin and Cork Children Courts.

The research noted that in Dublin, the morning list, which begins at 10.30 am, frequently contained more than fifty cases. This required that young people and their families wait for long periods before their appearance in court. The length of this list is thus frustrating the provisions of the Act whose objective is to mimimise the time young people are out of school or employment. It also has serious consequences for the efficiency of the entire court process.

Delay was also noted to be a problem in Cork where only one list, which begins at 10.30 am, was used. This required that all young people attending court that day be there at this time, even though their cases may not be heard until much later in the morning or, in some cases, in the early afternoon. In the context of these problems, it is vital that the organisation of the list is addressed as a matter of urgency to relieve the strain under which the courts currently work. Additional judges should be assigned to the Dublin Children Court to clear the backlog and a new approach to listing cases should be piloted, perhaps by grouping cases together in hourly or half-hourly intervals to keep the delay to a minimum.

Ineffectiveness of the Children Court

The potential of the Children Court to check offending behaviour is not currently being maximised due to the ineffective and inefficient operation of the court system. Charges against young people are continuously and persistently adjourned leading to a delay in the final determination of charges which causes many young people to enter a cycle of offending, broken bail conditions and court appearances which can be difficult to break without imposing a custodial sanction.[52] The delays which adjournments cause also reduce the connection between the offence and the sanction imposed meaning that young people are offered little incentive or support to check their offending behaviour. This, together with the lack of meaningful sanctions, has led to a culture of impunity among some young people.

The exercise of judicial functions in a range of areas – including granting adjournments and ordering benchwarrants – is not consistent within or between Children Courts. Some judges issue a bench warrant once it is requested by the Garda, while another shows flexibility by offering the young person the opportunity to show up later in the day. Judges' approaches to the absence of young people or their parents, and to other issues, vary; this leads to forum shopping by young people, and demonstrates a lack of awareness about best practice in other courts and more generally.[53] The practice of requiring individual judges to retain seisin (jurisdiction) over charge sheets but not over the young person means that several judges may be involved in a single case, a situation which frustrates a coherent or holistic response to the behaviour of young people. This is compounded by the irregular assignment of judges to the Children Court, particularly in Dublin. The lack of coordination between agencies and poor management of cases also leads to confusion and delay.

Practice in some courts is clearly designed to address these problems. For example, the judge of the Limerick Children Court organised a meeting with the Gardaí, the Special Residential Services Board, solicitors, the Health Service Executive (HSE) and the Probation and Welfare Service with a view to improving communication and co-operation between them. All agreed that this was a very worthwhile exercise which provided an important opportunity to exchange information and ideas and clarify any possible misunderstandings.[54] Clearly, this practice deserves to be replicated in all other Children Courts as well as between them. While the decision to remove the co-ordinating function from the Special Residential Services Board may have a negative effect here, the proposed development of Youth Justice Teams to support the Children Court at local level may have a more positive role to play in improving the co-ordination and communication between agencies.[55]

Training in all aspects of the Children Act 2001 as well as on an inter-disciplinary basis including psychology, criminology and youth justice should be undertaken by all court personnel including the judiciary, solicitors, Gardaí and both Probation and Welfare Service and HSE officers. As noted elsewhere, this is recommended by international standards.[56]

In Camera Rule

In compliance with international standards, which require that the child's identity and privacy be protected throughout court proceedings, the Children Act stipulates that the proceedings of the Children Court are heard *in camera*, in the absence of the public and those who are not directly involved in the proceedings. Section 94 provides that the Court has discretion to permit such other persons to attend the Court and this is often used to allow *bona fide* researchers, members of other government agencies such as the Special Residential Services Board, and members of the young person's family to attend the proceedings. Maintaining the privacy of the courtroom is thus a goal in itself, although it has also been linked to reducing the intimidating features of criminal proceedings for young people on trial.

Research into the Children Court has highlighted that one of the problematic issues arising in this context is the presence in the Children Court of members of An Garda Síochána not involved in the case being heard.[57] Apart from the manpower issue – over ten Gardaí frequently sit through proceedings for their case to be heard – their lack of involvement in the cases being heard means that this is an apparent breach of the *in camera* rule. Moreover, the fact that members sit together in some courts can make their presence an obvious and sometimes intimidating feature of the proceedings.

In contrast, in the Dublin Children Court, only the Garda prosecuting or giving evidence in the case is entitled to be present. With the exception of the Garda monitoring the door to the courtroom, Gardaí are not generally permitted to be present in the Court. This practice should be mainstreamed across the Children Court system.

The enforcement of the *in camera* rule is also an issue in some Children Courts where movement of people in and out of the courtroom is not closely monitored or controlled. In addition to this failure to police the *in camera* rule effectively, some courts, like the court in Smithfield, have a glass door or porthole which means that the privacy of those inside is not adequately protected. Every effort should be made to protect the privacy of those in the courtroom by covering up windows and doors.[58]

Location of the Dublin Children Court

The fact that only one, albeit full-time, Children Court sits in Dublin means that young people travel from all over the city to appear, resulting in a large daily congregation of young people, novice and experienced, at the courthouse. This has on occasion led to public order and other problems. Although these have been addressed effectively by the imposition of a standard bail condition ordering young people to stay away from the court unless appearing, consideration is also being given to moving sittings of the Children Court to areas of the city from where many young people who appear before the Court live. This is an apparently attractive proposition which would prevent young people from making new friends and renewing acquaintances outside the court and would also relieve young people of the long journey to Smithfield from Dublin's suburbs.

The advantage of retaining the Court in Smithfield should not be minimised however. As research shows, despite its problems, the Dublin Children Court reflects much in the way of best practice, and in particular, boasts a level of professionalism and expertise among court personnel that could be lost if the Court were moved to different locations. While it is undeniable that the building requires structural improvement – particularly the waiting area – it is not apparent that dividing the court list and moving it to other locations like Clondalkin, Tallaght and Ballymun would in itself solve existing problems with the operation of the Children Court. Indeed, it may in fact add to those problems by diversifying judicial practice further and undermining the expertise that has been built up in the Dublin Children Court.

TRIAL OF CHILDREN OUTSIDE THE CHILDREN COURT

Application of the Children Act

While most young offenders are tried by the Children Court, those charged with more serious offences appear before the Circuit and Central Criminal Courts either by transfer from the Children Court when it refuses jurisdiction or by direction of the DPP. As noted above, the Children Act 2001 makes provision for the Children Court to sit in private, at a different time and place to the ordinary courts and in a manner that keep adults offenders separate from children. According to section 2 of the Act, 'court' means the 'Children Court' in Parts 7 and 8. Accordingly, these provisions are limited to the Children Court and do not apply to proceedings involving children in the Circuit Criminal Court or the Central Criminal Court. This is despite the recommendation in the Kennedy Report in 1970 that the Circuit Courts should be specially constituted when hearing appeals from the Children's Court.[59]

In these situations, children in the higher courts are effectively tried as adults. They enjoy none of the informality of the Children Court – wigs and gowns are worn as normal, and the court is not adapted to take their age and understanding into account. None of the rules minimising their time at the courthouse apply, they are not prevented from mixing with adult accused and their parents are not required to attend. No legal provision exists requiring their age to be taken into account on sentencing and while the sentencing judge may well be mindful of this fact, this is a matter for his/her personal discretion.

Exercising Jurisdiction in Children's Cases

Importantly, section 96 of the Children Act is not limited to the Children Court and, consequently, the principles governing the exercise of criminal jurisdiction over children apply to all courts. Section 96 provides that 'any court when dealing with children charged with offences shall have regard to the principle that children have rights and freedoms before the law equal to those enjoyed by adults and, in particular, a right to be heard and to participate in any proceedings of the court that can affect them'. It goes on to recognise the desirability, wherever possible, of allowing the education or employment of a child to continue uninterrupted, to preserve and strengthen the relationship between a child and his/her family, to foster the ability of families to develop their own means of dealing with their child's offending and to allow to remain children in their own homes. It provides that, for this reason, 'any penalty imposed on a child for an offence should cause as little interference as possible with the child's legitimate activities and pursuits, take the form most likely to maintain and promote the development of the child and take the least restrictive form that is appropriate in the circumstances'.[60] More importantly, perhaps, section 96(3) provides that a court 'may take into consideration as mitigating factors a child's age and level of maturity in determining the nature of any penalty imposed', unless the penalty is fixed by law, but notes that the penalty imposed on a child should be no greater than that which would be appropriate in the case of an adult who commits an offence of the same kind and may be less.

Section 96 thus contains important mandatory principles which must be taken into account on sentencing and also gives the court discretion to attach importance to the child's age and maturity in the sentencing process. While intended to guide the court, the mandatory nature of the principles supports the view that failure on the part of a judge to adhere to these requirements may constitute or substantiate an argument based on irrationality or disproportionate grounds if a decision or order of the court is appealed or judicially reviewed.[61] In this regard, it is important that they encourage but do not oblige the court to take the child's age into account as a mitigating factor on sentencing, although the compulsory nature of other factors listed in the provision mitigate this to some extent. Crucially, however, this section has not yet been commenced.

Adapting the Adult Court for Children

No substantial research has been undertaken on the sentencing of children in the Circuit and Central Criminal Courts or on the extent to which children tried in these courts participate in proceedings against them. However, *ad hoc* observations of these courts and media reporting, including the trial of 16-year-old Darren Goodwin in the Central Criminal Court in 2004, raise some concern here. In this case, for example, the accused was described as 'chillingly calm'; his demeanour was reportedly described by the trial judge as 'one of scorn and contempt for the trial process in particular and society in general'.[62] However, the capacity of the accused to participate in the trial emerges as a pertinent issue, particularly given psychologists' reports describing him as deeply disturbed.

It appears therefore that young people on trial in the Circuit and Central Criminal Courts may not be treated in a manner that takes their age into account as required by international standards such as the CRC. Nor does there appear to be any attempt to adapt the court process to take their age and special circumstances into account as required by the ECHR and the Children Act 2001. This contrasts sharply with the Practice Direction of the Lord Chief Justice of England and Wales on the trial of children in the Crown Court, which makes very specific rules regarding the trial of children outside the youth court.[63] While the Courts Service does not appear to have given any formal consideration to these issues,[64] it is important that it does so without further delay. Training is recommended for Children Court judges on the trial of young people, including taking their age and maturity into account during the proceedings and in the sentencing process, should also be provided to judges involved in criminal cases involving children at all levels.

Privacy and Reporting

Neither section 93 of the Children Act 2001, which restricts reporting of cases in which children are involved, nor section 94, which provides for proceedings to be held *in camera*, apply to courts other than the Children Court. As a result, proceedings against young people under 18 years in the Circuit and Central Criminal Courts are held in public unless, for some other reason such as the nature of the charge, they are held *in camera*. Moreover, the names and photographs of the young people convicted in these courts may be and usually are released to the media on request. Arguments in a number of cases that it was not in the interests of justice or the young people themselves that they be named and photographed in the press subsequent to conviction (whatever about being named in court) were rejected.[65] Moreover, it has been confirmed that the constitutional requirement that justice be administered in public allows the court only a very limited discretion to minimise media coverage.[66] In a very narrow interpretation of relevant case law, Judge Barry White held in one such case that reporting restrictions could only be justified if they constituted a risk to the fair trial of the accused or in other exceptional circumstances.[67]

The names and photographs of all four young people (three 16 year olds and one 15 year old) convicted of the Cratloe Woods rape and sentenced on 31 July 2004 appeared on the front pages of all Irish newspapers that day. Also in 2004, two other young people, aged 16 and 17 years, were named and photographed in the newspapers following their respective convictions for murder.[68] The media coverage of these and other cases involving children convicted of serious crime plays an important role in the implementation of the principle that justice must seen to be done. However, apart from selling newspapers, it is difficult to see what the pictures of the convicted boys added to the media coverage of their trial and sentence.[69] Indeed, there is an argument that the publicity afforded to the young people in these cases put their own lives, welfare and rehabilitation at risk. In December 2004, the *Irish Times* reported 'a jail attack' involving one of the young people convicted in the Cratloe Woods case. Darragh Ryan had been transferred, for reasons unknown, from St. Patrick's Institution to Wheatfield Prison in the first week of October 2004. However, he was badly beaten by inmates there 'because of the nature of his conviction'. After receiving hospital treatment for his injuries, he was transferred back to St. Patrick's Institution, where he, and two of his co-accused were placed (and remain) in a segregated area of the facility 'for their own protection'.[70]

A far greater risk faced the two boys convicted of the murder of James Bulger in Liverpool in 1993 when the High Court made an injunction in 2001 for the duration of their lives restraining any publication of the boys' identities, including photographs, and their whereabouts after release.[71] The boys faced numerous threats to their lives, as well as a media campaign to discover their new identities following the trial judge's original decision to lift the reporting restrictions at their trial so that the public might be informed of the names and backgrounds of the two boys. While extreme in many ways, this case nevertheless highlights the extent to which the publication of the identity of the convicted young person not only fails to add anything to the legitimate discussion of the case and the trial, but in fact threatens to overtake the issue itself in importance. Thus, while media reporting of cases is vital for confidence in the administration of justice, it is not clear why identity of the convicted person is necessary to allow that debate to take place. While issues of public safety and security may be at issue, they were not in these cases given that the boys were being sentenced to long periods in detention. Moreover, where children are concerned, it is submitted, there are added considerations to be taken into account other than the public interest, namely the child's right to privacy and the right to be protected from harm. In the necessary balancing act, the interests of the young person, their welfare and their prospects for successful reintegration into society on release should take priority in all but the rarest of cases.

TRANSFER OF CHILDREN FROM THE CHILDREN COURT

While some offences must be tried in the Central Criminal Court (notably murder, manslaughter and rape), the Children Court has a broad jurisdiction to deal with minor and other more serious offences. Section 75 of the Children Act 2001 gives the Children Court a discretionary power to deal with such indictable offences in a summary manner in certain circumstances. Importantly, the Act sets out the criteria that the Court must take into account when deciding whether to retain or refuse jurisdiction over an offence. In this situation, the Court must take account of the age and level of maturity of the child concerned and any other factors that it considers relevant.

Given the concerns expressed above about the extent to which the rights of children to a fair trial are protected when they are tried outside the Children Court, particularly regarding their privacy and understanding of the process, it is significant that the Children Court is under a duty to take the child's age and maturity into account when deciding whether or not to send a case forward for trial to a higher court. In particular, this provision has the potential to act as a safeguard to protect young people who may not understand or be capable of participating in the process from being subjected to a trial in those circumstances.[72]

Despite the commencement of section 75 on 1 May 2002, research in the Children Court, which routinely sends children forward for trial in the higher courts, observed that the provision does not appear to be implemented in practice. In particular, the Children Court was not observed giving express consideration to the child's age and maturity when deciding to refuse jurisdiction in any individual case.[73] Indeed, the only factors taken into account in the cases observed were the seriousness of the crime and the level of damage or harm caused by the offender. The extent to which in practice children lose their right to be tried in accordance with their age and maturity when they are tried in the Circuit and Central Criminal Courts thus does not appear to be a factor given any consideration in the Children Court when refusing to try children summarily. This is the case notwithstanding that sixty-five young people, or 4 per cent of all cases determined, were returned for trial in the higher courts in 2004.[74]

It is arguable that section 96 of the Children Act, relating to the exercise of criminal jurisdiction over children, is also relevant here. In particular, it is submitted that the issue of whether the child will enjoy his/her rights recognised in this provision, including the right to be heard and participate in proceedings in the court to which he/she is being referred, should be taken into account by the Children Court when deciding whether to accept or refuse jurisdiction. This is permitted by the reference in section 75 to the court's duty to take into account any factors it considers relevant.

Section 75 (3) of the Children Act requires that the Children Court shall not deal summarily with an indictable offence where the child, on being informed by the Court of his/her right to be tried by a jury, does not consent to the case being so dealt with. An important factor, therefore, is the extent to which children genuinely understand this matter when it is put to them by the Court. Observations of the Children Court showed that this question – whether a child wished to be tried by jury in the

Circuit Criminal Court or by a judge in the Children Court – was not adapted in any way to make it comprehensible to children. Many young people – generally, it appeared, those who had heard the question before or were prepared for it – knew to reply 'this court' or 'here'. For others, however, the question was greeted with a confused look, a request to the judge to repeat it, and/or a searching glance to his/her solicitor or guardian for assistance. This raises further concern about the compatibility of the decision to retain or refuse jurisdiction with the Children Act and highlights the need to devise age appropriate explanations for children in the Children Court so as to vindicate their right to understand the process.

A further issue that arises under section 75 is the lack of entitlement to legal advice in advance of a decision to consent to be tried by the Children Court or by jury in the Circuit Criminal Court. While it is the exception rather than the rule that children do not enjoy the support of a solicitor in court, it nonetheless makes it even more important that the child understands the nature of consent given in this context.

Many jurisdictions have a formal process of sending children forward for trial to an adult court and the rate at which it is being used is on the increase in countries like the United States (whose 'judicial waiver' system is well established in many states), Belgium and the Netherlands.[75] This is a worrying trend insofar as adult courts may take little or no account of the child's age or welfare and the use of the transfer mechanism in such cases involves a worrying rejection of the principles of youth justice for serious crime or children above a certain age. Germany, on the other hand, allows for transfer 'down' from an adult to a youth court where maturity and social factors support such an approach.[76] Given the decision in the Criminal Justice Act 2006 to retain the age of criminal responsibility at 10 years for crimes of rape, murder and manslaughter,[77] for which children a fair trial cannot always be secured in an adult court, consideration should be given to developing such an approach in the Irish system also. With respect to refusing jurisdiction, the apparent failure to adhere to the Children Act 2001 in this context is a cause for concern which requires further research. The implications of sending a young person for trial in a court other than the Children Court should always be very carefully considered, not just from the perspective of the crime but from the perspective of the young person who is effectively waiving his right to trial as a child in the process. Judicial training should thus be undertaken as a matter of urgency on the implications of section 75 and the decision-making process by which jurisdiction is refused.

CONCLUSION

This chapter has raised a number of fundamental issues central to the administration of youth justice and the operation and effectiveness of the court within the youth justice system. It is clear that many of the serious problems in the system manifest themselves most acutely in the Children Court – delay, poor coordination between state agencies, a lack of consistency and a failure to engage with offenders about their behaviour. Moreover, the Children Court is failing to maximising its potential to address offending behaviour and is thus out of line with international standards and best practice in other jurisdictions. An overhaul of all Children Courts is required to transform them into a modern youth court system.

However, in some ways, a more worrying yet invisible problem may exist with regard to the trial of children for serious crimes. Although research is required to evaluate the extent to which the Circuit and Central Criminal Courts are operating in line with international standards of youth justice, initial indications are that these children are tried as adults with little mitigation for their age, maturity and other principles of youth justice. A full review of the operation of these courts in children's cases should be undertaken as a matter of urgency.

NOTES

1 This is in contrast to other systems such as in New Zealand, where only a minority of children end up before the court. See Morris, A., 'Youth Justice in New Zealand', 31 (2004), *Crime and Justice* 243–92, p. 267.

2 The need to protect children from the harm caused by undue publicity and the process of labelling is also required by Rule 8 of the UN Standard Minimum Rules on the Administration of Juvenile Justice (the Beijing Rules) 1985, adopted by General Assembly resolution 40/33 of 29 November 1985, available at www.ohchr.org (accessed 18 January 2006), which states that, 'in principle, no information that may lead to the

identification of a young person accused or convicted shall be published'. Further augmentation of other standards is also found in these Rules. See further the Introduction.

3 See further Zilli, L., 'Children's Rights to a Fair Trial under International law', 5 *Trinity College Law Review*, (2002) 224–50.

4 The Act may also provide a remedy for young people whose rights are infringed in the Irish youth justice system. See Kilkelly, U., 'Child and Family Law', in Kilkelly, U. (ed.), *ECHR and Irish Law* (Bristol: Jordans, 2004), pp. 111–50 and O'Connell, D., 'The ECHR Act 2003: A Critical Perspective', pp. 1–12 in the same volume.

5 Article 6 provides for the right to a fair hearing before an independent and impartial tribunal. See *Nortier* v. *Netherlands* (1994) 17 EHRR 273. Note in particular the concurring judgment of Judge Morenilla, which referred to Article 40 of the CRC and highlighted the need to set up 'juvenile courts under specific procedural rules'. See further, Kilkelly, U., *The Child and the ECHR* (Aldershot: Ashgate, 1999), pp. 56–8.

6 *T* v. *UK* and *V* v. *UK* (2000), 130 EHRR 121.

7 *Ibid.*, para. 180.

8 See further Kilkelly, U., 'The Human Rights Act: Implications for the Trial and Detention of Young People', 51(3) *Northern Ireland Legal Quarterly* (2000), 466–80.

9 For one view see Sentlinger, E.D., 'V. v. United Kingdom: is it a "new deal" for prosecuting children as adults', 16 *Conn. J. Int'l L.* (2000) 117–48.

10 *T* v *UK*, paras. 68–78. The Court held that setting 10 as the age of criminal responsibility did not constitute inhuman and degrading treatment contrary to Article 3, although its conclusion that this age is not inconsistent with European-wide state practice is questionable.

11 *Ibid.*, para. 84.

12 *SC* v. *UK*, judgment of 15 June 2004.

13 *Ibid.*, para. 29.

14 *Ibid.*, para. 32.

15 Judge Pelonpaa, joined by Judge Bratza, expressed the dissenting view that the domestic court's assessment of the applicant's ability to proceed and be tried in the Crown Court should have prevailed *inter alia* due to the absence of the aggravating factors present in the cases of T. and V., the lack of evidence that the applicant was unfit to plead, and the fact that the domestic judge, who made the assessment which was upheld on appeal, had personal contact with the young defendant.

16 *SC* v. *UK*, para. 35.

17 *RCTP* v. *West London Youth Court, the Crown Prosecution Service and the Home Secretary* [2005] EWHC 2583 (Admin). The High Court has also advised that those under 18 years should, where possible, be tried in a youth court, which was best designed for their specific needs. *Crown Prosecution Service v. South East Surrey Youth Court and Milad Leon Glansari* (2005) EWHC 2929 (Admin).

18 Practice Direction: (Crown Court: Trial of Children and Young Persons) (2000) 1WLR 659.

19 Home Office, *No More Excuses: A new approach to tackling youth crime in England and Wales* (London: Stationery Office, 1997).
20 *Ibid.*, para. 9.2.
21 *Ibid.*, para. 9.3.
22 Allen, C., Crowe, I., and Cavadino, M., *Evaluation of the Youth Court Demonstration Project*, Home Office Research Study 214 (London: Stationery Office, 2000), available at www.homeoffice.gov.uk (accessed 7 January 2006).
23 *Ibid.*, p. 73.
24 *Ibid.*, pp. 15–30. The research report contains a list of words and phrases (such as 'date of birth', 'concurrent' and 'compliance') which the research found incomprehensible to defendants and their parents. Alternative words were proposed. These are listed in Appendix F of the report.
25 *Ibid.*, pp. 31–42.
26 The Bench Book is available at-www.jsboard.co.uk (accessed 8 January 2006).
27 Morris, A., 'Youth Justice in New Zealand', pp. 267–9.
28 See Weijers, I., 'Requirements for Communication in the Courtroom: A comparative perspective on the Youth Court in England/Wales and the Netherlands', 4(1) *Youth Justice* (July 2004) pp. 22–31 at p. 28.
29 The Children Act 1908, s. 111 as amended by the Children Act 1941, s. 26.
30 For a more lengthy description of this area of law see Walsh, D., Juvenile Justice (Dublin: Thomson Round Hall, 2005), pp. 70–7.
31 Two members of the Task Force recommended in a supplementary report that distinct children's courts be established, staffed by specially qualified professional children's judges recruited by an independent body. See further Walsh, D., Juvenile Justice, p. 479.
32 Dáil Select Committee on Crime, Juvenile Crime – its Causes and its Remedies (Dublin: Stationery Office, 1992). See further Chapter Two above.
33 The same point was made with respect to the 1924 Act. See Mitchell, D., *A Report on the Law and Procedures Regarding the Prosecution and Disposal of Young Offenders* (Dublin: DPP, 1977).
34 O'Malley, T., 'Juvenile Justice' in Heffernan, L. (ed.), *Human Rights: A European Perspective* (Dublin: Round Hall, 1994), p. 314.
35 See Kilkelly, U., *The Children's Court: A Children's Rights Audit* (Cork, 2005) and McPhillips, S., *The Dublin Children Court: A Pilot Research Project* (Dublin: IASD, 2005).
36 Walsh, D. *Juvenile Justice*, p. 105.
37 Kilkelly, U., *The Children's Court: A Children's Rights Audit*, p. 33.
38 Ibid., pp. 34–5.
39 Weijers, I., 'The Moral Dialogue: A Pedagogical Perspective on Juvenile Justice' in Weijers, I. and Duff, A., *Punishing Juveniles Principle and Critique* (Oxford: Hart Publishing, 2002), pp. 135–54.
40 Kilkelly, U., *The Children's Court: A Children's Rights Audit*, p. 30.
41 *Ibid.*, pp. 62–5.
42 This has been described as 'one of the cornerstones of the Act'. See O'Donnell, T.E., 'The Children Act 2001: A practical analysis from a

judicial perspective', a paper presented at Law Society Criminal Law Committee Seminar for Judges of the District Court, 3rd December 2004, p. 10.

43 Kilkelly, U., *The Children's Court: A Children's Rights Audit*, pp. 42–5. See also Allen, C., Crowe, I. and Cavadino, M., *Evaluation of the Youth Court Demonstration Project.*

44 Dáil Select Committee on Crime, *Juvenile Crime – its Causes and its Remedies*, pp. 38–9.

45 McPhillips, S., *Dublin Children Court: A Pilot Research Project*, p. 25.

46 *Ibid.*, p. 27.

47 *Ibid.*, p. 26.

48 *Ibid.*, pp. 28–9.

49 Kilkelly, U., *The Children's Court: A Children's Rights Audit*, pp. S0-3.

50 *Ibid.*, p. 53.

51 *Ibid.*, p. 36–8.

52 *Ibid.* See also McPhillips, S., *Dublin Children Court: A Pilot Research Project*, pp. 17–30.

53 Ibid., pp. 53–8.

54 O'Donnell, T.E., 'The Children Act 2001: A practical analysis from a judicial perspective', p. 1.

55 *Report on the Youth Justice Review* (Dublin: Department of Justice, Equality and Law Reform, 2005) pp. 46–7, available at www.justice.ie (accessed 4 January 2006). *See Amendments to Children Act 2001 and Amendments to Criminal Justice (Legal Aid) Act 1962 for inclusion in the Criminal Justice and Children Bill*, available at www.justice.ie (accessed 16 January 2006).

56 See Chapter Three and also Kilkelly, U., *The Children's Court: A Children's Rights Audit*, pp. 4–5.

57 *Ibid.*, pp. 84–5.

58 *Ibid.*, pp. 38–9.

59 *Report of the Committee on Reformatory and Industrial Schools Systems* (Dublin: Stationery Office, 1970) prl 1342 (The Kennedy Report). See further Walsh, D., *Juvenile Justice*, p. 471.

60 See further Chapter Six.

61 McDermott, P.A. and Robinson, T., *The Children Act 2001* (Dublin: Round Hall, 2003), p. 112.

62 *Irish Times*, 16 October 2004.

63 See above.

64 A review of the courts did not consider it appropriate to consider the jurisdiction of the Children Court given the recent enactment of the Children Act 2001. See The Criminal Jurisdiction of the Courts (Dublin: Stationery Office, 2003), p. 12.

65 See *DPP* v. *Darragh Ryan*, 31 July 2004 and DPP v. Christopher Dunne, 20 December 2004.

66 *DPP* v. *Christopher Dunne*, Transcript of Evidence heard before Judge White on Wednesday 6 October, 2004, p. 8.

67 *Ibid.*, pp. 8–13.

68 Darren Goodwin (16) was sentenced to life in detention for the murder of Daragh Conroy (14) on 15 October 2004, the same day that Christopher Dunne (17) was convicted of the murder of Alan Higgins (17). *Irish Times*, 16 October 2004.

69 Some reporting was of questionable merit. See, for example, the report by Frank McNally of the Darren Goodwin case, who referred to the expression of the young accused, clearly a deeply troubled young person, as being on the 'polite side of neutral' and described him as seeming 'utterly indifferent to the proceedings'. *Irish Times*, 13 October 2004.

70 *Irish Times*, 18 December 2004.

71 *Venables and Thompson v Newsgroup Newspapers Ltd., Associated Newspapers Ltd. and M.G.M. Ltd*, Q.B.D., Dame Butler Sloss, 8 January 2001. See also *X., a woman formerly known as Mary Bell* v. *Newsgroup Newspapers and MGN Ltd.*, Q.B.D., 21 May 2003 where the identity of the daughter of Mary Bell, also convicted of murder as a child, was given life-long protection.

72 It is also relevant, as highlighted above, that failure to facilitate the child's participation in the trial may render the decision susceptible to review.

73 These observations were made by the author throughout the research. Kilkelly, U., *The Children's Court: A Children's Rights Audit.*

74 Courts Service, *Annual Report*, 2004, p. 98.

75 Van Dijk, C., Nuytiens, A., and Eliaerts, C., 'The referral of juvenile offenders to the adult court in Belgium: Theory and Practice' 44(2) *The Howard Journal of Criminal Justice* (2005) pp. 125–66; Junger-Tas, J., 'Youth Justice in the Netherlands' 31, *Crime and Justice* (2004), pp. 293–347, Arteaga, J. A., 'Juvenile (in)Justice: Congressional Attempts to abrogate the procedural rights of juvenile defendants' 102(4) *Columbia Law Review* (May 2002) pp. 1051–88; and Green, S., 'Prosecutorial Waiver into Adult Criminal Court: A Conflict of Interests Violation Amounting to the States' Legislative Abrogation of Juveniles' Due Process Rights, 110 *Penn St. L. Rev.* (2005). pp. 233–81.

76 Doob, A.N., and Tonry, M., 'Varieties of Youth Justice', 31 *Crime and Justice* (2004) pp. 1–201, p. 8.

77 See further Chapter Two.

Chapter Six

Sentencing of Young People

INTRODUCTION

Sentencing in the Children Court has long been a relatively simple affair. Most of the sanctions available are in place since the Children Act 1908 and consist of detention and a limited range of non-custodial options. Although there has been an increase of community-based schemes supported by the Probation and Welfare Service they are frequently over-subscribed. Moreover, this has been accompanied by an apparent increase in the use of detention, among children and adults alike.

Fortunately, this is one area where the Children Act 2001 has the potential to make a substantial improvement to the current system. Part 8 establishes the family conference under the aegis of the Probation and Welfare Service as a diversion from conviction and sentence, while Part 9 puts in place a wide range of community-based sanctions aimed to put the principle of detention as a last resort into practice. Significantly, too, the Act offers the courts strong guidance on the factors to be taken into account when choosing from this potentially dazzling array of sanctions. However, to this mix is to be added Anti-Social Behaviour Orders (ASBOs); although a civil order, if breached it will trigger the penal sanctions in Part 9 of the Act. This is undoubtedly a retrograde step in an area full of potential for positive reform.

This Chapter analyses the range of devices at the discretion of the courts when faced with a child charged with a criminal offence. It considers the contribution to be made by the family conference, non-custodial sanctions and ASBOs to prevent further offending by young people, and measures these initiatives by the benchmark of international standards.

INTERNATIONAL STANDARDS

International standards require the protection of children from the harmful effects of the formal justice system. They stipulate that any treatment children receive should be proportionate to their circumstances and the offence, and should promote the well-being of the child, his/her continued education and need to play a constructive role in society.[1] In accordance with Article 40(1) of the Convention on the Rights of the Child (CRC), young offenders have the right to be treated in a manner which takes into account their age and the desirability of promoting their reintegration and assuming a constructive role in society.

The Beijing Rules recognise that there are conflicting ideologies within youth justice as regards rehabilitation versus just desert; assistance versus repression and punishment; a reaction according to the singular merits of an individual case versus reaction according to the protection of society in general; general deterrence versus individual incapacitation. Rather than prescribing a single approach, these and other standards set out the approach most in line with best practice. They are 'practical guidelines that should ensure a common starting point', which could contribute considerably to ensuring that the fundamental rights of young offenders are protected, especially 'the fundamental rights of personal development and education'.[2]

The principal standard for the sentencing of young people is that detention should be used only as a measure of last resort and for the shortest appropriate period of time. This is recognised in Article 37(b) of the CRC as well as Rule 19.1 of the Beijing Rules. Underlying this principle is the recognition that the adverse influences of detention on young people cannot be outweighed by treatment efforts. Moreover, the negative effects, not only of loss of liberty, but also of separation from the usual social environment, are more acute for young people than adults because of their early stage of development. For these reasons, the Beijing Rules aim to restrict detention in both quantity ('last resort') and in time ('minimum necessary period') and assert the basic guiding principle that a young person should not be detained unless there is 'no other appropriate response'.[3] Standards also provide that the deprivation of liberty shall not be imposed unless the child is convicted of a serious act involving violence against another person or of persistence in committing other serious offences.[4]

Rule 17 recognises that strictly punitive approaches are not appropriate in children's cases and encourages the use of alternatives to detention to the maximum extent possible, bearing in mind public safety. Probation should be granted to the greatest possible extent and the competent authority shall have the power to discontinue the proceedings at any time. In order to implement the principle of detention as a last resort and to achieve proportionality in the treatment of the child, Article 40(4) of the CRC provides that 'a variety of dispositions, such as care, guidance and supervision orders; counselling; probation; foster care; education and vocational training programmes and other alternatives to institutional care' shall be made available.[5] Making available such a wide variety of measures is designed to ensure flexibility in individual cases and to avoid detention 'to the greatest extent possible'.[6] All such measures have in common 'a reliance on and an appeal to the community for the effective implementation of alternative dispositions'.[7]

The standards also require a holistic approach to the child's offending. Rule 24 of the Beijing Rules recommends that efforts be made to 'provide juveniles, at all stages of the proceedings, with necessary assistance such as lodging, education or vocational training, employment or any other assistance, helpful and practical, in order to facilitate the rehabilitative process'. In order to be effective, therefore, sanctions must serve these multi-dimensional objectives and must aim to support rather than punish.

IRISH LAW AND PRACTICE

An analysis of the compatibility of Irish law and practice with these standards must be undertaken from two perspectives: the current one and that when the Children Act 2001 is fully implemented. With regard to the latter situation, the Act clearly reflects the objectives set by the international standards, although the extent to which its provisions receive targeted and sustained resourcing will determine whether this positive conclusion extends to practice. With regard to the current situation, it is apparent that neither law nor policy complies with international standards; this will be even less so when Behaviour Orders are introduced.

SANCTIONS CURRENTLY AVAILABLE

Most of the sanctions currently available to the Children Court are found in the Children Act 1908. A full list of the ways in which a child may be dealt with is set out in section 107 in a consolidating provision. It is useful to outline these sanctions both to explain current practice as well as to place the sanctions contained in the Children Act 2001 in context. According to the Children Act 1908, the court may deal with the charge against the child in a number of ways, including by:

- *dismissing the charge*: this occurs in two possible circumstances, first when the child before the court is under the age of criminal responsibility or otherwise incapable of committing the offence with which he/she has been charged and second, where the Probation Act is applied. With respect to the latter, the Probation of Offenders Act 1907 makes specific provision for dismissing a summary charge when the court considers that it is inexpedient to convict or to inflict any punishment having regard, *inter alia*, to the age of the accused;
- *discharging the offender on his entering into a recognizance and/or placing him under the supervision of a Probation Officer (Probation Bond)*: Under the Probation Act, a child may be found guilty but discharged on condition that he/she enters into a recognizance to be of good behaviour. The child may also be placed under the supervision of a Probation Officer and be subjected to additional conditions necessary to prevent a repetition of the offence, including conditions with respect to residence and abstention from alcohol;
- *committing the offender to the care of a relative or other fit*

person: section 57 of the Children Act 1908 provides for a 'fit person order' i.e. that the court may place a child in the care of a relative or other fit person in lieu of sending him/her to an industrial or reformatory school. The 'fit person' order generally applies when the child's parent or legal guardian has been convicted of cruelty towards the child;[8]
- *sending the offender to an industrial school, reformatory school or a place of detention*: under the Act the choice of detention facility depends on the child's age and the nature of his/her offending/non-offending behaviour. Under section 65 of the 1908 Act, a child cannot be kept in an industrial school beyond the age of sixteen years;[9]
- *ordering the offender and/or his parent or guardian to pay a fine, damages or costs*: under section 99 of the 1908 Act, a child can be fined or charged to pay damages or costs if the court is of the opinion that the case would be best met in this way with or without any other punishment. Unless the parent cannot be found, he/she is actually fined or charged and no such order can be made without first giving him/her the opportunity to be heard, and
- *ordering the parent or guardian of the offender to give security for his good behaviour.*

In addition, it is open to the court to impose a Community Service Order on young people over the age of sixteen years under the Criminal Justice (Community Service) Act 1983.

SENTENCING IN THE CHILDREN COURT

As with other areas of the Irish youth justice system, there is a dearth of statistical and analytical data on the practice of sentencing young people in the Children Court and elsewhere. Very limited statistics are published on the outcome of individual cases. The Annual Reports of the Courts Service, first published in 2001, only contain data on the applications for the committal of children to special (Industrial and Reformatory) schools. Although the 2004 Report contains information on the determination of cases by the Dublin Metropolitan District broken down according to age, no statistics are available on cases determined by Children Courts in Limerick, Waterford, Cork, Galway or elsewhere. Nor does the report contain any commentary on these figures.

It is clear, therefore, that few statistics are available from official sources on the sanctions applied by the Children Court and virtually nothing of any historical value is available to enable the tracking of trends. The absence of official data and the difficulties involved in conducting research of this kind – highlighted in Chapter One above – are pertinent here also. The lack of evaluative studies considering the use of various sanctions and their impact is a major deficiency in the youth justice system. Two major sentencing studies were carried out in the Dublin Children Court in the 1980s and 1990s. O'Donovan conducted a study of 12,628 cases that came before the Court in 1985. His study found that of the 4,083 cases which involved summary offences, the vast majority of these, 83.7 per cent, were disposed of by way of supervision by the Probation Service, dismissal under the Probation Act or struck out. Only four cases were dealt with by way of Community Service Order, 10.3 per cent by way of fine, and the remaining 5.8 per cent were sentenced to detention. His study also noted that this incarceration rate showed an increase from 4.9 per cent in 1982.[10]

A more recent, unpublished and otherwise unavailable study, carried out for the Department of Justice, Equality and Law Reform in 2001/02, considered nearly 2,500 charge sheets and found that 10 per cent of children appearing before the Dublin Children Court, whose cases were disposed of during the study, received a custodial sanction. When the researchers measured case outcome according to charge sheets rather than individual offenders, they found that custodial sanctions represented the most frequently used penalty for male offenders.[11]

More recent research, based on observation of the Children Court, has also pointed to an increasing use of custody as well as the lack of meaningful sanctions overall. While only 793 cases of the 944 observed in this research in 2003 and 2004 involved a final determination of the charges faced, of the 151 that were resolved, the most common sanction imposed (33 per cent) was a Probation Bond, with a sentence of detention a close second at 23 per cent. Fines were imposed in 13 per cent of cases, and both suspended sentences and Community Service

Orders were received in 6 per cent of cases.[12] While the rate at which fines are imposed as a sanction has not changed significantly since previous studies, the rate at which detention is imposed appears to show a significant increase.[13] Further support for this view can be found in research published by the Irish Association for the Study of Delinquency (IASD) in 2005.[14] This analysis of 50 cases before the Dublin Children Court between January and October 2004 found that 18 of the young people (36 per cent) were given a custodial sanction – nine of the young people were sent to St Patrick's Institution and the other nine were sent to Children Detention Schools – while a further four young people had previously been in detention. When the charges sent forward for trial (four) and discharged (ten) are removed, however, the figures are even more worrying. Of the young people convicted by the Children Court, half (18), were sent to detention – nine (or a quarter) received a Probation Bond, and the remaining nine young people received a suspended sentence (three), a Community Service Order (two), a Peace Bond (two) and a fine (two). This research also carried out a more superficial analysis of 751 cases decided by the Dublin Children Court via the Criminal Case Tracking System and classified them according to outcome (detention, sent forward for trial, non-custodial sanctions and not convicted).[15] According to this analysis, detention was ordered in 9 per cent of cases and a non-custodial measure (Probation Bond, suspended sentence, fine or Community Service Order) was applied in a further 30 per cent of cases. The Courts Service statistics actually indicate the detention rate to be much higher – 14 per cent in 2004[16] – with non-custodial sanctions being applied in approximately 28 per cent of cases by the Dublin Children Court.[17] A point of consistency between the Courts Service data and the IASD research is the high number of cases not ending in prosecution or conviction. According to both sources, charges against young people were struck out, dismissed or otherwise did not end in conviction in almost 55 per cent of cases. The lack of commentary accompanying these figures means that they leave an open question over *half* of the cases heard by the Children Court.

There are clear difficulties with the available data here which frustrate any attempt to draw definitive conclusions. In particular, the presentation of data in different ways makes it difficult to accurately identify trends in the use of particular sanctions – for example, one custodial rate emerges from the analysis of cases in which a sanction was imposed (50 per cent according to the IASD research), while a lower rate of 14 per cent (according to the Courts Service Annual Report) is identifiable when all the cases heard are taken into account. Either way, two points are clear: first, the use of custody is increasing and would appear to be the sanction of choice in the Children Court and second, and related, it is apparent from the research that there is a distinct lack of meaningful alternatives to custody. Neither position reflects the international standards and instead stands in stark contrast to the principle of detention as a measure of last resort. However, the context of these statistics is worthy of greater analysis. In particular, it is clear that the lack of early intervention and the inadequate availability of meaningful sanctions means that the offending of young people is not checked promptly when they arrive into the children court system. Problems of delay and endless remands mean that young people drift through the system with many collecting further charges while on bail, including for breach of bail conditions. The net result of this failure – which is systemic – is that for these young people, all too soon, the last resort arrives and detention is the only option.

The data from the prisons system is also grossly inadequate and makes it impossible to verify the above conclusions with regard to the use of custody with any real certainty.[18] From the data available, Walsh concludes that there has been an underlying trend (between 1976 and 1994) upwards in the committals to St Patrick's Institution (which accommodates young people between 16 and 21 years) with an increasing emphasis on the older age groups.[19] He notes that most young people under 18 years appear to have been sent to St Patrick's for larceny; while their share is lower, it would appear that juveniles convicted of offences against the person (or 'other offences') are more likely to receive a custodial sentence than if they were convicted of a property offence.[20] It is also important to note (although not surprising given the lack of a dedicated detention centre for girls over 16 years) that imprisonment is used less frequently in the sentencing of females than males.[21]

Regarding children under 16 years, it is clear from the data that the number in detention continues to fall; boys constitute 97 per cent of this group although the number of girls detained in Children Detention Schools is increasing. Boys also enjoy a larger share (83 per cent) of remands. The divergence between the number of girls committed (3 per cent of the total) and detained on remand (13 per cent of the total) suggest that remand is being used as an end in itself. While a focus on detention as a measure of last resort may reduce the number of young people committed to detention on conviction, clearly more sophisticated measures – including the introduction of bail schemes – are required to reduce the use of detention as a preventive measure, especially for girls.

THE CHILDREN ACT 2001

Sentencing Principles

One of the single most important contributions of the Children Act 2001 is the provision made for sentencing principles to be applied by all courts deciding cases against children.[22] Section 96 details the factors that must be taken into account by courts when sentencing children and young people. In particular, it recognises that it is desirable wherever possible to prevent interruption of a child's education, training or employment, to strengthen the relationship between children and their families and to allow children to reside in their own homes. For these reasons, it provides that any penalty imposed on the child for an offence should:

- take into account as mitigating factors the child's age and level of maturity;
- interfere as little as possible with the child's education, training or employment;
- take the form most likely to maintain and promote the child's development;
- take the least restrictive form appropriate in the circumstances and in particular, be no greater than that imposed on an adult for the same offence;
- respect the principle of detention as a last resort; and

- have due regard to the interests of any victims of the child's offending.

This is a rare statement of the principles and objectives of youth justice in the Children Act and a welcome articulation of the important factors that all courts must take into account when sentencing children. It is unfortunate that these principles do not also bind the other agencies – An Garda Síochána, the Probation and Welfare Service, the Health Service Executive – involved in the delivery of services in the youth justice system.[23] Moreover, the absence of guidance as to how these sentencing principles are to be applied leaves judges to use their own discretion as to how to approach the sentencing process when one or more of the above factors conflict. While it is likely that a particular sanction will involve detention as a last resort while also interfering as little as possible with the child's education or training, for instance, other factors may not sit so easily together. In particular, it will not always be easy to reconcile the interests of any victims of the child's offending, to whom the child's age may not matter, with the duty to take the child's age and maturity into account as mitigating factors. For this reason, it is strongly recommended that judicial consideration be given to how section 96 might be implemented, giving special attention to how to overcome the practical challenges of balancing the interests involved. Priority should be given to developing guiding materials for the judiciary in this area. This is particularly important for the Children Court where these principles are most likely to be pertinent (see below), but they also have general application given that a judge's failure to adhere to its requirements may constitute or substantiate an argument based on irrationality or disproportionate grounds if a decision or order is appealed or judicially reviewed.[24]

While the difficulties involved in applying section 96 in principle may be one reason for the failure to commence this section to date, the failure to put in place the community sanctions under Part 9 of the Act may more fully explain the delay. How are judges to implement the mandatory sentencing principle of imposing detention as a measure of last resort when there are few meaningful alternatives to custody available? As Seymour notes, 'while these principles represent an important departure from the Children Act (1908), they will be rendered effectively meaningless without the full enforcement of the provisions of the Act relating to community based sanctions'.[25]

The Range of Sanctions

In order to implement the principle of detention as a last resort, the Children Act 2001 provides for a range of community sanctions as alternatives to detention. When a court finds a child guilty of an offence, it may impose one or more of the sanctions out in sections 108-141. The sanctions can be categorised as follows:

- *An order for fines, costs or compensation* (ss. 108-110): the court must have regard to the ability of the child to pay a fine, compensation or court costs;
- *An order imposed on parents, such a parental supervision order or an order that a parent be bound over* (ss. 111–114): Binding over the parent requires him/her to enter into a recognizance to exercise proper and adequate control over the child. Forfeiture of the bond (up to £250/€317) occurs if the child commits another offence within the period of the order and the court is satisfied that the failure of the parents to exercise adequate control was a factor. A parental supervision order may be imposed also where the court is satisfied that a wilful failure of the child's parents to control the child contributed to the child's criminal conduct. It may require the parent to comply with any instruction of the court including to participate in a substance abuse programme or a parenting course and a Probation and Welfare Officer is appointed to supervise, assist and monitor the parents. Failure to comply will be treated as a contempt of court;
- *A community sanction, such as a probation order, a day centre order, an order requiring supervision by a suitable person or mentor* or *an order restricting movement* (ss. 115–141): the court may impose a variety of community sanctions and attach conditions such as attending school, limited contact with specified individuals, attending certain places and staying away from alcohol or drugs. The community sanctions include the basic Probation Order,

where the child agrees to be supervised by a Probation and Welfare Officer and three variations on this order. The first of these is the Probation (training or activities programme) Order where a child can be referred to a specific programme with the agreement of the programme manager. The second is the Probation (intensive supervision) Order where the child is closely supervised, must attend an educational or training course or undergo treatment, and reside at a specific address for a period up to 60 days. The third is a Probation (residential supervision) Order which provides for residence in a place other than the child's home, such as in a hostel approved by the Probation and Welfare Service. Two further orders provide for the child to be placed in the care of a person other than a family member – the Suitable Person (care and supervision) Order, according to which the court may, with the parents' consent, assign an offender to the care of a suitable person where the parent is unable to cope or the home environment unsuitable and the Mentor (family support) Order which allows the offender to stay in the home but receive help and advice from a suitable person while under the supervision of a Probation and Welfare Officer. A Restriction on Movement Order is similar to a curfew insofar as it prevents the child from attending certain places and requires him/her to be at home between certain hours[26] and a Day Centre Order provides for attendance at a day centre (for the purposes of leisure, sporting or other constructive activities) to be approved by the Minister for Justice. A maximum attendance of 90 days, not necessarily consecutive, can be required;
- *An order placing a child in detention or combining detention and supervision in the community (ss. 142–156):* In addition to placing a child in detention, the Act introduces an important sanction, which requires the offender to serve half his sentence in detention and the other half in the community. It is to be hoped that this would develop as the normal type of sentence to be imposed where detention is deemed appropriate given its potential to successfully reintegrate the offender into the community on release.

Part 9 of the Act thus consolidates the sanctions available under other legislation. While the question as to whether these sanctions are genuinely new or just repackaged is discussed below, the principal function of Part 9 of the Children Act, like section 107 of the Children Act 1908 before it, is that it brings all the sanctions together in one place. This is not an insignificant contribution as it is likely to draw the attention of all those involved in the system to the range and combination of measures available to meet the situation of a particular child in a given case.

The range of sanctions provided for under the Act is designed to ensure that there is an appropriate measure available for each child regardless of his/her needs or problems. Emphasis is placed on care in the community, varying the level and type of care and supervision in accordance with the needs of the child and of society, and ensuring that detention is imposed only as a last resort. Under the Act, the choice of sanction for each child is made by the court following a Probation and Welfare Officer's Report and/or a Victim Impact Report. The Act lays down a number of conditions with regard to the preparation of the report requiring, in particular, that the place where the report is undertaken be accessible to the child and the times he/she is required to attend do not interfere with education or work schedules. Importantly, also, the Act places strict duties on Probation and Welfare Officers with regard to young people placed under their supervision. In particular, section 141 provides that they have a duty to visit, assist and advise the child, and where feasible his/her parents; see that the child observes the terms and conditions of the supervision, and when necessary and appropriate, try to find the child suitable employment and accommodation. In addition, section 200 of the Act provides that where their child is placed under supervision, parents must not exercise their rights and powers in a way which would interfere with that supervision. The constitutionality of such an interference with the exercise of parents' rights, given express recognition in Article 42 of the Constitution, has yet to be tested.

The Act also provides for a sentence of detention to be deferred *inter alia* if it is in the interests of justice to do so or a place is not available in a Children Detention School (for children under 16 years). According to O'Dwyer, 'deferred detention gives statutory recognition to a practice that has built up in recent years whereby the court chooses to defer sentence on condition that the offender complies with supervision from a probation and welfare officer' and is designed to avoid the creation of the 'revolving door' where offenders are 'released prematurely to make room for newcomers'.[27] He warns that there may be a need for more detention places if an unwarranted build-up of detention deferrals is not to occur. Seymour expresses a different concern about this provision 'in light of the argument that delays and postponements in the criminal justice system impact on its effectiveness and especially on the effectiveness of the punishment'.[28] She also questions the equal treatment of children 'if in one set of circumstances a child is detained immediately, while in another identical case a child is required to wait until a place becomes available' or indeed has a community sanction imposed due to the lack of a place in a Children Detention School. In many respects, she notes, this may leave the legislation open to a 'wider interpretation that was originally envisaged in the drafting of the Act'.[29]

New or Just Repackaged?

While the range of community or non-custodial sanctions set out in the Act seems extensive, appearances can be deceptive. In fact, many of the measures set out in Part 9 are already in place either under the Children Act 1908 or through established practice. In particular, section 107 of the 1908 Act, which allows a case to be dealt with by ordering the offender to pay a fine, damages or costs or making such an order against the child's parent or guardian, is merely reiterated in sections 108–9 of the 2001 Act. Sanctions against parents contained in the 2001 Act are not new either – provision was made in the 1908 Act for parents to be ordered to give security for their child's good behaviour. At the same time, the parental supervision order contained in section 111 of the 2001 Act is a new twist on making parents shoulder responsibility for their child's offending[30] insofar as it can require parents to undergo parenting courses or receive treatment for drug addiction. In this way, it has been criticised for applying double standards given that the state is 'immune from prosecution' when it fails children, whereas parents, clearly, are not.[31]

The range of community sanctions contained in the 2001 Act has been heralded as new and innovative. However, in the same respects, they may be considered a repackaging of the 1908 Act. In particular, three of the eight community sanctions set out in Part 9 of the 2001 Act represent variations on the theme provided for in section 107 of the 1908 Act, which allows a child to be placed under the supervision of a Probation Officer. Far from being new, the Probation (training or activities) Order, Probation (intensive supervision) Order and the Probation (residential supervision) Order can be said to be simple Probation Orders with their purpose set out in more detail. Similarly, the 1908 Act provided for an order committing the offender to the care of a relative or other fit person – this is reflected in the provisions of the 2001 Act including the Suitable Person (Care and Supervision) Order which orders the child to live in a fostering type arrangement with a suitable person, and the Mentor (Family Support) Order which assigns the child to a person, who may be a relative, who will help, advise and support the child and his or her family in its efforts to prevent the child re-offending – a more detailed and specific version of the century year old provision.

Of the remaining provisions in the 2001 Act, the Day Centre Order is arguably the only provision with any real innovation (certainly the restriction of movement order is not ground-breaking in so far as it aims merely to contain young people and may indeed be 'unenforceable'[32]). Section 198 requires the child to attend 'a day centre' (any centre designated for this purpose) for up to six months to participate in an occupation or activity, or receive suitable and beneficial instruction. There is no real limit on the type of activity that a day centre can provide and this Order is clearly designed to secure the child's positive involvement in some sporting, leisure or educational activity available in his/her community. Availability or access to such activity is key therefore. So, as with all of the community sanctions, it is clear that the availability of resources, both human and material, will be central to their successful implementation.

As stated above, the only orders in force to date (commenced in 2002) are those restricting movement and ordering the child to pay a fine or compensation. Despite this, data from the Courts Service Annual Report of 2004 indicate that neither type of order was made by the Dublin Children Court in 2004.[33]

DETENTION AS A LAST RESORT

Translating the Principle into Reality

Under section 143 of the Children Act 2001, the Children Court shall not make an order imposing a period of detention on a child unless it is satisfied that detention is the only suitable way of dealing with the child and, in the case of a child under 16 years, that a place in a Children Detention School is available for him/her. According to McDermott and Robinson, this provision should be read together with section 96 which provides that 'a period of detention should be imposed only as a measure of last resort'.[34]

The experience of other jurisdictions makes it clear that a number of factors are necessary to fully implement the principle of detention as a last resort. While the availability of meaningful alternatives is an obvious pre-condition, convincing the courts to use these alternatives is also vital. Yet the argument against detention is persuasive. Behind the political mantra that 'Prison Works', it is well documented that incarceration is ineffective as a solution to the problem of youth crime. Apart from the resources wasted on detention, the rehabilitative and deterrent effects of imprisonment have been greatly exaggerated. For young people, whose crimes are frequently opportunistic, unpremeditated and undertaken without any thought for their consequences, a more pertinent consideration should be the amount of damage detention actually causes to the children sent there.[35]

The other dimension missing from efforts to implement the principle of detention as a last resort is an examination of what is needed to translate this theoretical principle into reality. Many have argued that a range of community sanctions is in itself insufficient to bring about a decrease in the numbers sentenced to detention. For instance, Bateman notes that during the 1980s when the numbers of children in custody in England and Wales fell, the 'alternatives to custody movement' had developed 'an almost crusading zeal', whereby 'local courts were not infrequently persuaded of the importance of keeping children in the community wherever possible'.[36] Advocating community sanctions as a real alternative to custody will only work, however, where well resourced infrastructure exists to deliver these sanctions on a multi-disciplinary basis. Even then, as currently in England and Wales, where that infrastructure is well placed to deliver holistic responses, Bateman notes: 'the new punitiveness (which favours custody) appears to have taken a toll on operational practice too.'[37] Thus, what is also required, in addition to the political commitment to community sanctions – which appears currently to be absent in Ireland – is the undertaking to engage with young people, including those whose offending is serious and persistent, in order to maintain them outside penal establishments.[38] This engagement is a two way process, of course, and although some would dismiss young people as being uninterested or unwilling to change, others more rightly put the onus on the adults and practitioners in the process. As Batchelor and McNeill have put it: 'Commitment to desistance from crime on the part of the young person appears to be generated by personal and professional commitment on the part of workers, whose reasonableness, fairness and encouragement is seen by young people to demonstrate an understanding of, and genuine concern, for them as people.'[39]

To some extent, therefore, it is irrelevant whether or not the non-custodial measures set out in Part 9 of the Children Act 2001 are considered novel. It is their implementation that is the real challenge. In this context, what is important is the political support for the view that community sanctions, parental support and measures which divert young people from custody have the potential to prevent young people from re-offending. The fact that few of these provisions have been implemented to date is unfortunate if not understandable given the training, resources and infrastructure necessary to make them work effectively. At the same time, it is vital that an immediate commitment be given to commencing the remainder of Part 9 and that plans to resource their implementation be expedited.

The Challenge of Serious Crime

Section 96 of the Children Act makes it discretionary rather than mandatory for the court to take the child's age and maturity into account during the sentencing process. Its discretionary nature is relevant in light of the fact that while the principle applies to all children and in all courts, in reality, judges in sentencing children for minor offences are likely to give greater weight to it than those sentencing children for more serious crimes. This appeared, for example, from the sentencing in 2004 of four young people convicted of rape, and two others convicted of murder. In the former case, Judge Paul Carney, sentencing Thomas O'Neill (16) to ten years, Dean Barry (16) to nine years, Darragh Ryan (16) to eight years and Jason Ring (15) to four years, suspended the last year of their sentence as a result of their 'guilty pleas'.[40]

As to what weight was attached to their young ages, Judge Carney made a number of insightful comments during sentencing. First, he noted that he was 'fully conscious' of the fact that he was 'dealing with children' who 'must be rehabilitated if that is at all possible'. This, he noted, was 'a primary consideration'. However, he then went on to note that he also had a 'concern for the protection of society', which he said was 'very much present to my mind'. He held that, in his view, the accused represent 'a continuing danger'. While indicating that he was treating them as children, and having regard to his obligations in respect of children, 'that does not necessarily mean', Judge Carney continued, 'that I have to deal with them by way of very short sentences because rehabilitation in their case is clearly going to take a very great deal of time and the community is going to require to be protected from their propensities for a very long period of time'.[41] It is not clear from these statements, therefore, what precise weight was given to the age and maturity of the accused in their sentencing. What is clear, and perhaps not surprising given the seriousness of the crimes, was that the risk they posed to society appeared to be given far greater weight by the sentencing judge than the personal circumstances of the young accused. Ironically, although the judge noted the need to impose a long sentence to allow rehabilitation to take place he failed to take into account that few if any facilities exist to address offending behaviour in St Patrick's Institution, to which three of the four boys were sent.

In 2005, the fifth member of the gang, a 24-year-old male, received twenty-one years for his role in the attack. According to Judge Carney, it was no form of mitigation that the man was not the ringleader as 'he was going around the countryside taking orders from a child'. His sentence thus reflected the fact that he did not 'take control and stop what was going on'.[42] If his co-accused were not treated leniently because of their young age, it appears he was treated more severely because of it.

It is equally unclear whether any account was taken of the young age of Darren Goodwin when he was sentenced in 2004 for the murder of 14 year-old old Daragh Conroy. 'Notwithstanding your youth', Judged Barry White reportedly said, 'the only sentence is one of imprisonment for life, and I now impose that sentence on you'.[43] He went on to note that Goodwin's sentence would be reviewed in ten years time.[44]

When Christopher Dunne was sentenced at age 17 in December 2004 for the murder of Alan Higgins, he too was given a sentence of life imprisonment. Arguments from his lawyer to have him treated as a child under the Children Act 2001 were unsuccessful. 'For the purpose of sentence, Mr Dunne is not a young person', Judge Abbot held.[45] His appeal against his life sentence was unsuccessful.[46]

Apart from the decision of the judges in these cases not to allow the age and maturity of the young people to serve as mitigating factors in the sentencing process, no regard would appear to have been given to the other factors set out in mandatory form in section 96, namely the requirement to choose the least invasive sanction appropriate taking into account the child's education, development and family relations and to impose detention as a last resort. While more comprehensive research is clearly needed here, it appears, nonetheless, that these factors will not normally be considered relevant where children have been convicted of violent crime. While an important provision in theory, therefore, section 96 may thus be of questionable relevance in practice especially for judges sentencing children with respect to serious or violent crime. Here, protection of society and the punishment of the accused are likely to remain dominant factors.[47]

COMMUNICATING THE SENTENCE TO YOUNG PEOPLE

The importance of communicating expectations to young people is an important role for the Children Court as was highlighted in

Chapter Five. The value of communicating with young people in the court was acknowledged in the Probation of Offenders Act 1908, section 2 (3) of which required the juvenile court to make sure that the offender fully understood the conditions of a Probation Order by requiring the Order to be given to the young person in writing in 'simple terms'.[48] This is reiterated in the Children Act 2001, which places a duty on the court to explain the sanction imposed on the child. According to section 116, when ordering a community sanction, the courts must explain the following to the child in open court and in language appropriate to the child's level of understanding:

- why it is being imposed;
- its terms and conditions;
- that the child is expected to behave while the sanction is in force;
- possible consequences of failure to comply; and
- that the child's parents or guardian are expected to help the child to comply and not to commit further offences.

Observations of the Children Court have highlighted that few judges explained anything to the young people before them and in cases where a sentence was imposed, it was almost impossible to understand the reason beyond the judge's choice of a particular sanction.[49] Judges who did explain the conditions being attached to a probation or bail bond rarely did so in age appropriate language. The young person frequently left the Children Court without an understanding of what had been decided.[50] Current practice does not suggest, therefore, that all judges in the Children Court have the necessary skills to communicate effectively with young people as required by the Children Act. Training is clearly required to ensure that judges are appropriately equipped to communicate with young people that come before them, many of whom may have poor capacity to understand formal legal language. It is also recommended that serious consideration be given to developing a Bench Book, similar to that adopted by the Judicial Studies Board of England and Wales, with proposed wording to be used by the judge in particular situations.[51] These measures would all bring the Court's operation closer in line with international standards.

THE FAMILY CONFERENCE

In addition to the new sanctions, the Children Act 2001 also added an entirely new layer to the youth justice system in the form of a family conference. Section 78 provides for a court-directed and supervised family conference which is to be convened by the Probation and Welfare Service. Similar in many respects to the Garda conference held as part of the Diversion Programme,[52] the Probation-led conference can be ordered by the Children Court where a child accepts responsibility for his/her behaviour, the child's parent/guardian agrees to participate in and support the activities of the conference and the Court believes that it may be the appropriate response. The conference is thus convened as an alternative to proceeding to a finding and it thus gives the court 'an important discretion to achieve a balance between issues of accountability and the best interests of the child'.[53] The advantage for the child is that it offers an opportunity to avoid a conviction, while at the same time aims to address the causes of his/her offending.

According to the Act, the Probation and Welfare Officer convenes the conference by bringing together the child, his/her family and any other person (teacher, community worker, representatives of state agencies) likely to contribute to an attempt to address the child's offending behaviour. This comes in the form of the action plan, which the conference supports the family to draw up, which is designed to help prevent the child from offending. The action plan formulated by the family conference and consented to by the child is approved and supervised by the court. If it is completed according to the court's satisfaction, the charge against the child may be dismissed. If the child has failed to comply with the action plan, the court may resume the proceedings against the child.

The provisions relating to this model of the family conference were commenced in July 2004[54] and so are only in the early stages of implementation. Many factors are important to their success not least that the Children Court have sufficient awareness of and confidence in the mechanism to use it. The success of the family conference also depends on good working relationships between all the state agencies involved, as well as their ability to support the family, particularly those who may have difficulty communicating and working together.[55] Finally, the successful implementation of an action plan requires the availability of those resources and services that the conference believes should be directed at the young person's offending. If the action plan proposes counselling for addiction problems, therapeutic intervention for mental health difficulties, vocational training or education or a new hobby or leisure activity for the young person, and none of these services is available within a reasonable timescale and convenient to the child's home, fulfilment of the terms of the action plan will be very difficult. The fact that these measures are court-ordered, by its sanctioning of the action plan, may facilitate the arrangements necessary here. Ultimately, however, if the peripheral services are not available then the family conference, and the young person whose offending it is designed to address, will fail.

ANTI-SOCIAL BEHAVIOUR ORDERS

The failure to commence and fully resource all these provisions of the Children Act means that their potential to address young offending is not yet known or understood. Current methods of data collection make it difficult to evaluate the effectiveness of the sanctions already in place. Despite this, the Minister for Justice, Equality and Law Reform announced in December 2004 that he considered further measures in this area to be necessary. He announced that ASBOS were coming to Ireland.

The UK Experience

A New Labour invention, ASBOs were introduced in England and Wales in 1998 (under the Crime and Disorder Act 1998) and subsequently, amid much controversy, in Scotland and Northern Ireland.[56] An ASBO is a civil order made to prohibit anti-social behaviour which is defined as 'behaviour which causes harassment, alarm or distress'.[57] In the UK they can be imposed on anyone over ten years-of-age and they involve the court attaching to the order as wide a range of conditions as it deems appropriate in order to restrict the actions and behaviour of the impugned individual with a view to protecting the community from further anti-social acts. Although an ASBO is a civil order, breach is a criminal offence which, on indictment, has a maximum penalty of five years imprisonment.

In the UK, the introduction and increasing use of ASBOs has been described as forming part of 'a growing apparatus of exclusion and social control introduced in the name of protecting communities'.[58] Opposition to them has been led by groups like the Howard League for Penal Reform and has also included Britain's leading professors of criminal law, legal practitioners, the National Association of Probation Officers and a range of individuals and community groups.[59] The Council of Europe's Commissioner for Human Rights has also expressed his criticism of the impact of the Orders on young people.[60]

ASBOs have been subjected to detailed research in the UK since their introduction with increasing conclusions as to their disproportionate, arbitrary[61] and harmful effects, particularly on children and young people on whom the majority of Orders are imposed. Their impact on already marginalised young people has been dramatic, and in 2004, led to the first increase for some time in the numbers of young people in custody in England and Wales.[62] Despite the apparent problems with the measure in practice – the relevant legislation has had to be amended several times – the police and local authorities have come under increasing political pressure to apply for ASBOs, contrary to community policing and youth diversion strategies. Thus, while the number made was low when they were first introduced in 1999 (104 orders), more than 7,300 orders were made before September 2005.

ASBOs can be criticised from a number of different perspectives including the criminal law and human rights. The wide definition of anti-social behaviour has lead to concerns about arbitrariness and ASBOs being the solution to fit every problem. This is of particular concern considering that the normal rights of due process do not apply[63] given that proceedings to apply for an ASBO are civil in nature. This makes an application for an ASBO difficult to defend as the fact that hearsay evidence can be used reduces the burden on the police to provide evidence that can be cross-examined.[64] An application for an ASBO is thus rarely refused.[65]

In the making of an ASBO, the courts have a wide discretion as to the nature and breadth of the conditions to be attached. They need not be limited to the behaviour proved, and can be wide-ranging and punitive in nature. Research for the Youth Justice Board (YJB) in 2005 found that a wide variety of conditions was attached to ASBOs, although the majority were standard, such as 'non-association with certain people, not behaving anti-socially, geographical restrictions and curfews'.[66] ASBOs have been used to prohibit young people from using certain language/words, from wearing certain clothes (e.g. hoodies and baseball caps), ordering them to stay away from public places such as shopping centres and parks, and from meeting named individuals anywhere.[67] These conditions are not only disproportionate – and may raise an issue of incompatibility with various provisions of the European Convention on Human Rights in this respect[68] – but for many young people, these conditions are so restrictive that they are impossible to keep. According to the YJB research, the conditions most commonly breached included 'non-association' and 'geographic restrictions' leading to questions about the applicability and reasonableness of these conditions. Moreover, the data bear out how unrealistic many of the ASBO conditions are: the YJB study found that of the ASBOs breached, 31 per cent of conditions were found to have been breached within the first month, with 85 per cent of all the breaches occurring in the first quarter of the term of the Order. According to the research, 'breaches sometimes occurred within the first week, and in a few cases on the first day: there was a couple of incidents related where the young person breached as they walked out of the court, either by talking to someone they were prohibited from associating with, or for making an obscene gesture at the local press'.[69] This suggests that these young people were either never going to be able to abide by the order, or that the ASBO imposed excessive or unsuitable restrictions, or both. The research noted that many of the young people involved were 'persistent offenders who are unlikely to abide by the conditions of an ASBO, probably as a result of a lack of respect for authority'.[70] However, a related factor is undoubtedly the extent to which young people understand 'why they are not allowed to see their friends or go to a place where they have spent a lot of time before'.[71] Overall, the level of breach raises serious questions as to whether ASBOs simply setting up young people to fail.

Failure in this context means that a criminal offence has been committed. The YJB research found that the rate at which ASBOs are breached lies at 36 per cent, that 45 per cent of all breaches will result in custody (for behaviour that was not imprisonable of itself) and, therefore, that 15.5 per cent of all ASBOs imposed on young people will result in detention.[72] Related to this is the complaint that ASBOs are being used to circumvent the criminal law. According to Ashworth, their combined effect means that 'people are being sent to prison for committing a non-criminal act (such as entering a part of town when banned) or for an offence which has a maximum penalty of a fine'. Such provisions 'turn the criminal law upside down'.[73] The ASBO is thus increasingly used for more serious offences in lieu of prosecution and has lead to the increased criminalisation of young people.[74] In the YJB research, for instance, 34 per cent of the 50 cases for which data were available were found to involve a restriction from committing a criminal act, such as carrying offensive weapons, theft, burglary and assault. Although an argument may be made that this is indeed anti-social behaviour, it raises the possibility that a young person may be sentenced more severely due to both the commission of a criminal offence and the breach of the ASBO. Clearly, in this instance, both offences arise from the same act.

Another concern about ASBOs – at the other end of the scale – is that they lead to net-widening, i.e. bringing into the criminal justice system those who have not committed a criminal offence.[75] This is often linked directly to the range, detail and number of conditions imposed and the rate at which custody is imposed for breach of those conditions.[76]

There are also substantial children's rights grounds for opposing ASBOs. In the UK, reporting restrictions are lifted for the making of an ASBO; indeed, publicising the identity of the young person (including name, address and picture) and the conditions attached to his/her ASBO is seen as central to their effectiveness insofar it assists the policing of the Order. Newspapers have published pictures of young people with the conditions of their ASBO on their front pages notwithstanding that they have not committed a criminal offence.[77] This directly challenges international law, including Article 40 (2)(b) of the CRC which recognises the absolute right of the child to have his/her privacy fully respected at all stages of proceedings.[78]

ASBOs also run counter to international standards on youth justice, which advocate, *inter alia*, the need for progressive delinquency prevention policies, which avoid criminalising and penalising a child for behaviour that does not cause serious damage to the development of the child or harm to others.[79] In this regard, the guidelines recommend that states should prioritise education, safeguard the rights of young people, prevent labelling and consider that youthful behaviour that does not conform to overall social norms and values is often part of the maturation and growth process and tends to disappear spontaneously in most individuals with the transition to adulthood. Rather than adopting punitive responses, states are encouraged to adopt measures to address such behaviour which should be consistent with respect for the rights of the child, should be a holistic, multi-agency response which supports the child and his/her family and should protect the privacy of the child.

According to Millie et al, who carried out research on ASBOs in the UK in 2005, the general population tends to equate anti-social behaviour with problems they associate with young people including graffiti, drug use or simple rowdiness.[80] Those questioned for the research linked this behaviour to 'poor parenting, alcohol and drugs' and 'low respect for others', while another major cause was thought to be boredom and not enough to do.[81] However, the researchers cautioned against the lack of conceptual clarity regarding anti-social behaviour; because ASBOs can powerfully curb the freedom of those on whom they are imposed it is important to be clear about the limits on the use of such powers.[82] Overall, the research recommended that both 'national and local anti-social behaviour strategies should aim for a balance between enforcement and prevention and that more care is needed in defining anti-social behaviour and in deciding the limits on the use of civil remedies'.[83] The report also acknowledged that while ways need to be found to tackle the sense of powerlessness among residents, 'parachuting solutions into these communities and fuelling public concerns about social order through campaigns to garner support for ASBOs should be avoided'.[84]

Overall, a persuasive argument can be made out that ASBOs encourage net widening, involve the labelling and criminalisation of young people and fail to employ positive approaches and supports to divert young people away from behaviour that could lead to criminal activity but is not in itself criminal. The ease with which applications are granted, the punitive and restrictive nature of conditions, which set up young people to fail, and the employment of the media to encourage the public to police the Orders involve multiple breaches of the rights of children and young people, who have not necessarily committed even a minor criminal offence. In short, ASBOs are an extreme measure for an undefined problem.

THE IRISH MODEL

Understandably, therefore, the announcement of the Minister for Justice, Equality and Law Reform of his intention to introduce ASBOs into Ireland was greeted with dismay. A broad range of non-governmental groups and individuals including the Irish Penal Reform Trust, Children's Rights Alliance, the Irish Traveller Movement, the Jesuit Centre for Faith and Justice, the National Youth Council and a range of academics, practising lawyers and community groups formed the Coalition against ASBOs to voice their opposition.[85] The Minister for Children, Brian Lenihan T.D., and the Ombudsman for Children, Emily Logan, also expressed concerns in regard to the possible impact of ASBOs on children.

Having earlier committed himself to introducing ASBOs along the line of the UK model, in July 2005, Mr McDowell subsequently modified his position.[86] Acknowledging the problems with the application of ASBOs to young people in particular, as highlighted by the Coalition against ASBOs, he undertook to alter the British model for children. According to the proposals published in January 2006, ASBOs are to be integrated into a new Part 12A of the Children Act, along with a new preliminary stage of a 'Behaviour Warning' to be issued by a Garda and subsequently, a Good Behaviour Contract (GBC), to be drawn up between a child, his/her parents and a Garda Superintendent on the fulfilment of certain conditions.[87]

Failure to comply with a GBC may result in the child being diverted to the Garda Diversion Programme (admission to which has also been extended to children who commit anti-social behaviour), or alternatively an application for an ASBO being made.

Under the proposals, ASBOs are made by the Children Court in civil proceedings on application by a Garda of at least Superintendent rank setting out what steps have already been taken to prevent the child from committing further anti-social behaviour. The Court may make an ASBO if it is satisfied that, despite the warning and the Good Behaviour Contract, the child, who is over 12 years, has continued or is likely to continue to behave in an anti-social manner, and the order is necessary in all the circumstances. Presumably, section 96 of the Children Act applies to both the proceedings for a Behaviour Order and proceedings for breach, requiring the Court to have regard to the rights of the child, the principle of detention as a measure of last resort and to give discretion to take the child's age and maturity into account.

The Court can make an Order for up to two years and any child behaving in conflict with an ASBO can be arrested without warrant. Breach of an ASBO is a criminal offence which triggers section 98 of the Children Act, namely the custodial and community sanctions in Part 9 of the Act.

Although modified from the UK model, many of the worrying elements of ASBOs are still present in the version intended for application against children here. The fact that they are accompanied by a further system of warnings and formal interventions and the overall extension of the Garda Programme to include anti-social behaviour means that what is proposed has the potential to be even broader in reach than the UK system. The other problems remain: the lack of certainty as to what is anti-social behaviour, the possibility of using this approach when a prosecution with the attendant safeguards is more appropriate and the failure to address the underlying causes of anti-social behaviour. Moreover, the Minister has reneged on his commitment not to apply ASBOs to children under 14 – they are to apply to children over 12 years – and more worryingly, perhaps, the Children Act's reporting restrictions, which protect the identity of the child from being published or broadcast, are to be lifted to the extent that enforcement of an ASBO requires. As one of the more damaging elements of the UK model, this represents an erosion of the child's right to privacy in criminal proceedings in favour of the public's spurious right to name and shame. Regardless of the modifications,[88] then, the ASBO as it is proposed to be integrated into the Children Act 2001, raises serious concerns about its consistency with the European Convention on Human Rights (ECHR) and international law on children's rights as outlined above. There may also be constitutional difficulties here.[89]

Political statements suggest that ASBOs are to be used as a last resort and that exceptions to the child's right to privacy will be allowed only to make ASBOs known to those who need to be aware of them rather than to the media at large. Regardless of these refinements, the fact remains that the case for ASBOs has simply not been made. With stable levels of youth crime, and a raft of measures underway to improve the effectiveness of the youth justice system, it is unclear what need ASBOs are intended to meet. They will be hugely resource-intensive to secure (given the necessary preliminary steps) and to enforce and if applied for in any numbers will undoubtedly put An Garda Síochána and the courts under further pressure. At the very least, it appears that a further and completely unnecessary layer has been added to the youth justice system without any evidence that the existing (and uncommenced) laws are inadequate.[90]

CONCLUSION

The Children Act contains a wide variety of progressive measures to respond to the individual needs of offending children. The family conference offers particular potential to promote family support of the child with constructive and long-term consequences. The Act also introduces an impressive range of non-custodial and community sanctions, which should present clear opportunities to address the causes of offending behaviour. However, failure to fully commence Part 9 of the Children Act 2001 means that the courts have continuously little scope for responding to young offenders in a meaningful way and this undermines their duty to impose detention as a measure of last resort. The lack of timely intervention and appropriate and meaningful responses to young offending also has a knock-on effect on the youth justice system as young people enter an endless cycle of offending resulting in one court appearance after another. For all these reasons, it is regrettable that ASBOs will be introduced into this mix even if the model has been modified somewhat. A cynical view may be that if, as with previous initiatives, the ASBO remains unimplemented it may, for once, be not so bad.

NOTES

1 See Rules 5 and 17 of the UN Standard Minimum Rules for the Administration of Juvenile Justice (the Beijing Rules) adopted by General Assembly resolution 40/33 of 29 November 1985, available at www.ohchr.org (accessed 18 January 2006).
2 *Ibid.,* Commentary to Rule 17.
3 *Ibid.* See the Commentary to Rule 19.
4 *Ibid.*, Rule 17 (1)(c).
5 See also Rule 17 (1)(d) of the Beijing Rules.
6 *Ibid.*, Rule 18(1).
7 *Ibid.*, Commentary to Rule 18.
8 The failure to use the fit person order was criticised by the Kennedy Report, but explained by the unwillingness of friends or relatives to undertake responsibility especially where there is no financial assistance. It recommended that the Health Authority consider fulfilling this role. See The Kennedy Report at para. 10.10 in Mitchell, D., *A Report on the Law and Procedures Regarding the Prosecution and Disposal of Young Offenders* (Dublin: DPP, 1997) pp. 28–9.
9 On the slightly complicated rules in this area see further Mitchell, D. *ibid.*, pp. 29–45.
10 O'Donovan, M., *Report* (Dublin: Probation and Welfare Service, 1987) in Bacik, I., 'The Practice of Sentencing in the Irish Courts' in O'Mahony, P., *Criminal Justice in Ireland* (Dublin: IPA, 2002), pp. 362–3.
11 McLoughlin, E., Maunsell, C., and O'Connell, D., *Children in the Irish Juvenile Justice System*, cited in Bacik, I. *ibid.*
12 Kilkelly, U., *The Children's Court: A Children's Rights Audit* (Cork, 2005), p. 26.
13 However, these figures were collated on the basis of observation of the Children Court only and were not independently verified by a parallel case file analysis. Although they must be treated with caution for this reason, they nonetheless suggest an increased trend in the use of detention

consistent with other research in this and other jurisdictions.

14 McPhillips, S., *Dublin Children Court A Pilot Research Project* (Dublin: IASD, 2005) pp. 23–5.

15 *Ibid.,* pp 82–7.

16 The Courts Service, *Annual Report 2004*, p. 20, available at www.courts.ie (accessed 19 January 2006).

17 It may be relevant that the Courts Service statistics cover the full calendar year, whereas the IASD research undertook to analyse files between January and October 2004.

18 As Walsh notes, the Annual Prisons Reports were only published annually up to 1994, when they ceased. Although two composite reports have been published (covering 1995–98 and 1999–2000) these include only limited statistics on the prison population. See Walsh, D., *Juvenile Justice* (Dublin: Thomson Round Hall, 2005) pp. 431–63.

19 *Ibid.*, pp. 431–51.

20 *Ibid.,* pp. 452–3.

21 *Ibid.,* pp. 441–8.

22 The provision has been described as 'the cornerstone of the Act'. See O'Donnell, T. E., 'The Children Act 2001: A practical analysis from a judicial perspective' a paper presented at the Law Society of Ireland Criminal Law Committee *Seminar for Judges of the District Court*, 3 December 2004, p. 10.

23 See further Chapter Two above.

24 McDermott, P.A., & Robinson, T., *Children Act 2001* (Dublin: Thomson Round Hall 2003), p. 112.

25 Seymour, M., 'Juvenile Justice in the Republic of Ireland', Prepared for the Thematic Working Group on Juvenile Justice European Society of Criminology available at www.esc-eurocrim.org (accessed 11 January 2006), p. 13.

26 Under amendments to the Children Act 2001, a Garda who finds a child in breach of this order will be permitted to arrest the child without warrant. See the Criminal Justice Act 2006.

27 O'Dwyer, K., 'Juvenile Crime and Justice in Ireland' in Bala, N., et al. (eds), *Juvenile Justice Systems: An International Comparison of Problems and Solutions* (Toronto: Thomson Educational, 2002), p. 176.

28 Seymour, M., 'Juvenile Justice in the Republic of Ireland', p. 16.

29 *Ibid.*

30 See Arthur, R., 'Punishing Parents for the Crimes of their Children' 44(3) *Howard Journal of Criminal Justice* (July 2005), pp. 233–53.

31 Shannon, G., *Child Law* (Dublin, Thomson Round Hall, 2005), p. 394.

32 For criticism of this order see O'Dwyer, K., 'Juvenile Crime and Justice in Ireland' in Bala, N., et al. (eds) *Juvenile Justice Systems*, p. 177.

33 The Courts Service, *Annual Report* 2004, p. 98.

34 McDermott, P.A., and Robinson, T., *Children Act 2001*, p. 147.

35 See Moore, S., 'Child Incarceration and the New Youth Justice', in Goldson, B., *The New Youth Justice* (London: Russell House, 2000), pp 15–128. For a disturbing account of the damage and harm inflicted on

young people in detention in Britain see Goldson, B., *Vulnerable Inside Children in Secure and Penal Settings* (London: The Children's Society, 2002). See also Kilkelly, U., et al., *In our Care, Promoting the Rights of Children in Custody* (Belfast: NIHRC, 2002) available at www.nihrc.org (accessed 18 January 2006).

36 Bateman, T., 'Reducing Child Imprisonment: A Systematic Challenge', *Youth Justice* 5(2) (October 2005), 91–105, at p. 98.

37 *Ibid.*, p. 99.

38 See Squires, P. and Stephen D.E., *Rougher Justice: Anti-social behaviour and young people* (Devon: Willan Publishers, 2005), p. 81.

39 Batchelor, S., and McNeill, F., 'The Young Person – Worker Relationship', cited in Bateman, T., 'Reducing Child Imprisonment: A Systematic Challenge', p. 102. See also Bateman, T., and Pitts, J. (eds), *The RHB Companion to Youth Justice* (Lyme Regis: Russell House Publishing, 2005).

40 DPP v Thomas O'Neill, Dean Barey, Darragh Ryan, Jason Ring, Transcript of the sentence delivered by Mr Justice Carney, on Friday, 30th July 2004. The sentence of Jason Ring could not be suspended because he was to serve it in Trinity House (a Children Detention School for those under 16 years). *Irish Times,* 31 July 2004.

41 *Ibid.*, p. 118.

42 *Irish Times,* 28 June 2005.

43 According to the Central Criminal Court, it has the power to impose either a determinate sentence or an indeterminate sentence (detention at the pleasure of the court) in the case of a young person convicted of murder. See Walsh, D. *Juvenile Justice*, pp. 155–7.

44 *Irish Times*, 16 October 2004.

45 *Irish Times,* 21 December 2004.

46 *Irish Times,* 15 November 2005.

47 On issues of sentencing for indictable crimes see further Walsh, D., *Juvenile Justice*, pp. 118–58.

48 Mitchell, D., *A Report on the Law and Procedures Regarding the Prosecution and Disposal of Young Offenders*, p. 23.

49 Kilkelly, U., *The Children's Court: A Children's Rights Audit,* p. 67.

50 *Ibid.*, pp. 64–5. In one case, a child who had confirmed that he understood his bail conditions was asked to explain them back to the judge but could not articulate what they meant. Others demonstrated a clear lack of understanding of 'curfews' and orders excluding them from certain places.

51 The Youth Court Bench Book, drafted in 2002 and revised in 2005, can be found on the website of the Judicial Studies Board of England and Wales at www.jsb.gov.uk (accessed 18 January 2006) see further Chapter Five above.

52 See further Chapter Three.

53 The Law Society's Law Reform Committee, *Rights-based Child Law: The case for reform – Part 1*, (Dublin: Law Society, December 2005), p. 98

54 SI no 468 of 2004.

55 See the proposal to develop a pilot in this area. The Law Society's Law Reform Committee, *Rights-based Child Law*, p. 98.

56 In Northern Ireland, their introduction was challenged unsuccessfully by the Northern Ireland Commissioner for Children and Young People on the basis that children and young people, those most likely to be affected by the Order, had not been adequately consulted under s 75 Northern Ireland Act, 1998. Re Application of the *Northern Ireland Commissioner for Children and Young People* [2004] NIQB 40. They were also judicially reviewed unsuccessfully in *In the Matter of an application by Peter Neill for Judicial Review,* unreported Queen's Bench Division (Girvan J) , 7 October 2005.

57 See further Ramsay, P., 'What is Anti-social Behaviour? *Criminal Law Review* (2004) 908–25.

58 Burney, E., 'Still the wrong approach', 23(1) *Howard League Magazine* (February 2005) p. 5.

59 ASBO Concern is the umbrella group for those opposed to ASBOs in the UK. See www.asboconcern.org.uk (accessed 11 January 2006).

60 Report of the Commissioner for Human Rights on his visit to the United Kingdom, 11-14 November 2004, (Strasbourg: Council of Europe, 2005) pp. 36-40 available at www.echr.coe (accessed 18 January 2006).

61 See Fletcher, H., 'An analysis of the first six years of the use of ASBOs' (April 2005) at www.napo.org (11 January 2006). See further research discussed below.

62 The figures are available on www.youth-justice-board.co.uk (11 January 2006). For an explanation see Morgan, R., 'Anti-social behaviour: getting to the root of the problem' 23(1) *Howard League Magazine* (February 2005) pp. 13–14.

63 Guinchard, A., 'Fixing the Boundaries of the Concept of Crime: A Challenge for Human Rights' 54(3) *International and Comparative Law Quarterly* (2005), pp. 719–34.

64 See also Hamilton, C., 'Anti-Social Behaviour Orders and the Presumption of Innocence', 23 *Irish Law Times* (2005), pp. 215–21.

65 One study quotes 98.3 per cent. See Rowlands, M., 'The state of ASBO Britain – the rise of intolerance' ECLN Essays no 9 available at www.ecln.org (accessed 11 January 2006). ASBO concern reports that only 62 applications have been rejected (www.asboconcern.org.uk) accessed 19 April 2006.

66 The research also noted the more 'ridiculous' conditions such as being prohibited from wearing gloves or from leaving home without socks on. Brogan, D., *Anti-Social Behaviour Orders An assessment of current management information systems and the scale of Anti-Social Behaviour Order breaches resulting in custody* (London: Youth Justice Board, 2005), available at www.youth-justice-board.co.uk (accessed 18 January 2006), p. 26.

67 See Scraton, P., 'Disrespecting Children's Rights', 23 *Safer Society,* forthcoming Winter 2005/06.

68 See Kilkelly, U., 'ASBOs: A Human Rights Challenge' paper delivered at a seminar *ASBOs: Social Policy and Human Rights* in Trinity College Dublin, 22 June 2005. See also Human Rights Commission Observations

on Proposals for Amendments to the Criminal Justice Bill 2004 (Youth Justice) 30 March 2006 available at www.ihrc.ie (accessed 19 April 2006), p. 23.

69 Brogan, D., *Anti-social Behaviour Orders*, p. 24.

70 *Ibid.*, p. 26.

71 *Ibid.*, p. 33.

72 *Ibid.*, p. 20

73 Ashworth, A., 23(1), *Howard League Magazine* (February 2005), p. 6.

74 Rowlands, M., 'The state of ASBO Britain – the rise of intolerance'.

75 See Hopkins Burke, R., and Morrill, R., 'Anti-Social Behaviour Orders: An infringement of the Human Rights Act 1998?' 11(2) *Nottingham Law Journal* (2002), 1–16, p. 13–14.

76 According to Rod Morgan, Chair of the Youth Justice Board of England and Wales, the Board is 'concerned that the number of children being received in custody for breach of an ASBO is rising. In early 2004, it was approx 25 per month; it is now (in Feb. 2005) double that rate'. Morgan, R., 'Anti-social behaviour: getting to the root of the problem'.

77 Scraton, P., 'The denial of the liberties and rights of children in the UK and the North of Ireland' *ECLN*, no. 14 (2005), p. 5 available at www.ecln.org (accessed 11 January 2006).

78 Report of the Commissioner for Human Rights, p. 39.

79 UN Guidelines for the Prevention of Juvenile Delinquency, 1990 (the Riyadh Guidelines) para. 5, adopted by General Assembly resolution 45/112 of 14 December 1990, available at www.ohrhc.org (accessed 18 January 2006).

80 Millie, A. et al., *Anti-social Behaviour Strategies: Finding a Balance* (London: Policy Press, 2005) p. 13.

81 *Ibid.*, p. 13.

82 *Ibid.*, p. 2.

83 *Ibid.*, pp. 36–7.

84 *Ibid.*, pp. 37–8. The Government's appeal to the narrative of declining standards, and in particular how it was marketed, was the subject of strong criticism amid the conclusion that the political and media debate about anti-social behaviour has been oversimplified. In the Irish context see Woulfe, J., 'Crime fears: anti-social behaviour tops list' *Irish Examiner*, 22 March 2005.

85 The press release launching the Coalition expressed its aims to publicly highlight the potential problems if ASBOs are introduced in Ireland and the need for alternative ways of tackling anti-social behaviour which do not criminalise people for behaviour that is not in itself criminal; to bring together those concerned about the way ASBOs might be used in a joint campaign; to advocate for the full and immediate implementation and adequate resourcing of the Children Act 2001 and to publicly highlight the existence of options other than ASBOs in alleviating the difficulties caused by anti-social behaviour. 4 May 2005, available at www.youth.ie (accessed 11 January 2006).

86 Address by Michael McDowell TD, Minister for Justice, Equality and Law

Reform to a Forum on ASBOs, 6 July 2005.

87 See further Chapters Two and Three above.

88 The Human Rights Commission noted that many of the problematic aspects of the UK system have not been replicated here. The Human Rights Commission, Observations on Proposals for Amendments to the Criminal Justice Bill 2004 (Youth Justice).

89 Binchy, W., 'Anti-Social Behaviour Orders and the Constitution' paper delivered at a seminar *ASBOs: Social Policy and Human Rights* in Trinity College Dublin, 22nd June 2005.

90 See the Irish Youth Justice Alliance, 'Recommendations on the Proposed Amendments to the Children Act 2001', 25 May 2006, available at www.iprt.ie (accessed 25 May 2006). See also the Criminal Justice Act 2006.

Chapter Seven

Young People in Detention

INTRODUCTION

International law is clear that the detention of children must be a measure of last resort. The Children Act 2001 makes it clear that this principle applies here too although translating it into practice is a challenge that has not yet been fully met. While the use of detention was discussed in Chapter Six, this chapter is concerned with what happens to those who are sent to detention in Ireland.

Detention is known to be harmful to children and to encourage rather than address offending behaviour; indeed, some have made a convincing case for it to be abolished altogether.[1] International standards provide that where it is required, detention should be used to maximum advantage to address the child's educational, health and behaviour problems and prepare him/her to participate in society in a constructive manner on release. In Ireland, while those under 16 years are detained in the educational and care environment of Children Detention Schools (CDS), those over sixteen are held in the penal environment of St. Patrick's Institution, where children mix with adults in circumstances which address neither their offending behaviour nor their educational disadvantage. In reality, little is known about either regime, or the extent to which it operates in line with international requirements. This Chapter aims to fill this gap. It describes the places of detention for children in Ireland – first for those under 16 years and then for those over that age – and considers whether the treatment of children there meets international standards and indeed the domestic regulations that mirror them.

INTERNATIONAL STANDARDS

International consensus was reached on the detention of children in conflict with the law far earlier than on any other principle of youth justice. Both Article 10 of the International Covenant on Civil and Political Rights 1966 (ICCPR) and Article 37 of the Convention on the Rights of the Child 1989 (CRC) recognise the right of the child to be detained separately from adults.[2] The CRC goes further by establishing the principle of detention as a last resort and for the shortest appropriate period of time,[3] while also providing that in detention children must be treated with humanity and respect, in a manner which takes into account the needs of persons of his/her age and with a right to maintain contact with his/her family through correspondence and visits. In 1998, the Committee on the Rights of the Child reviewed Ireland's compliance with the CRC and noted with concern 'the treatment of children deprived of their liberty, particularly in light of the principles and provisions of the Convention and other relevant international standards'.[4]

In recognition of the danger of 'criminal contamination', Rule 13 of the Beijing Rules recommends that whenever possible, detention pending trial shall be replaced by 'alternative measures, such as close supervision, intensive care or placement with a family or in an educational setting or home'.[5] If a young person must be placed in detention, loss of liberty should be restricted to the least possible degree, priority should be given to 'open' over 'closed' institutions and any facility should be educational rather than penal in type.[6] While in detention, children must receive care, protection and all necessary individual assistance in view of their age, gender and personality.[7]

The most coherent and detailed body of rules on the detention of children are the UN Rules for the Protection of Juveniles Deprived of their Liberty.[8] In addition to setting out fundamental principles – detention must be used as a measure of last resort, the juvenile justice system must uphold the rights and safety of juveniles and promote their physical and mental well-being – the Rules also provide detailed guidance on the management of detention facilities and the rights of children detained there. They are usefully divided into sections concerning record-keeping, admission and transfer procedures, conditions of detention, physical environment and accommodation, education and work, recreation, health and medical care, contacts with the wider community, disciplinary and restraint procedures, inspection and complaints, qualifications of personnel and return to the community. While non-binding in nature, the effectiveness of the Rules demands that they are circulated among all personnel working in the system and incorporated into legislation.[9] Altogether, they provide a practical set of guidelines for the management of detention facilities, recognise the rights of children in detention, and explain the means by which to implement those rights effectively in order to maximise the potential of detention to address offending behaviour and its underlying causes. The Rules provide an important benchmark against which the treatment of children in detention can be measured.[10]

THE CHILDREN ACT 2001 AND REFORM

Part 10 of the Children Act 2001 provides for places of detention for children and young people under 18 years. The Act provides for those under 16 years to be detained in Children Detention Schools – formerly industrial and reformatory schools – under the remit of the Minister for Education and Science, while those over 16 years are to be detained in Children Detention Centres, of which St. Patrick's Institution is the only one, under the remit of the Minister for Justice, Equality and Law Reform. While Part 10 of the Act was never commenced, it has begun to be implemented in practice.

However, the current arrangement will change substantially under the Criminal Justice Act 2006, which moves all young people under 18 years to Children Detention Schools and transfers responsibility for the Children Detention Schools to the Department of Justice, Equality and Law Reform as recommended by the Youth Justice Review in 2005.[11] While it is logical that responsibility for the detention of all children should rest with one authority, there are genuine fears that moving responsibility for all Detention Schools to the Department of Justice will result in their current educational focus being replaced with a more punitive ethos.[12] In this regard, it is important that the Review specifically envisages that the opposite effect will be achieved namely that 'The outcome of bringing sixteen and seventeen year old offenders into this new framework should be to allow the education-focused model of the detention school to become the objective for all children under eighteen years in detention'.[13] Compliance with international standards demands that this be the case.

While these proposals make provision for the eventual transfer of St. Patrick's population to Children Detention Schools, it is clear that this is a long-term objective. Although it may not be possible to move young people from St. Patrick's immediately, the continuing use of a prison environment to detain children is wholly out of line with international standards, as is explained further below. The failure to address this issue in definitive terms and within a finite time schedule is particularly problematic.

The changes proposed also require reform of other provisions of the Children Act. In particular, while the provisions dealing with the management and operation of Children Detention Schools remain relatively unchanged, it is significant that responsibility for education in the Schools will be given to the local Vocational Educational Committees. While this is positive as it should ensure the integration of educational services in the schools with those in the community, the expertise currently in the schools regarding the educational needs of children in detention must not be lost. The drafting of the new educational policy by the Youth Justice Service must work to this end.

A further proposed amendment to the Act relates to its provision for an Inspector and a Visiting Panel for the CDS. These provisions had not been commenced and it is now proposed to repeal them and replace them with an 'authorised person', to be appointed by the Minister for Justice, Equality and Law Reform, with limited powers of investigation and inspection. In particular, while the Inspector was required to inspect the schools every six months, the authorised person must only do so annually. On a positive note, however, the 'authorised person' appears to have a more specific function to hear complaints by children and to have access to school records in order to investigate these complaints.[14] While the issues of inspections and complaints are dealt with below it is important to highlight here that international standards require the establishment of an independent office to receive and investigate complaints made by children in detention. These proposals should thus be amended as a matter of priority.

Change is also proposed with regard to the role of the Special Residential Services Board. This is discussed below.

DETENTION OF CHILDREN UNDER SIXTEEN YEARS

An Overview of the Children Detention Schools

The detention of children in Ireland has a complicated and dark past being intertwined with the industrial and reformatory schools which were set up in the mid-nineteenth century to cater for neglected children and offenders respectively.[15] These remain in existence today: the two main industrial schools are St. Joseph's in Clonmel and Finglas Child and Adolescent Centre in Dublin, while the reformatory schools are Oberstown Boys School, Oberstown Girls School and Trinity House School all based at Lusk, Co. Dublin. All schools currently fall under the remit of the Department of Education and Science[16] and between them they offer detention, remand and assessment for children under 16 years. They are managed by administrative Boards of Management pending the appointment of newly composed Boards under the Children Act 2001. One board is responsible for the three schools on the Lusk campus, while individual boards of management are in place for the Finglas and St. Joseph's Schools.

Referrals to Trinity House School and Oberstown Boys School are made only from the courts. The other three units also take referrals from the Health Service Executive for assessment and, in the case of St. Joseph's, residential care. St. Joseph's is an open unit and Trinity House is classified as a secure unit. The other three units have the capacity to restrict the movement of young people within the buildings but the units and the campuses are not totally secure.[17]

The capacity of the schools has decreased in decent years in line with the decreasing demand for places. Oberstown Boys School has a capacity of twenty beds, of which eight are remand; Trinity House School has a capacity of twenty-seven beds (nineteen committal, five remand and three step-down) and Oberstown Girls School has a capacity of fifteen beds, seven of which are for remand and assessment purposes.[18] All units cater for children between 12 and 16 years, although Oberstown Girls School has the capacity to take girls aged 17 years. Finglas Child and Adolescent Centre has a capacity of twenty-six beds, but it currently caters for approximately twelve young people referred mostly from the Children Court, with six beds dedicated to assessment purposes. St. Joseph's School in Clonmel has a capacity of forty beds for both offending and non-offending children, although the majority falls into the latter category.[19]

In 2004, the total spend of the Department of Education and Science on the operation of the five Children Detention Schools was €33.4 million and the average annual cost of maintaining a detention place for a young person (based on average occupancy) was as follows:

> Finglas Child and Adolescent Centre €507,407
> Oberstown Boys School €282,505
> Oberstown Girls School €454,320
> St. Joseph's Clonmel €233,378[20]
> Trinity House €362,206.[21]

Many of the schools are based in old buildings whose state of repair and unsuitability for their purpose has been the subject of comment.[22] In 2000, the then Minister for Education and Science, Dr Michael Woods, TD, announced a £21 million (€26.6 million) development plan for the Schools to include a major refurbishment and updating of facilities at Trinity House, the replacement of facilities at Oberstown Boys and Girls Schools and the development of a new highly specialised unit at the Lusk campus.[23] According to Minister Woods, 'it is important that these facilities cater for the special needs of the young people referred to them by the courts and are of the highest quality to facilitate the excellent work which the staff in these centres are engaged in'. This work is still on-going and, so far, has included the purchase of St. Joseph's by the Department, the provision of a specialised unit at Trinity House catering for six boys with challenging behaviour, the provision of step-down facilities at Trinity House and Oberstown Girls School, the provision of a security fence at the Lusk Campus and the refurbishment of the Care and Education Unit at Finglas.[24]

The Children Act 2001: Aims and Objectives of the Schools

As explained above, Part 10 of the Children Act makes provision for the running of the schools including their day-to-day operation. The pivotal section of the Act in this area is section 158, which sets out the aims and objectives of the schools: to provide appropriate educational and training programmes[25] for children referred to them by a court having been convicted of an offence. In particular, the CDS must aim to promote the reintegration of children into society by having regard to their health, welfare and interests; providing proper care, guidance and supervision for them; preserving and developing relations between them and their families; exercising proper moral and disciplinary influences on them and recognising their personal, cultural and linguistic identity. From a practitioner's perspective, these positive non-punitive principles are 'clear and understandable' and 'helpful guiding principles which will permeate the ebb and flow of day to day life in the schools'.[26]

When looked at closely, section 158 offers a 'singular, attainable blueprint on which management and staff of the schools can build policies, procedures and programmes to benefit those children who, for one reason or another, find their way through the various diversionary nets into the detention schools'.[27] For some, it presents a stark contrast between the industrial and reformatory schools of the past whose aim was to accommodate, feed, clothe and educate children to the modern Children Detention School, whose functions are more holistic. Accordingly, it has been noted that 'the aspiration in 158 is that the children who find themselves committed to a CDS will, as a result of having experienced 'appropriate educational and training programmes ... take their place in the community as persons who observe the law and are capable of making a positive and productive contribution to society'.[28]

Further provisions of the Act set out the rights of young people in the CDS. Section 213, for example, recognises the right of the child to receive religious assistance and instruction and to have the opportunity to practise his/her religion while section 200 provides for the right to receive adequate medical attention.

Section 204 of the Act recognises the importance of mobility trips to the child's reintegration into society by making provision for authorised absences from the school for education, recreation, therapeutic and developmental purposes.[29] For the same reason, the Act makes provision for temporary leave and supervision by a Probation and Welfare Officer in the community (effectively allowing the Director to authorise the child's release); importantly, the Director of each school must formulate a temporary leave programme for every child in the school for whom this is appropriate (s. 205). The Act also makes provision for aftercare, where the child is supervised by a Probation and Welfare Officer on release from the school. Unfortunately, the Act does not make this a compulsory part of every sentence (unless the Children Court makes a Detention and Supervision Order under section 151) and it can only be undertaken with the child's consent and where the Director considers that this would further assist the child's reintegration into society. Given the likelihood that every child needs this basic level of assistance both to reintegrate and to prevent further offending, it is regrettable that the Act fails to make aftercare a right of every child. In practice, the provision of step-down facilities is very much a priority for the CDS.[30] Both Oberstown Girls School and Trinity House School have step-down units and aftercare programmes designed to facilitate young people's successful return to society from detention.

The treatment by the Children Act of the important practical issues of permitted absences, temporary leave, mobility and unconditional release has been welcomed and the relationship of these provisions to the aims and objectives of the CDS in section 158 is clear.[31] As Howard notes: 'reflected throughout these often contentious, demanding and delicate areas' of decision-making is the children's 'safety, welfare and interests including their physical, psychological and emotional wellbeing'.[32] The best interests principle is implicit, if not explicit here.

Operation of the Children Detention Schools

All five Children Detention Schools have varying functions, accommodate children with different needs, and provide care at different points along a continuum of open to secure. While this diversity is a positive feature, the fact that they operate as 'separate organisational units' without an 'overarching strategic plan' or, common formal policies and procedures' has been the subject of concern.[33] A review of the existing residential provision, including the schools, commissioned in 2001, recommended that the lack of coherence between the schools be urgently addressed *inter alia* by the appointment of a single management structure. While this recommendation was never implemented, the adoption of *Standards and Criteria for the Children Detention Schools* to guide a common inspection process of all schools, was a step in the right direction in this regard.[34] Although the management of the sector was 'kept under review'[35] this recommendation is now likely to be overtaken by bringing the schools under the umbrella of the newly created Youth Justice Service in the Department of Justice, Equality and Law Reform.[36]

Little is published or widely available about the schools, their policies and procedures and how they treat young people. Until recently, in fact, there was no 'detailed baseline information about the quality of care and education currently provided and the policies and procedures underpinning them'.[37] However, Care Inspections have recently been carried out on all five schools and these and other sources are used in the analysis which follows to evaluate the extent to which the schools operate in line with international standards.[38]

St. Joseph's School, Clonmel

Originally in the care of the Rosminian Order, this School was taken over by the Department of Education and Science in June 2002. It is an open residential care centre catering for boys from both an offending and a non-offending background who are detained together. Although its operational capacity is forty, average occupancy is thirty-two. At the time of the Care Inspection in December 2003, there were twenty-six boys residing there: eighteen young people from nine different Area Health Boards, seven on foot of Court Orders while one boy was the subject of a High Court Order.[39] This shows the complexity of need for which schools like St. Joseph's are expected to cater. It also highlights that offending and non-offending children are detained together in the Irish system. This practice is not consistent with international standards for a variety of reasons and should be discontinued.

Apart from these diverse backgrounds and needs, the team which inspected St. Joseph's in December 2003 noted that the length of stay of young people during the time of the inspection ranged from one day to twenty-seven months. The average stay for each boy over the previous three years (2001–03) was 2.2 years.[40]

St. Joseph's does not have traditional institutional characteristics: the building complex is comprised of six residential units, four of which are used as residential quarters, while one is a close supervision unit for boys requiring 'extra specialised supervision' away from their peers (presumably meaning isolation).[41] There is also a very sophisticated gym, which is part of a leisure centre, a purpose-built school, a dining block and a chapel on campus. A purpose-built residential facility at a seaside resort near Waterford City is used as a summer camp. The boys purchase their own clothing and footwear under supervision in local shops from a fixed budget. The normalising effect of this practice is difficult to underestimate when compared to boys in St. Patrick's Institution, who cannot wear, let alone buy, their own clothes.[42]

Despite the mutual respect witnessed between staff and boys, and the positive atmosphere in the School, the Inspection Team expressed a number of concerns regarding issues of 'care and control'.[43] In particular, concern was expressed regarding the protracted period of time over which several physical restraints had lasted (one lasted between 91 and 100 minutes). The school was also urged to reconsider use of the boys' bedrooms for time-out purposes, given that this is his only personal and private space. The Inspection Team was also concerned at the use of

Therapeutic Crisis Intervention (TCI) to make a young person comply with a directive; they considered this a wholly inappropriate use of the restraint technique because it teaches the boys that 'it is ok to have your way by using physical force'.[44]

With regard to the rate of absconding, the Inspection Team noted that there had been several abscondings in the previous years: eighty-two in 2001, sixty-eight in 2002 and sixty-eight in 2003. While it was clear that staff knew the procedures to be followed in this event, it criticised the lack of written procedures, which are vital to maintain a consistent approach to reporting and responding to such events.[45]

Regarding the young person's access to information, the Inspection Team found that while the *Booklet for Young People* received by young people on admission was comprehensive, consideration should be given to simplifying the language in the section on 'rights and responsibilities' in order to ensure that this is fully understood.[46] Moreover, although the young person's right to privacy was mentioned here, it was absent from the main *Policies and Procedures* document. The young person's right to access personal information held by the School is also absent from this document, which should outline what information the young person is entitled to view, e.g. entries in personal diaries, log books, etc. These procedures for gaining access to information should also be incorporated in the *Booklet for Young People*[47] in order to comply with international standards.[48]

Regarding the complaints procedures, both staff and young people appeared to be familiar with the procedures and expressed confidence in them. However, it was noted that the School did not have any system in place to facilitate a young person wishing to invoke the help of an independent person should he feel unable to speak to a member of staff regarding a complaint or child protection issue. This was found to be inconsistent with the *Standards and Criteria for Detention Schools* and although it was being examined, the importance of ensuring every young person has 'access to an independent channel of advocacy' was stressed.[49] The Inspection Team similarly found that there was no adequate formal arrangement in place in the School to ensure that young people were involved in preparing for meetings and reviews that concern their own welfare.[50] Although comprehensive care plans were available on each young person, it was not always clear from the records if the objectives had been reached and it was also recommended that 'the young people should be involved on a more formal basis in case conferences and reviews in line with current approaches in best practice in care'.[51] Participation in discharge plans was not a problem, however as both the Keyworker and the After Care Officer were noted, to help the young person through this process before, during and after discharge, for as long as is necessary.[52]

The Inspection Team acknowledged the importance of education to the young people at the School. However, it found that efforts to create educational profiles on each student are often hampered by a lack of information from previous schools.[53] International standards provide for the right of children in custody to have education suited to their needs and abilities and designed to prepare them for return to society. To this end, they emphasise the need to provide education through programmes integrated with the education system.[54] It is vital therefore that a mechanism be developed to improve co-ordination in this area and in particular, that nothing should frustrate the development and implementation of individual educational programmes.[55]

Regarding curriculum, the Inspection Team noted that there was considerable emphasis on practical and vocational subjects while a work experience programme also operated with local work centres. Overall, staff were commended for the high levels of dedication and commitment to the welfare of the boys in this area.[56]

More generally, the staff in St. Joseph's School were noted to be highly qualified – a high percentage hold a third-level qualification and the average length of service – 10.5 years – lends stability to staffing arrangements at the School.[57] Not surprisingly, the Inspection Team noted the high morale among staff and commented that they are now 'more confident and self-assured in dealing with emerging problems among the boys' than at the time of the last inspection in 2000.[58] Records and files were also found to be maintained in excellent condition and the Inspection Team concluded that the management and staff were making the best possible use of the wide array of resources at their disposal.

In addition to good record keeping, the Inspection Team noted that health needs – dental and optical care for example – were regularly identified on admission and addressed while the young person was at the School in line with international standards. This is very important given that many children arrive into detention with poor health and related problems and that detention often presents the first and only opportunity to have these needs identified and addressed. Moreover, the fact that these problems may be due to children's offending behaviour makes resolution of them essential to their successful reintegration into society upon release.[59] International standards also recommend that children in detention access the medical services in the community.[60] This is precisely what happens in St. Joseph's where specialist services – including psychiatric support, speech therapy and drug/alcohol counselling – are all accessible in the Clonmel area, where local services respond quickly to requests from the school. In this regard, the long history of the School as part of the wider local community helps greatly in helping to uphold the rights of children to health care in line with international rules.[61]

According to international standards, every effort should be made to encourage young people to individualise their own private space.[62] A further positive feature of the School is the extent to which young people are permitted to decorate their rooms. Within reasonable limits, they can personalise their rooms through the use of posters, musical instruments, radios and notice boards and each of the residential units is decorated and maintained to a very high standard and in a way that gives the boys an experience of 'good quality home-type comforts'.[63]

However, while the boys are aware that authorised searches take place as part of routine security, the Inspection Team criticised a lack of 'detailed policies, procedures and guidance that include keeping appropriate records on room and clothing searches'. It also noted 'the lack of written information available showing the means by which searches will be carried out and in what circumstances'. Apart from being inconsistent with the *Standards and Criteria for Children Detention Schools*, this is also inconsistent with international standards and rules. In particular, it is likely to be in breach of Article 8 of the European Convention on Human Rights (ECHR), which requires that such interferences with a person's private life be in accordance with law.[64] The inspection report recommended that the single reference to searches in the *Booklet for Young People* be clarified and expanded.[65] It is also recommended that consideration be given to putting such searches on a statutory basis.

Regarding individual work on offending behaviour, it was noted that the residential psychologist sees every young person regularly but on the basis of self-referral only. The main programme undertaken by young people to deal with offending behaviour is the Copping On programme, which is delivered by a multi-disciplinary team. While conversations with young people highlighted that the knowledge and understanding they had gained was of great importance,[66] the lack of published data on whether such young people stay out of trouble on release makes it difficult to confirm the programme's success. The Inspection Team recommended that an evaluation take place to ensure that the content of the programme is relevant to the changing population of young people resident at any given time.[67]

Oberstown Girls School

Oberstown Girls School accommodates girls aged between 12 and 17 years for remand and/or remand and assessment, and detention purposes. With a capacity of 15 beds, it was occupied at almost 50 per cent of its capacity in 2004 when altogether 28 young people were detained there.[68] The objectives of the school are to protect the community from crimes that might be committed by the girls if they were not detained; to promote the safety, well-being and purposeful development of those detained; to reduce the likelihood of the young girls re-offending following their release and to equip them with appropriate skills for living in the community under supervision.[69]

A Care Inspection carried out in late 2004 was largely positive in its conclusions and observations about the operation of the School. Good relations based on mutual respect were observed between staff and young people, and young people were noted to be 'very much involved in all decisions relating to both their current and future care'. They did not appear to have been involved in the development of the School's *Policies and Procedures* however.[70]

According to the Inspection Team, young people were clearly

aware of their rights but they were equally cognisant of the responsibilities that attached to such rights.[71] Staff, too, were found to be fully aware of 'the rights of the young people resident at the school' and according to the Inspection Team, 'it was evident, both in the day-to-day interactions with the girls and at the formal reviews, that the rights of the young people are of paramount importance in all considerations.'[72] As the international standards make clear, qualified professional staff are key to promoting and protecting the rights of children in detention,[73] and in Oberstown Girls School, 93 per cent of the permanent staff had or were pursuing a third level qualification in 2004, while all temporary and relief staff were already qualified to this level.[74] The average length of service among care staff was over six years, which lends stability to the staff body within the school.[75]

At the time of the inspection the School had ten full-time staff and a part-time teacher for three days per week (for twenty boys and six girls). With reference to the international standard that a child in detention has the right to have education suited to their needs and abilities,[76] the School was found to offer a broad and balanced curriculum for those of primary school age, while those of post primary age were noted to attend classes in a wide range of subjects and sit for the certification examinations. The introduction of FETAC (Further Education and Training Awards Certificate) programmes was a welcome development at the School given that continuous assessment allows the young people to gain credits over cumulative short periods of time. A range of Life Skills programmes integrated into individual care plans[77] is also provided on a co-operative basis by school and care staff, augmented by outside experts.[78] There is adequate opportunity for leisure activities.

Significantly, each student was found to have an individual education plan and it was noted that a very satisfactory level of co-operation existed between care staff and teachers.[79] However, while all students are assessed psychologically on entry to the school and ongoing assessment is undertaken as required, the Inspection Team noted the difficulty accessing reports from previous schools attended by the young people. This appears to be a common problem which needs to be addressed by all CDS on a collective basis.

Regarding health care, the Inspection Team noted that the medical staff always meet the young person on admission taking a full history and recording any medical condition needing treatment. A medical report is then compiled by the medical officer and submitted as part of the documentation for the meetings. While medical records held in the School are sufficient, concern was expressed about 'the lack of medical history which accompanies a young person when she is sent to the School, especially if she is on a prescription at that time'. Overall, staff felt that 'the flow of information on health and medical data that comes to the School after a young person is admitted is often very slow'.[80] This is clearly out of line with international standards which reflect the importance of providing integrated health care to those in detention and efforts should be made to resolve this difficulty at a management level.[81] Moreover, while specialist support in the form of psychiatric and psychological services is available to the School on a sessional basis through the Mater Child Guidance Clinic, 'a serious flaw in psychiatric services for girls of sixteen years of age and under', 'deplored' by the Director, has resulted in the need to buy in psychiatric nursing support for some young people. Providing these services at the School on a sessional basis is clearly inadequate to meet continuing needs and falls far short of international standards which require the health care provided to children in detention to be adequate to meet their needs.[82]

In relation to work on offending behaviour, the Inspection Team noted that while a range of programmes were offered to young people, no reviews had taken place with regard to their effectiveness. Similar to St. Joseph's, it was recommended that an in-depth evaluation be carried out to ensure that the programmes are effective for the present population.[83]

Regarding the use of force, the number of such incidents has steadily declined along with the number of girls detained at Oberstown; in 2004, only ten incidents involving six girls were recorded.[84]

The Inspection Team noted that the complaints procedure is contained in the *Young Person's Information Booklet* issued to them on admission. Moreover, it was observed from a review of past complaints that 'the procedures are well known both to the young people and the staff; young people were found to be both 'aware of the procedures' and 'had full confidence that staff adhere to them at all times'.[85] Overall, the booklet was praised for being 'very well laid out' and 'easy to follow' and containing 'all of the main areas relating to advice and procedures'. The young person's right to access information in their files was also found to be observed in practice[86] and the care plans of the young people are reviewed at least weekly with the keyworker taking responsibility for ensuring that deadlines set are adhered to and that the young person is fully involved in the review process.[87] The inspection report welcomed the fact that while the new *Policies and Procedures* document made a commitment to providing each young person with a child-friendly version of both their care plan and education plan, this had not been implemented.[88]

Regarding matters of child protection, the School was found to follow the written procedures for appointing a Designated Child Protection Officer, reporting concerns, processing allegations or suspicions of abuse and carrying out staff training.[89] However, the Inspection Team expressed some concern that some dates were missing in a small number of files. This was recommended to be addressed 'as a matter of urgency' given that without a date, 'the submitted report cannot be contextualised time-wise'.[90] Otherwise, the Inspection Team reported file-keeping to an excellent standard, although it recommended that serious consideration be given to electronic storage of files.[91]

Regarding the physical environment, the Inspection Team found that, in general, the units were 'unsuited to modern demands and to current health and safety requirements'.[92] The poor ventilation in the rooms was criticised as was their lack of 'personality', particularly in the Remand unit where young people tend to stay for short periods. It recommended that future building take into account the need to facilitate the individualising of rooms.[93]

Finglas Child and Adolescent Centre

Finglas Child and Adolescent Centre (CAC) comprises a Care and Education Unit and an Assessment and Remand Unit both of which were established in the early 1970s. The campus is open with one secure wing. Seventy five per cent of its twelve available beds were occupied in 2004, when sixty-eight young people were detained there.[94] The CAC was the first residential school to be inspected in 2002 under the then draft *Standards and Criteria for CDS*.[95]

A number of important issues arose during the inspection process many of which could be traced to the Centre's Statement of Purpose. In particular, it was found to define neither the target group served by the Centre nor its relationship to the courts, the other schools and the Health Boards.[96] Ownership by the staff of the Statement was weak because it had been drafted by senior management.[97] At the heart of the problems faced by the Centre was, according to the inspection report, the fact that the demands presented by a number of young people admitted to the Centre were 'very severe', while those whose level of stated problematic behaviour would seem not to warrant a residential placement were also accommodated there. The fact that the Centre experienced such a wide range of referrals 'reflects the national paucity of viable alternative provision and serves to underline the importance of the Centre being clear about its role'.[98]

The inspection of the CAC found that how staff related to the young people in their care varied, principally because there was no understood and commonly agreed approach to working with young people. The lack of a commonly agreed approach to care and control was identified as going to the root of the problems facing staff and young people in the Centre. As the Inspection Team noted, 'the lack of consensus and clarity about, for example the setting of limits, what constitutes unacceptable behaviour and what sanctions should be applied and in what circumstances, leads to inconsistencies in practice from one care team shift to another and within teams'.[99] The high number of inexperienced staff, the lack of appropriately qualified staff and the high turnover of staff within the Centre all contributed to these problems.[100] Other issues of serious concern which emerged during the inspection were: the lack of a comprehensive care plan for every young person subject to a systematic and regular review;[101] inconsistent quality of record-keeping and inadequate access by young people to their file;[102] a lack of consensus among and leadership from management regarding key aspects of care including use of the safety room; sanctions and the lack of a care and children's rights culture;[103] the lack of a separate complaints procedure for recording and processing the complaints made by young people;[104] the failure to integrate education and care plans;[105] inadequate and unsafe arrangements for the storing of medicines;[106] the poor standards of personal living accommodation in the Assessment Unit (including no natural light) and overall a building inadequate for its purpose; the failure to address young people's offending behaviour.[107] The report's concluding observation was that the organisation was in 'acute crisis' lacking 'direction', 'not meeting a number of basic requirements', resulting in a situation where young people were 'not receiving the level of care, control and education they require' and on occasions, being 'unsafe for young people and staff'.[108] Responsibility for this situation was not placed on the Centre alone, rather the report identified that the 'professional isolation of the Centre and the other residential schools has left them all in a policy and practice vacuum'.[109] Thus, while the CAC was found to be 'crisis driven' and lacked a coherent plan, it was also clear, according to the report, that 'a national strategic plan' was required.[110]

The inspection report set out a number of strict conditions that would have to be met if the Centre was to recover its capacity to function effectively. However, over eighteen months later, in February 2004, the Department of Education and Science considered it necessary to commission a further review of the Centre with the aim of identifying and making recommendations to address the continuing problems where feasible. The report, published in April 2004, was a brief document, which drew the ultimate conclusion that due to a variety of problems with the staffing/management relationship, a change in the population of the Centre and a number of other complex issues, the capacity of the staff in the day-to-day delivery of care to troubled young people had been lost and the Centre could not continue to operate in its current state.[111] Recommendations were divided into short-, medium- and long-term and included a complete restructuring of management, a re-establishment of protocols, procedures and professional care practices with essential training to underpin these developments and, in the long-term, to carry out inspection and monitoring of the Centre, reviewing and monitoring implementation of the recommendations with a view to developing a five-year strategic plan. To facilitate this rebuilding and restructuring process, the Minister of State with Special Responsibility for Children, Brian Lenihan, TD, agreed in May 2004 to a further reduction in the operational capacity of the Centre to twelve beds.[112]

In September 2004 a new Board of Management was appointed and a new Director was appointed in October 2004 with a clear mandate to restore trust, confidence and build an organisation for the future. The Centre was inspected by the Department of Education and Science Inspection Team in February 2006 who noted that 'provision for young people has been transformed in a remarkably short period of time'.[113] Improved staff relations and morale have led to dramatically lower absconding rates and fewer complaints by young people. Achievements are also noted in the areas of staff training and development, care plans and reviews including the involvement of young people and their parents, discharge and aftercare, education, including the work of the educational psychologist, and health care.

The Inspection Team was critical, however, of the failure to finalise the Centre's statement of purpose and all its policies and procedures although it was apparent that staff were aware of the content of these documents and related protocols.[114] The young people's information booklets were recommended to include sections on rights and responsibilities and further recommendations were made regarding the monitoring of the use of separation and complaints. Consideration was also recommended to be given to the establishment of a step down unit to prepare young people for return to the community.

Overall, the operation of the Centre has improved dramatically since 2004 when it faced closure. The Director is rightly singled out for praise in this respect. The high level of care provided to the admittedly small number of young people detained in Finglas is particularly noteworthy and the attention paid to the young people's right to privacy and private space appears worthy of replication by other schools. Overall, it is clear that a positive framework for the sustainable future of the Centre has been developed based on respect for the rights and needs of young people. This work is continuing.

Oberstown Boys School

Oberstown Boys School is an open Detention School for boys between 12 and 16 years sent there by the Children Court for remand or committal purposes. In 2004, its twenty beds were occupied at 96 per cent of its capacity and seventy boys were detained there throughout that year.[115]

According to its Statement of Purpose, the School provides 'care, education and re-integration in an open setting for challenging young people who commit criminal offences'.[116] The School is committed to individual programmes designed specifically for each young person admitted and actively promotes the ongoing development and education of its staff with a view to developing best practice care. The Remand Unit specialises in the care of boys under 16 years at the time of admission providing a short-term programme of care, education and reintegration for young people who are awaiting disposal of their case by the courts.

According to its Director, care programmes in Oberstown are designed to bring about a change in the lives of the young people accommodated there.[117] For this reason, whether or not the boys have been assessed before, a further in-house assessment lasting about eight weeks is undertaken on admission in order to identify the strengths and weaknesses in the boy's character and to provide a 'benchmark' from which to measure any future progress. While this assessment is in progress, the boy's Keyworker will make contact with his parents, to encourage them to visit the centre and become involved in his care programme. The Keyworker will also liaise with the Probation and Welfare Officer and the Social Worker allocated to the case and convene a case conference once the assessment is complete to draft the intervention plan for the young person. The main focus of the plan is usually the development of the young person's self-esteem through participation in a series of individually designed programmes and by encouraging positive relationships with the adults in their environment. Both group work and individual work are used in the Centre, and all the boys attend the Education Centre and develop work-place skills.[118]

According to the Team who inspected the School in October 2005, the reports detailing young people's care plans contain much useful information but do not make it clear what goals are being set for each young person. A specific section requiring the identification and recording of goals was recommended to be included.[119] The lack of success in addressing offending behaviour was also queried by the Inspection Team which noted that no evaluations of the offending behaviour programmes had been undertaken. To improve this situation, it recommended that management enter discussions with the Probation and Welfare Service about accessing programmes that can be used to address the offending behaviour of young people.[120]

The school has a *Young Person's Guide*, which every boy receives on admission. According to the *Guide*, the school operates a system of rewards for behaviour whereby each boy is given a mark by the staff in the unit and the teachers in the school. Boys' behaviour is marked in eight areas: Room; Hygiene and Appearance; Unit and School; Verbal behaviour; Physical Behaviour; Mobility; Problem Solving; Night/ Morning.[121] While much depends on how the system is operated and explained to young people, these categories appear at first glance to be inconsistent – for example they measure 'behaviour' as a category in itself while also measuring behaviour at different times (night/morning) and in different places (unit/school). It might, at least in theory, be possible that a young person who is verbally aggressive in the unit at night-time is marked down under three categories (unit and school; verbal behaviour and night/morning). As international standards require that no juvenile should be sanctioned more than once for the same disciplinary infraction,[122] it might be preferable to measure behaviour to categories that are transparent and less arbitrary such as behaviour, personal appearance and state of room. Moreover, it appears from the scale (from zero to five) that it is easier to fare badly than well. In particular, the fact that the scale includes three negative awards – not acceptable, poor and fair – but only two positive awards – good and excellent – does not give young people a fair chance. According to the *Guide*, 'if you earn a high level you get more pocket money and you may go on trips to the cinema, horse riding, adventure centres etc'. However, it is not clear what sanctions are imposed on those who do not perform well according to this system: are they simply denied these opportunities? If so, this would not appear to be compatible with international standards which recognise the importance of leisure and recreation for all young people as an important part of the process of reintegrating young people into society from detention. For this reason, international standards recommend providing full access to sport and recreation facilities as a matter of right not privilege earned through good behaviour.[123] This is also acknowledged in the Children Act, notably from the requirement that the Director develop a temporary release programme for every child in the school; the notion of permitting only those who behave to receive such benefits, while logical on its face, contradicts this.

In the main, the Inspection Team drew positive conclusions from its inspection of Oberstown Boys School in 2005. It was generally supportive of staff working in the School but recommended that members of the Board of Management undertake inspections of the School on a more regular and systematic basis. Although it praised the efforts of staff to plan the discharge of young people from the School, it recommended that consideration be given to developing a step-down unit there. It also noted that the Policies and Procedures document (with regard to bullying and absconding) and the Statement of Purpose and function (which should be child accessible) required revision.[124] However, its sharpest criticism was reserved for the state of repair of the buildings, which were found to be outdated and unsuitable for an institution that provides care for young people.[125] Pending replacement or refurbishment of the School it recommended that the maintenance of existing premises be improved.

Trinity House School

Trinity House School is the most secure unit for young offenders under the age of 16 years and as a result, it arguably receives the most persistent and serious offenders of that age group. This is represented in the fact that thirteen out of twenty-one young people discharged from the school in 2000 were in prison in 2002.[126] In 2004, Trinity House was occupied at 68 per cent of its capacity and fifty young people were detained there during the year.[127] Its capacity of twenty-four is divided into three living units of eight beds and an Education Unit. House one is the admission unit, in which young people spend the first part of their stay: they are also assessed there to form the basis of the placement plan. Houses two and three are where most young people spend the duration of their stay. Trinity House also has a step-down unit, with three places, which provides a six month programme of preparation for independence, including an outreach service, tracking system and a work placement programme for those leaving the school.[128]

A care inspection of Trinity House School was carried out in November 2005. This document together with the School's Annual Reports and Outcomes documents and the 2002 report of the Council of Europe Committee for the Prevention of Torture, Inhuman and Degrading Treatment or Punishment (CPT)[129] provide a clear view of life in the school.[130]

In their Reports the CPT and the Department of Education and Science welcomed the fact that the staff appeared to be motivated and well equipped to work with the young people and that they treated the children with respect and in a manner likely to enhance their individual self-control.[131] This is supported by the commitment of Trinity House School to ensure that all care staff have a minimum child care qualification (NVQ level 3).[132]

Regarding the material conditions, the CPT noted that young people were accommodated in 'good-sized, personalised single rooms grouped in units', that the rooms had good access to natural light and ventilation, and were adequately furnished. Each unit had a homely and comfortable television/sitting room, a dining room, a kitchen, a 'quiet room', sanitary facilities: they were clean and in a good state of repair.[133] Satisfaction with the physical environment in which they are detained has also been expressed by the young people themselves,[134] and this is clearly something which is advocated by international standards.

The step-down unit, opened in 2001, is a particularly important feature of Trinity House. Bearing in mind that those leaving the school are particularly vulnerable young people, the unit aims to provide a range of supports to them both before and after they return to the community. These include a work placement programme (currently with six employers), Safe Pass, (a programme focusing on safety in the construction industry), and help to set up a bank account. Several young people successfully completed these programmes in 2003 and 2004. The School also uses a tracking system, which helps staff to monitor young people through a series of meetings up to twelve months after they leave. This process not only supports young people on their return to the community, it also allows staff to get feedback on young people's experiences and to collect data on the long-term life chances of people detained there.[135] The outcomes recorded are not necessarily positive, although trends are difficult to draw. In 2004, seven of the sixteen boys who had left the school were in prison. In 2003, twenty-four of the fifty-seven young people who left were in prison, while twenty-five were living at home within six months of their release.[136] This was a slight improvement on 2002, however, where 50 per cent of the admittedly small number of young people released through the step-down programme were in prison. And this showed a further improvement on 2001, when the step-down facility opened, when six of the seven young people released ended up in prison.[137]

In 2004, only three young people of the sixteen released were reported as employed and one young person was in training. Practically all the young people reported having picked up charges since leaving the school.[138] This was an increase on the re-offending rate of 50 per cent recorded for 2003. In the 2003 *Outcomes Report*, it was noted that eight young people who picked up new charges since leaving the School would have gone to prison, but for the direct intervention of the step-down unit. While this is a significantly positive issue for these young people, it raises the question about the arbitrary way in which support is provided to young people before the Children Court. In particular, if support staff are not in a position to intervene and persuade the Court that prison is not appropriate, then the young person may serve a further sentence of detention. The availability of this support is also a factor which should be taken into account when considering the numbers of young people sent to detention following their release from Trinity House.

The re-offending of this group of young people following their time in detention thus remains very high despite the efforts of the step-down unit to prepare them for release. Although more extensive longitudinal research is required to confirm this trend and to cross reference it with a range of factors including the duration of the placement, how time is spent there and whether there are any comparative lessons to be learned from other Detention Schools, the data point to a clear pathway to prison.

While this is a complex issue, the question must nonetheless be raised about the purpose served by detaining this group of young people in the first place, if all detention does is contain them until they are released to return to their offending. As the *Outcomes Report* for 2003 notes, those who are sent to Trinity House have 'operated consistently, and some for a long time, outside the bounds of reasonably acceptable behaviour'.

> While a lot of work is done with the young people while in Trinity House School, it is accepted that it is easier to contain the young people's behaviour while they are living in the secure environment of Trinity House School. However, when they are released and make contact with outside agencies they find it very difficult to cope with the very rigid guidelines, such as with having to attend at specific times, and so on.[139]

The young people themselves have also expressed concern about leaving Trinity House and those interviewed following return to the community reported 'missing the structure and security which they felt when living there'. They also missed 'the activities and sports that were made available'. The most frequently cited difficulty for young people on leaving the School was to get back into a routine without ongoing support and encouragement, which they felt they had received from the staff there. The young people also referred to the difficulty of being able to hold down a job.[140] In response, the staff have recommended providing a drop-in centre for young people, developing activity-based programming in the community and providing a residential facility in the community.[141] While these are important and positive initiatives, it is questionable whether this is an area in which the staff of the Detention School should be involved, not least given that similar developments are all envisaged as part of the community sanctions under the Children Act 2001 and arguably fall within the remit of the Probation and Welfare Service.[142] Closer co-ordination with the Service should be developed in order to attempt to provide young people with seamless support on release from detention.[143] However, only the full implementation and resourcing of community sanctions under the aegis of the Service will ensure there exist meaningful alternatives to detention in the first place.[144] This may be facilitated by the move to the Department of Justice, Equality and Law Reform.

Regarding education in Trinity House, the CPT noted that the school offered individualised programmes of activities to children, with the objective of assisting them in catching up on any delay they may have experienced in their basic education in the community. The Annual Report for 2004 confirms that eleven boys, 65 per cent of those at the school in June, sat one or more subjects in the Junior Certificate.[145] The Inspection Team noted in 2005 that the curriculum includes a good range of academic and practical subjects, but highlighted the views of the Principal that greater attention be given to literacy and numeracy.[146] The boys are required to attend classes (which included literacy/numeracy, woodwork, metalwork, art, cookery, physical education, horticulture and computing) in small groups during normal school hours and found that sports and other facilities are of a high standard. Other activities, including drug awareness, offending behaviour programmes and sex education, are available.[147] According to the school, 'young people continue to be actively involved in their reviews/case conferences' which has 'been a major development and has seen a marked improvement in that many of our young people have gained the skills to make decisions about their futures.'[148]

On the matter of discipline, the CPT expressed concern in 2002 about the use of a padded room as a cooling off device and sought confirmation that, according to Trinity House policy, this had been phased out.[149] In 2005, the Department of Education and Science Inspection Team noted significant improvements in this area. In particular, the introduction of a 'chill-out' room, training on TCI and the monitoring of the use of physical restraint have all combined to reduce recourse to both 'physical restraint and use of time-out'. Separation is now only used where the behaviour poses a danger to the young people or others.[150]

The CPT was also concerned about the lack of an effective complaints mechanism for children in detention. According to the CPT, given that 'effective complaints procedures are basic safeguards against ill-treatment in institutions where children are deprived of their liberty, children in such institutions should have avenues of complaint open to them, both within the establishment's administrative system and to outside bodies, and be able to have confidential access to an appropriate authority'. In this regard, it noted that at Trinity House School, new arrivals are provided with a comprehensive guide setting out in detail the rules of the establishment and explaining the ways to lodge complaints, and there is a child protection scheme laying down the procedures for dealing with complaints.[151] However, the CPT expressed concern at the intention to exclude children in detention from the remit of the (then) proposed Ombudsman for Children.[152] This concern about the complaints procedures was also raised by young people themselves when interviewed on release in 2003. Contrary to the other elements of the survey (relations with staff, state of buildings, programmes offered, etc.) the vast majority of young people rated the complaints procedures 'really bad' (in 2003)[153] or 'okay' (in 2002).[154] In 2005, the Inspection Team also highlighted the need for independent intervention should a young person lack confidence in using the internal complaints mechanism[155] as this is clearly an issue demanding urgent attention (see below).

The CPT expressed satisfaction with the standard of medical care available at the school but was concerned that no psychologist was attached to the health care team given the prevalence of behavioural and/or emotional problems among detained children.[156] The Government responded by stating, simply, that 'the School engages psychological and counselling services on a consultative basis as required'.[157] Clearly this situation is not satisfactory and, as with Oberstown Girls School, it must be addressed to provide an in-house psychology service designed to meet the particular needs of these young people.

Reflecting international standards, the CPT noted the importance for children in detention to maintain contact with the outside world, and welcomed that importance is attached to this issue at Trinity House School. In particular, it noted that children were encouraged to correspond with, and make telephone calls to their relatives, who could also visit them freely. In appropriate cases, visitors were offered practical assistance such as accommodation and local transport. This approach was welcomed by the CPT, which noted that the active promotion of such contacts can be very beneficial for children deprived of their liberty, many of whom may have behavioural problems related to emotional deprivation or a lack of social skills.[158]

Best Practice and a Collective Approach

In summary, it is clear that the Children Detention Schools measure relatively well against the *Standards and Criteria for Children in Detention Schools* as well as against international standards. Staff are highly qualified and settled, they are focused on the education and well-being of the young people in their care and provide for their needs within the school in an integrated manner. Some concerns exist around the provision of information to young people, and the involvement of young people in the design and implementation of their care and education plans. Difficulties accessing medical and educational information on the young people must also be addressed if international standards are to be met. There are obvious problems in preparing young people to return successfully to the community and work on offending behaviour and the evaluation of such work deserves much greater attention given the reasons why young people are in detention in the first place.

There is much in the way of good practice taking place in the schools notwithstanding the policy and legislative vacuum in which they have operated for many years and the poor state of their buildings. Moreover the level of communication between them, and between them and the other agencies in the youth justice system is improving, as practice and policies continue to be mainstreamed across the schools. For example, in 2002 the schools agreed a policy on the separation of young people and prepared a booklet jointly on child protection and welfare procedures. The schools are also continuing to engage in a structured and co-ordinated way with external agencies, including the Probation and Welfare Service and educational and health authorities. This will undoubtedly be an area that the new Youth Justice Service will be keen to address and consolidate further. It must do so if international standards are to be properly implemented.

SPECIAL RESIDENTIAL SERVICES BOARD

Co-ordination between schools is not an area that falls within the scope of the Special Residential Services Board (SRSB) established under Part 11 of the Children Act. Designed to address the chaos that had existed hitherto, where the courts sentenced young people to detention but places could not be found, the SRSB is an independent body with a particular duty to assist the courts in identifying suitable places in Children Detention Schools for children found guilty of offences. As guardian of the principle of detention as a last resort, section 227 of the Act also provides that it is the duty of the SRSB to ensure the appropriate and efficient utilisation of Children Detention Schools with regard to this principle. It is also responsible for ensuring the efficient, effective and co-ordinated delivery of residential accommodation and support services for children detained in schools, although it does not have any executive authority in respect of any of these services.[159]

The SRSB also has broader duties in areas of monitoring, policy development and research that reach beyond detention (including both offending and non-offending children) and include support services. For example, it is responsible for monitoring and reviewing the level and nature of residential accommodation and support services, it has a remit to advise the Government on policy relating to the remand and detention of children in schools and Special Care Units, to promote, organise and take part in seminars, conferences and demonstrations in Ireland and elsewhere on the issue of detention and delinquent behaviour of children, and to collect, maintain, research and evaluate statistics and other data relating to the detention of children. Interestingly, this duty does not appear to be limited to the detention of children under 16 (i.e. in the schools and units) but could be found to apply to children generally.

Since it came into operation on a statutory basis on 7 November 2003,[160] it has established itself as an efficient and progressive organisation which is committed to maximising the potential of its mandate in line with best practice and the highest professional and international standards. The Board has six court officers liaising with the courts and set up a 24/7 On-Call Service available for the key stakeholders in May 2004.[161] It is developing an impressive research profile – it has commissioned research into the admission criteria for Special Care Units,[162] the impact of placement in Special Care Units on children and their families[163] and the definition and usage of high support units in

Ireland[164] – and in 2005, it established a scholarship scheme to promote postgraduate research in the area.

As one of the innovations of the Children Act 2001, the work of the SRSB has highlighted the importance and need for efficient co-ordinating infrastructure in youth justice to support a partnership approach. This was acknowledged by the Youth Justice Review which recommended greater inter-agency working supported by a single non-statutory body, together with the streamlining of the detention estate.[165] One of the consequences of these proposed changes, however, is that the SRSB is to lose its co-ordinating role and be confined to policy matters. This is a regrettable decision. However, the priority must be that the experience and experience built up within the SRSB is not lost, but rather utilised in some form by the Youth Justice Service, to whom its function in this area will presumably pass. It remains to be seen whether removing the co-ordinating function from an independent statutory agency like the SRSB will have wider consequences for the system.

DETENTION OF YOUNG PEOPLE OVER SIXTEEN YEARS

Children over 16 years are detained in places of detention under the remit of the Department of Justice, Equality and Law Reform and within the scope of the Irish Prison Service. While the principal place of detention is St. Patrick's Institution in Dublin, young people over 16 years have occasionally been placed in prisons and in other facilities now closed.

Fort Mitchel

Fort Mitchel (Spike Island) in County Cork accommodated young people between the ages of 16 and 24 years when it played an important role in providing appropriate detention for children over 16 years particularly from the Southern region until its closure on 31 January 2004.[166] Since then, all young people over 16 years must be sent to St. Patrick's Institution in Dublin creating a significant geographical barrier between young people, their families, and the communities to which they must eventually return. Anecdotal evidence suggests that life in St. Patrick's can be difficult for those outside of Dublin,[167] and apart from the rural/urban issue, young people from Cork and Limerick find it isolating to be detained so far from home.[168] Visits are relatively infrequent due to factors of time and cost.

Fort Mitchel also had a significant positive feature in its Education Unit which offered an enviable range of academic and vocational training delivered by experienced and qualified staff.[169] Its success in this area is evident from the fact that before its closure in 2003, young people's rate of participation in education was 92 per cent.[170] Here, it stands in stark contrast to St. Patrick's.[171] For these reasons, the closure, which was a casualty of the row between the Prison Service and the Prison Officers Association over the payment of over-time,[172] was extremely regrettable and clearly not in the interest of young people detained there. It has also created difficulties for St. Patrick's which now has no alternative places of detention to which those unsuited to detention there can be sent.[173]

Cloverhill Prison

Possibly the reason why overcrowding has not been a problem at St. Patrick's Institution is the opening of Cloverhill Prison, a remand prison in 1999. Cloverhill accommodates young people over 16 years and occasionally 15 and 16 year olds declared unruly or depraved under the Children Act 1908.[174] This is clearly an adult facility which accommodates young people over 16 years detained on remand. Apart from mixing adults with children, the unsuitability of the facility is clear from the lack of recreation facilities and the absence of a fully operational school.[175]

Limerick and Cork Prison

Despite the prohibition in the Children Act on the imprisonment of children, they are occasionally detained in Cork and Limerick prisons. While both places of detention officially accommodate those over 17 years, young people under that age are occasionally sent there particularly for remand purposes. This arises in Limerick because it is the only place outside Mountjoy Prison which accommodates female offenders, and in both Cork and Limerick in preference to sending a young person to St. Patrick's Institution some distance away in Dublin.[176] Both situations give rise to serious concern about the extent to which the rights of young offenders, who are particularly vulnerable, are protected.

St. Patrick's Institution

St. Patrick's Institution is thus the principal place of detention for young people over 16 years. It is a closed, medium-security place of detention which accommodates males between 16 and 21 years of age. It has a capacity of approximately 220 and since 1999, has accommodated a relatively consistent number of young people every year, with an average occupancy of 192.[177] On 21 September 2005, there were ten offenders aged 16 years and forty-five aged 17 years in St. Patrick's;[178] on average, one third of its population is under 18 years.[179] In January 2006, forty-five young people under 18 years were serving sentences in St. Patrick's for a variety of crimes including burglary (five), rape (three) car theft (thirteen).[180] Eleven of these young people were serving sentences of between three and six months, eight of between six months and one year, fifteen between one and two years and eleven over two years including one for life.[181]

St. Patrick's comes under the auspices of the Department of Justice, Equality and Law Reform and the Irish Prison Service, and as Walsh notes, 'the regime is more like that in a prison as distinct from that in an industrial or reformatory school'.[182] Both the regime and the physical environment of St. Patrick's Institution have been subjected to long and sustained criticism by international and Irish organisations despite 'professional management'.[183] In 1984, the Whittaker Committee was 'highly critical' of St. Patrick's Institution as a detention centre for young offenders considering it to be 'outdated, lacking in educational and recreational facilities and an environment that would contribute to the further delinquency of the juvenile rather than any rehabilitative function'.[184] It referred to its 'demoralising effect' and noted that the conditions of detention, including the fact that residents spent at least seventeen hours a day locked in their cells, were allowed only one visit and two outgoing letters per week, could 'easily lead to the psychological deterioration of the juvenile offenders in the institution'. It recommended that it be closed down as soon as possible and did not consider the renovation of the institution as an option.

Many – including the Council of Europe Committee for the Prevention of Torture (CPT), the Inspector of Prisons and St. Patrick's Visiting Committee – have reiterated these concerns in the twenty years since the Whittaker Report and more recently. Many of the problems in St. Patrick's stem from the age and general unsuitability of the buildings (lack of open green spaces, etc.), together with severe resource restrictions, which have led to the scaling back of recreational and vocational opportunities for young people.[185]

The workshops, or rather lack of them, have been a source of particular concern for some time. Their limited availability was highlighted by the Governor in his annual report for 2000[186] and the situation has continued to deteriorate. In 2003, the Visiting Committee identified a severe problem with the lack of adequate training facilities which it believed was militating against the boys' preparation for release: it identified the provision of 'proper workshops' as a 'number one priority'.[187] Despite this, the workshops were completely withdrawn in 2004 for health and safety reasons (a lack of proper ventilation in the relevant building) and due to a 'reallocation of resources'.[188] Efforts to reinstate them have not yet been successful although buildings being renovated for that purpose are expected to be operational in 2006.

Reallocation of resources was also noted to be responsible for the restricted opening hours in the gym in 2003, which is otherwise well equipped and staffed by dedicated staff. Indeed, high use of the gym facilities was reported by the Inspector of Prisons in 2004, although attention was drawn to the old building and its limited capacity.[189] While there has been a long tradition of very positive interaction between groups in the community and young people in St. Patrick's in competitive matches of chess and football, for example, in 2004 this was discontinued due to manpower constraints.[190] Overall, the impact of cutbacks and limited resources in the area of education, vocational training and leisure is stark.[191] Apart from the consequences for the young people's rehabilitation, the reduction of vocational and leisure opportunities has resulted in a high level of boredom – up to 100 young people are idle at any one time – and an increase in the level of conflict and assaults on young people and between young people and staff has been the result.[192] The Governor himself has acknowledged that the increased use of the exercise yard caused by the withdrawal of the workshops has led to 'increased disciplinary difficulties'.[193]

The education facilities have been found by the Visiting Committee to be adequate and a small number of boys were reported to be taking formal state examinations at post-primary level.[194] However, the rate of participation in education (counted as participation in at least one structured class per week) in St. Patrick's lags consistently and, in some cases, dramatically behind that in adult prisons.[195] Moreover, contrary to practice in the Children Detention Schools, a review of each person's education is not routinely carried out on committal,[196] and it is recommended that, in line with international standards, all young people have their educational ability assessed on admission and their needs identified as part of a process of drawing up and implementing an individual educational plan.[197]

This is particularly important in light of the concern, consistently expressed, about the level of illiteracy and innumeracy among the population in St. Patrick's. According to the Visiting Committee 'basic literacy continues to be a problem' and a substantial number of the inmates are unable to read or write and have very poor language skills.[198] Many of those who come to St. Patrick's arrive with 'a long history of educational neglect'; literacy is believed to be at 50 per cent and only 20 per cent can sign their name.[199]

Despite the apparent scale of this problem and the extent to which it must hamper the young people's attempts to spend their time in detention constructively, it does not appear to be addressed as a matter of priority or strategy within St. Patrick's. Although a channel with literacy instruction programmes is available on the television in the boys' rooms, in 2003, work on literacy was reported to be carried out largely by volunteers; nor does it appear to be integrated into each boy's educational plan. While it may be defensively argued that the boys detained are beyond the age of compulsory education and thus cannot be forced to learn, it is no doubt the case that the culture of St. Patrick's – which is a penal rather than an educational institution – does not encourage such a focus. Poor morale among staff may also play a role; the lack of pro-active leadership from the teachers was highlighted by the Inspector of Prisons although the syllabus was also criticised for its 'predictable and somewhat uninspiring' nature with 'little evidence of new initiatives or of confidence that much could be done to extend greatly the educational horizons of inmates who had been denied good educational opportunities in their earlier life'.[200] Despite this, both the Governor and the Inspector of Prisons have recommended that 'a bigger effort be made to get more inmates involved in education, especially re illiteracy problems'.[201] Greater co-operation between St. Patrick's and the Children Detention Schools – as all facilities are brought together under the new reforms – should be used to encourage this process.[202]

A further issue of serious concern to both the Visiting Committee and the Inspector of Prisons as well as within St. Patrick's Institution itself was the failure to implement the CONNECT project in the Centre. CONNECT is an action-research project which focuses on prisoners' transition from custody, through training, on to reintegration in the community and labour market participation. Despite a commitment by the Prison Service to implement the project in every Irish prison between 2000 and 2006, in 2004, the Visiting Committee reported that the project was now 'unlikely to occur in St. Patrick's despite its importance in light of the profile of its inmates'.[203] At the same time, it is important that some of the young people in St. Patrick's have participated in some of the courses on offer although their choice in 2004 at least was for courses which were not accredited: Computers, Guitar and Cookery, for example.[204] There appear to be no programmes on offending behaviour in St. Patrick's and the young people do not have individual plans designed to address their offending or to prepare them for release.

International standards recognise that staying in touch with family and friends is vital to young people in detention, both for their well-being while serving their sentence and their reintegration into the community on their release. Research into the impact of detention on young people has found that family relationships are extremely important to young people and they often 'missed their families considerably'.[205] However, opportunities for young people to communicate with their families are limited, arguably due to the sheer numbers of people in St. Patrick's. In particular, young people are entitled to one visit per week of a half-hour duration, although special visits are accommodated on request.[206] All letters are censored coming in and out and, according to the handbook *Information for Persons in Custody*, young people must make a request in order to communicate with their solicitor. Both situations are in clear breach of Article 8 of the European Convention on Human Rights insofar as they constitute disproportionate and possibly also illegal interferences with the right to respect for private and family life.[207] Similarly, the allocation of a daily telephone call of six minutes' duration, while reasonable, is limited to only two people nominated by the prisoner for the duration of his stay. Overall, these arrangements, while supported as 'liberal' by the Visiting Committee in 2003, appear very restrictive. While special arrangements are made for those travelling long distances to see family members in St. Patrick's, overnight visits are not possible.

Visits take place in a large bright area where tea/coffee facilities are provided by a voluntary organisation. However, cutbacks in budget allocation have resulted in a refurbishment of a section for children's play/creche facility being discontinued. As many prisoners have children and/or siblings who could use this facility, it is recommended that this be re-opened immediately.[208] A second visiting area is provided for those not permitted to have direct contact with their visitors.

There is a clear and serious problem with drugs in St. Patrick's Institution, which persists despite efforts by the Governor (installing netting and CCTV in the exercise yard) to physically keep drugs out.[209] While these measures, taken in 2004, have greatly reduced the illegal drug supply in the Centre, they have led to an apparent increase in bullying between young people with boys being intimidated into receiving drugs for others through visits.[210] To counteract this situation, the Governor introduced a controlled visitation system whereby each young person must nominate four visitors who must produce photograph proof of their identity to gain entry. Initial reports are that this has reduced the level of bullying in the Centre[211] although young people clearly continue to inflict injuries on each other.[212] Moreover, it is important that a flexible approach is taken to this arrangement and names can be changed with relatively ease so that the rules do not have a disproportionately negative effect.

The issue of protecting the physical integrity of boys in detention is an extremely serious one. Evidence of bullying and physical injury is apparent among young people appearing before the Children Court[213] and co-ordinated and urgent action must be taken to reduce bullying in St. Patrick's and to protect the boys' well-being on a collective, as well as on an individual basis. Every effort should be made to provide effective protection for those who are particularly vulnerable or at risk.[214] The fact that, at the time of the Inspector of Prisons' visit in 2004, ten young people were accommodated in the 'C' wing, a unit below ground level in St. Patrick's – which houses up to thirteen disruptive or protected young people in isolation from the main population – is evidence of the need for this protection on a broader scale.[215] In this regard, failure to take the action outlined in the St. Patrick's Business Plan 2003 with regard to recording and auditing assaults between young people is a matter of serious concern.[216] Critical too is the failure to implement recommendations regarding suicide prevention within the Centre[217] (there were seven incidents of self-harm in 2004),[218] although a decline in incidents in self-harm is welcome and believed to be at least partly attributable to the introduction of televisions into the boys' rooms.[219]

The Inspector of Prisons also expressed serious concern about the level of disciplinary problems in St. Patrick's. While this issue was not seriously addressed in the body of his report, it was noted in the conclusion that 'in the previous six months 861 disciplinary reports (P.19's) were dealt with by the Governor and, of those, 247 forfeited remission of sentence. In the previous twelve months, seventeen inmates were on report (P.19's) for assault on staff while 198 were reported for assault on fellow inmates. There were 368 inmates on P.19's in the previous six months for smuggling or attempting to smuggle illegal substances (drugs) into the institution and, of these, 233 were placed on 'screen' visits arising from the disciplinary reports. The number of inmates on disciplinary reports, four–five per day on average, appears quite high for a population of approximately

200, which gives me some cause for concern'.[220]

The Inspector of Prisons also appeared to be seriously concern about the level of bullying and assault alleged to be on-going in St. Patrick's, and concluded that 'Management and staff should be fully aware of its existence and a combined effort made to stamp this malpractice out. There are procedures and guidelines relating to dealing with bullying which should be applied as soon as possible. All of the services and agencies involved with the inmates within the institution should be involved in helping to eliminate this problem'.[221]

The existence and size of the Drug Free (D) Wing in St. Patrick's, while a positive measure, is evidence of the scale of the drug problem in the Centre. Opened in 2000 with a capacity of 76,[222] at the end of 2004, it had a waiting list for admission.[223] The young people admitted to this Wing are those who want to stay or get drug-free; they are admitted having provided a number of clean urine samples and undertaken to remain drug-free and be subjected to random sample tests. They sign this undertaking prior to acceptance onto the Wing. Positive sentence management programmes are also implemented on the D Wing[224] and other perks – such as fresh fruit, additional television channels and use of a playstation are also available.[225] However, young people, who must be drug-free before being placed on D wing, receive no assistance in reaching this position. The current approach thus favours those who have never used drugs and appears to reward them with 'perks' like bigger meal portions, which should be available to all young people in detention.

Closure of St. Patrick's Institution

Despite the damning criticisms of St. Patrick's, facilities with potential – like Fort Mitchell and the Shanganagh Castle – have been closed, while St. Patrick's Institution remains open. Although the flack is picked up by St. Patrick's – which now has no alternative facility to which young people requiring or deserving a more open regime or one closer to home can be sent[226] – the resources saved through these closures do not appear to have been diverted to St. Patrick's. In the meantime, €10 million was spent on a facility, originally for 14 and 15 year olds, that lies idle on the same grounds.[227]

These decisions are illogical at best, and they are difficult to square with any level of commitment to the welfare of young offenders and the need to maximise the potential for successful reintegration into society on release. As the Inspector of Prisons wrote in his first annual report: 'when one compares the facilities in St. Patrick's which has absolutely no open green spaces and is a complete concrete jungle with that of Shanganagh, one wonders which centre should be closed?'[228]

The maintenance of St. Patrick's Institution as the only facility in the state for the detention of children over 16 years is completely at odds with international standards. As the above material highlights it stands in devastating contrast to the operation and ethos of the Children Detention Schools. Threats to the boys' physical integrity and welfare through drugs and by the assault of other young people are real and the lack of workshops, meaningful and motivating leisure activities and interaction with the outside world reduce dramatically any likely effectiveness of detention in St. Patrick's to address offending behaviour. The detention of boys sentenced for life for murder, alongside those sentenced for shorter periods and less serious crimes is also questionable.

The balance is difficult to draw between acknowledging the serious failures of St. Patrick's – described as a 'disaster' by some – and accepting that with ever limited resources, continued cutbacks and a steady population of demanding and challenging young people little more can be done. The reality is that both facts are true. St. Patrick's is a disaster, or at least one waiting to happen, as it is only in the future that the true neglect of the young people who spend time there will be realised. Responsibility for this will not lie with the staff of the institution, however, but with the Prison Service, the Department of Justice and the Government who allowed such inhumane and detrimental treatment of young people to go relatively unchecked on their watch. At the heart of this lies an abject policy failure to appreciate that like their deeds – young people carry out certain types of crime in a certain way – young people's needs are also different and demand special treatment, highly qualified staff and dedicated services if the experience of detention is to bear any positive results.

In 2003, the Minister for Justice, Equality and Law Reform announced the closure of all prisons on the Mountjoy complex and their replacement with a new super-prison built on a greenfield site.[229] While a site has been purchased and plans are under way to build this facility, no decision appears to have been taken on provision for those over 16 years which must, under the (further) new proposals, be accommodated within the Children Detention Schools. Indications are that the removal of 16 and 17 year olds from St. Patrick's will take a decade to complete. Even given the need for planning, this is an outrageously long period of time and will mean that a further generation of young people will suffer its conditions and have little chance to address the behaviour and circumstances which gave rise to their detention in the first place.

SEPARATING ADULTS FROM YOUNG PEOPLE IN DETENTION

International law requires that children be separated from adults in detention[230] and section 156 of the Children Act 2001 also prohibits the imprisonment of children. This provision has not yet been commenced, however, and thus detaining children alongside adults is lawful despite being incompatible with Ireland's international obligations. The extent to which the separation of adults and children in detention is an aspiration is apparent from the (non-statutory) Prison Rules 2005, Rule 77 of which provides that, where practicable, young prisoners should be kept separate from adults.

Detaining children and adults together is not only a feature of St. Patrick's Institution. In 2002, the Inspector of Prisons noted with regard to Cloverhill Prison that 'juveniles should not be mixed with or sharing cells with adult prisoners'.[231] This issue had, in fact, been raised by the prisoners themselves as a concern. Moreover, according to the Irish Prison Service, 147 young people aged between 15 and 17 were placed in adult places of detention including St. Patrick's Institution, Cloverhill and Limerick persons between January and October 2005. A total of 166 young people were placed in Irish prisons in 2004.[232] While it is not illegal, the blatant inconsistency of this practice with Ireland's international obligations must make its elimination a priority.

SIXTEEN YEARS – THE WATERSHED IN THE IRISH YOUTH JUSTICE SYSTEM

Related to this issue is the arbitrary distinction made by the Irish youth justice system between young people under and over 16 years of age for the purpose of detention. While this has historical origins, it has been consolidated by the Children Act 2001, which provides that children under 16 years remanded or sentenced by the Children Court shall be sent to Children Detention Schools under the remit of the Department of Education and Science, while those over 16 years are sent to a Children Detention Centre (currently St. Patrick's Institution) under the remit Department of Justice, Equality and Law Reform and the Irish Prison Service. While Part 10 of the Act, which makes this provision, has not been commenced, the practice of sending those under 16 to an education and care focused secure unit and those over that age to a prison-like institution is well established. As the above analysis shows, it has resulted in those over 16 years – for no reason other than their age – being subjected to a much harsher regime than those sent to Children Detention Schools, with less educational and vocational opportunities, greater risks to their health and well-being than younger offenders and detention alongside adults contrary to international standards. While the basis for the distinction, i.e. that children under the school-leaving age fall within the scope of the Department of Education and Science may be correct, it is difficult to see the justification for effectively including 16- and 17-year-olds in the adult prison regime with so little consideration for their special needs, lack of maturity and vulnerability. The result is that although the Children Act 2001 establishes 18 years as the age of majority, those sent to detention are subjected to the harsh treatment of the adult system two years earlier. The distinction is one of the unjustified anomalies of the Irish system.

It is an ironic fact that even though the regime to which young people are subjected in St. Patrick's Institution is harsher than in the Children Detention Schools, they enjoy fewer safeguards. The remit of the SRSB with regard to ensuring the appropriate and efficient utilisation of places, including detention as a last resort, is limited to Children Detention Schools, and does not apply to St. Patrick's or any Children Detention Centre.[233] Moreover, the detailed and positive provision made in the Act for the objectives of the schools, the rights of young people to education, health care and religion, and the establishment of a statutory inspector to monitor their operation are similarly limited to the schools.

While St. Patrick's has been subjected to inspection by the Inspector of Prisons and Places of Detention since his appointment in 2002,[234] this is a non-statutory office (despite being established formally under the Prison Rules 2005) which does not apply child-specific criteria during the inspection process. Rather, it applies standards relating to the quality of the regime, the attitude of staff and inmates, the health, safety and well-being of prisoners, the conditions of the buildings and questions of humanity and propriety, which are inherent to an adult prison regime and take no account of the specific needs and rights of young offenders. Thus, in addition to being subjected to a harsher regime in St. Patrick's Institution, the regime itself is not subjected to any child-specific monitoring or review process. In this context, it is particularly worrying that the remit of the Ombudsman for Children to receive and investigate complaints excludes this particularly vulnerable category of young people.[235]

DETENTION OF FEMALE OFFENDERS

Given that St. Patrick's Institution is an all-male detention centre and Oberstown Girls School only accommodates girls under 16 years, there is no dedicated place of detention for female offenders above that age. This is a serious gap in current provision, which has resulted in girls being detained alongside adults in the Dóchas Centre (female prison) on the Mountjoy complex and in the female section of Limerick Prison. This arose before the courts in 1998 in the case of *The People (DPP)* v *W.*[236] In this case, the trial judge had sentenced a 16-year-old girl, who had pleaded guilty to murder, to seven years imprisonment. A problem identified by this sentence by O'Flaherty J. in the Court of Criminal Appeal was explained as follows:

> The difficulty about that sentence is that there is no place of detention for young women as opposed to young men. They can be sentenced to a period of detention in St. Patrick's Institution. There is a clear discrimination against women in the failure to provide similar facilities for young women as there are for young men. Miss W has been in Oberstown Girls Centre, Lusk, Co Dublin, since 6th May last and the Court is told that in one week's time she will have to leave there although she will not be 17 years of age until the 27th August. The only place she can go is to the women's prison in Mountjoy. We are quite satisfied that that is a totally unsuitable environment.

Accordingly, the Court of Appeal affirmed the sentence of seven years detention, but suspended the remainder of it on condition that the accused be on probation for three years.[237]

This is a practical illustration of the differential treatment which young women over 16 years enjoy in the criminal justice system. While the reality is that this female offender served three years of her sentence in the community instead of in detention, were the Appeal Court not so aware of the unsuitability of Mountjoy, the case would have ended differently.

In the eight years since the Court of Criminal Appeal expressed its concern about the lack of appropriate facilities for the detention of girls over 16 years, nothing has been done to address the needs of this group of young women although the fact that Oberstown Girls School occasionally accommodates 17-year-olds is a practical solution. Urgent attention must be given to the needs of girls under 18 years in detention with appropriate facilities put in place as a priority.

INSPECTION AND COMPLAINTS MECHANISMS

Part 10 of the Children Act makes provision for the appointment of an Inspector of Children Detention Schools. As discussed above, the nature of this role has been altered by the Criminal Justice Act 2006. The appointment of an inspector (or 'authorised person' under the new proposals) is an important safeguard necessary to protect the rights of children in detention and to promote their interests, welfare and treatment. These are very positive elements of the Children Act and while it is regrettable that these sections were not commenced before, it is welcome, at least, that the issue of putting in place an officer with statutory powers to inspect the schools is now finally being addressed. It is important also that this role will cover children currently detained in St. Patrick's (as young people are transferred eventually to the schools), although it is very worrying that this is to be an *ad hoc* rather than a permanent independent office.

Until now, the process of inspecting the schools has fallen to an Inspection Team in the Department of Education and Science. Importantly, they have been inspecting the schools in accordance with the Department's *Standards and Criteria for Children Detention Schools,* drafted in 2002 and revised in 2004. This document is an impressive and detailed statement of the rights and treatment to which young people are entitled in the CDS, which also sets out the criteria which must be fulfilled to ensure that these standards are met. Standards relate to the areas of the school including the care of young people, children's rights, child protection, education, health, tackling offending behaviour, contact and visits with family, staffing and premises. They compare very favourably with the UN Rules for the Protection of Juveniles deprived of their Liberty highlighted above[238] and should, it is submitted, form the basis for the new inspector's role.

Despite the positive nature of these mechanisms, they do not currently apply to young people detained in adult prisons or in St. Patrick's Institution. While a Visiting Committee for St. Patrick's was set up in 1960,[239] a recent report of the Inspector of Prisons commented on its 'ineffectual' nature.[240] The strong similarity between various passages in the 2003 and 2004 Annual Reports of the Committee supports this. A more serious example of the Committee's questionable merit is found in its 2003 Annual Report where the only comment it made on the death of an inmate in custody was to express sympathy to his family. In startling contrast, the Committee placed formally on record that it had received no complaints regarding the food in St. Patrick's in 2003 or indeed in previous years.[241] A further mark of the ineffectiveness of the Visiting Committee is the lack of influence it has. In 2003, for example, the Committee identified the full operation of the workshops as a matter of priority. In 2004, it reported that the workshops had been withdrawn altogether. There is also a sense from the Committee's reports that the staff and management are 'trying their best' and should not be criticised for this reason.

As the *Standards and Criteria for Children Detention Schools* show, inspecting places of detention for children is a complex process requiring specialist knowledge and experience of youth justice and residential care issues. From this perspective, the Visiting Committee, while well intentioned, is a grossly inadequate model, and the lack of detailed standards to govern the inspection process also further undermines its potential to identify problems and gaps in the system.

A similar criticism can be made of the Prisons Inspectorate, although he, at least, has a broader remit across all of the prisons and greater experience and expertise at his disposal regarding the adequacy of the custodial environment being inspected. His reports to date have been informative and practical accounts of the reality of prison life. In the case of young people, however, the inspection process does not involve the application of criteria and standards specific to residential care for children. This is a serious flaw.

International standards highlight the right of children to have access to independent, effective complaints mechanisms to address their grievances.[242] While complaints procedures exist in both the Children Detention Schools and St. Patrick's Institution, they are not independent from the management there. Indeed this is highlighted by the recommendation of the Department of Education and Science Inspection Team that young people should have access to an independent external complaints mechanism, although which such mechanism is envisaged is unclear.[243] With regard to the St. Patrick's booklet providing Information to young people in there explains, 'if you are not satisfied with the outcome locally you may appeal to the Visiting Committee, the Minister for Justice or a member of his Department or the Courts'.[244] The vulnerability of children in St. Patrick's Institution is clearly highlighted by this information. It is further compounded by the fact that such young people are also excluded from the remit of the Ombudsman for Children. The Ombudsman, appointed under the Ombudsman for Children Act

2002, has an otherwise broad role to promote and protect the rights of children, including the investigation of individual complaints.[245] Despite meeting with great criticism, the decision to exclude young people in prisons and places of detention from the Act was unchanged. Whatever the justification for excluding children in detention over 16 years from the remit of the Ombudsman, the Government has clearly failed to respond fully to the concerns of the Committee on the Rights of the Child, which expressed concern in 1998 about the lack of an independent monitoring mechanism to deal with complaints and violations of the rights of all children.[246] Regardless of the fact that implementation of current proposals for reform will mean that all children under 18 years will eventually be detained in a place of detention that is inspected by an authorised officer so appointed by the Minister for Justice, Equality and Law Reform, the position remains that this person is not independent from the Department, has no power to compel change; nor has he/she a specific mandate to hear and resolve the complaints of individual children. Accordingly, the remit of the Ombudsman for Children, which has the power to investigate individual complaints and to take action on behalf of children in this regard, should be extended immediately to receive complaints from all children under 18.[247] Moreover, pending the closure of St. Patrick's Institution, the Inspector of Prisons is recommended to ensure that an expert in residential care or the detention of children accompanies him on his next inspection.

CONCLUSION

This Chapter presents a descriptive and analytical overview of the places of detention for children in Ireland. Two distinct regimes currently exist: Children Detention Schools for those under 16 years and St. Patrick's Institution for those over that age. While it is clear that the schools are challenged by a varying population and a lack of a common approach, in the main they are positive environments where qualified staff not only are committed maximizing the positive potential of the young person's experience in detention, but also enjoy the support and resources to implement that commitment. Areas of concern include work on offending behaviour, the poor state of repair of buildings, the lack of an independent complaints mechanism and making policy and other documentation accessible to children detained there. St. Patrick's Institution is staffed principally by prison officers, rather than care workers, and this, together with the penal nature of the institution and the relentless cost-cutting imposed by the Department of Justice, Equality and Law Reform, continues to reinforce the punitive nature of the environment and its failure to protect and promote the rights of young people detained there.

The implementation of the recommendations of the Youth Justice Review provides an important opportunity as well as a threat to the future of this part of the youth justice system. It is regrettable that the Special Residential Services Board, which spent the last three years coming to terms with its role, will no longer have a mandate over the Detention Schools. The Youth Justice Service, which will presumably undertake this function, must set about developing a common strategy and approach to the treatment of children in all places of detention and to use the international standards as the benchmark for this purpose.[248] The proposed reform thus offers a significant opportunity to ensure the implementation of high standards across the detention estate. The danger, however, is that moving the Schools from the Department of Education and Science to the Department of Justice, Equality and Law Reform will have a negative effect on them, rather than a positive effect on St. Patrick's Institution. Moreover, while an expert is to be appointed to oversee the removal of 16 and 17 year olds from St. Patrick's, there is a real danger that this process, while aimed at 'getting it right' will simply take far too long. There is no need to reinvent the wheel here. International standards and best practice in Ireland and abroad clearly identify how detention for children should be organised and run. Only the political and administrative will is required to implement these standards and to ensure that detention both protects and promotes the rights of young people while also addressing their offending behaviour.

The extension to all the places of detention for children of child-focused standards and criteria will be vital throughout this process, as will the implementation of effective inspection and independent complaints procedures. In addition, however, it is crucial that the remit of the Ombudsman for Children be extended to include all children in detention. If implementation of the Youth Justice Review ended this anomaly, that really would be an achievement.

NOTES

1 Goldson, B., 'Child Imprisonment: A Case for Abolition' 5(2) *Youth Justice* (October 2005) 77–90.
2 Ireland entered a reservation to Article 10 of the ICCPR when it ratified the Covenant on 8 December 1989 stating that it would implement this provision 'as far as practically possible' while also making a commitment to 'progressive implementation'. In 1993, the Human Rights Committee reviewed Ireland's compliance with the Covenant and emphasised with concern that the segregation of juvenile offenders is required under the Covenant. See the Concluding Observations of the Human Rights Committee: Ireland. 3 August 1993, CCPR/C/79/Add.21 para 14. In 2000, the Committee recommended that Ireland withdraw its reservation and implement the Covenant in full. See the Concluding Observations of the Human Rights Committee: Ireland. 24 July 2000, A/55/40, paras 422–51. No reservation was entered to the equivalent provision in the CRC on ratification of that Convention in 1992.
3 See also Rule 17 of the UN Standard Minimum Rules for the Administration of Juvenile Justice (the Beijing Rules) adopted by General Assembly resolution 40/33 of 29 November 1985, available at www.ohchr.org (18 January 2006). See further Chapter Six.
4 Committee on the Rights of the Child, *Concluding Observations of the Committee on the Rights of the Child: Ireland*, 4 February 1998, UN Doc CRC/C/15/Add.85, para. 23, available at www.ohchr.org (accessed 18 January 2006).
5 Rule 13.2 of the Beijing Rules.
6 *Ibid.*,Commentary to Rule 19.
7 *Ibid.*,Rule 13.5.
8 Adopted by General Assembly resolution 45/113 of 14 December 1990 available at www.ohchr.org (accessed 19 January 2006).
9 *Ibid.*, Rules 6 and 7.
10 See, for example, Kilkelly, U., et al., *In Our Care Promoting the Rights of Children in Custody* (Belfast, NIHRC, 2002) available at www.nihrc.org (accessed 2 January 2006).
11 *Report on the Youth Justice Review* (Dublin: Department of Justice, Equality and Law Reform, July 2005), p. 7, available at www.justice.ie (accessed 4 January 2006).
12 Human Rights Commission, Observations on Proposals for Amendments to the Criminal Justice Bill 2004 (Youth Justice) 30 March 2006, pp. 13–15, available at www.ihrc.ie (accessed 19 April 2006).

13 *Repeat on the Youth Justice Review*, p. 7.
14 See Criminal Justice Bill 2004, Second composite List of Amendments, 16 May 2006, available at www.oireachtas.ie (accessed 16 May 2006). See further below regarding complaints mechanisms.
15 For background see Walsh, D., *Juvenile Justice* (Dublin: Thomson Round Hall, 2005) p. 239.
16 Following the recommendations of the Youth Justice Review, responsibility for the Children Detention Schools is to be moved to the Department of Justice, Equality and Law Reform. See above.
17 *Residential Provision for Children under the Auspices of the Department of Education and Science: A Preliminary Review* (Department of Education and Science, 2002) p. 32 available at www.education.ie (accessed 2 January 2006).
18 Department of Education and Science, *Care Inspection Report, Oberstown Girls School*, (Dublin: Department of Education and Science, 2004) p. 7, available on www.education.ie (accessed 3 January 2006).
19 *Residential Provision for Children*, at pp. 34–60.
20 The relatively low cost involved in St. Joseph's reflects the fact that as an industrial school, dealing with younger and less difficult cases, it requires less intensive staffing levels and due to its size enjoys economies of scale that cannot be availed of by the other centres. *Report of the Comptroller and Auditor General*, 2004, p. 89.
21 *Report on the Youth Justice Review*, pp. 21–2.
22 In 2004, a care inspection found that the various units in use in Oberstown Girls' Schools were 'unsuited to modern demands and to current health and safety requirements'. See Department of Education and Science, *Care Inspection Report Oberstown Girls School*, p. 7.
23 Press Release of 9 March, 2000 – *Woods Announces Major Developments at Childrens' Centres*, available at www.education.ie (accessed 3 January 2006).
24 Comptroller and Auditor General, 2004 *Report on the Department of Education and Science*, p. 88.
25 This section has been amended to refer here to 'appropriate educational and *other* training programmes and facilities' (emphasis added). See the Criminal Justice Act 2006.
26 'Children Detention Schools: the impact of s 158' by Noel Howard in Special Residential Services Board *Bulletin* Summer 2005, p. 3, available at www.srsb.ie (accessed 4 January 2006).
27 *Ibid.*
28 *Ibid.*
29 Currently, children who are remanded on the first court order are not permitted mobility trips, but can be allowed court-ordered mobility on the next or any subsequent remands but only at the discretion of the Director of the school.
30 Oberstown Girls School and Trinity House School both have step-down facilities. Indeed, in the case of Oberstown, staff have been criticised for spending 'too much time' on the aftercare of girls who had left the school,

a function which other agencies such as health authorities should assume. Department of Education and Science, *Care Inspection Report Oberstown Girls School,* p. 16. However, see the comments of the Inspection Team on aftercare in Department of Education and Science, Core Inspection Report: Oberstown Boys School (Dublin: Department of Education and Science, 2005) p. 19 and Department of Education and Science, Core Inspection Report: Trinity House School (Dublin: Department of Education and Science, 2006) p. 20.

31 Howard, N, 'Children Detention Schools'.

32 *Ibid.*

33 *Residential Provision for Children,* pp. 32–3.

34 *Standards and Criteria for Children Detention Schools* (Department of Education and Science, 2002 and 2004) available on www.education.ie (accessed 3 January 2006)

35 Comptroller and Auditor General, p. 90.

36 See further Chapter Two.

37 *Residential Provision for Children*, p. 4.

38 See also Kilkelly, U., 'Children in Detention Schools: Learning from International Best Practice' 13(2) *Irish Journal of Criminal Law* (2003) 15–19.

39 Department of Education and Science, *Care Inspection Report: St Joseph's, Ferryhouse, Clonmel* (Department of Education and Science, April 2004) p. 7 available at www.education.ie (accessed 4 January 2006).

40 *Ibid.*, p.4.

41 *Ibid.*, p.7.

42 See Inspector of Prisons and Places of Detention, *St. Patrick's Institution Inspection*: *15th–19th November 2004*, p. 65, available at www.justice.ie (17 January 2006).

43 Department of Education and Science, *Care Inspection Report: St Joseph's,* pp. 10–11.

44 *Ibid.*, p. 11.

45 *Ibid.*, p. 12.

46 *Ibid.*, p. 15.

47 *Ibid.*, p. 15.

48 Rule 25 of the UN Rules for the Protection of Juveniles deprived of their Liberty require that young people should be given details of the complaints procedures and advised as to methods of seeking information, including legal advice.

49 Department of Education and Science, *Care Inspection Report: St Joseph's,* p. 14. It is not clear what is envisaged here.

50 *Ibid.*, p. 15.

51 *Ibid.*, p. 29. This is also required by Article 12 of the CRC, which recognises the right of the child to participate in decision-making concerning him/her.

52 Department of Education and Science, *Care Inspection Report: St Joseph's,* p.17.

53 A similar conclusion was reached with regard to children in Special Care Units under the care of the Health Service Executive. See Hanlon, N., and

Riley, L., *The Impact of Placement in Special Care Unit Settings on the Wellbeing of Young People and their Families A Summary Report 2004* (Dublin: SRSB: 2004) p. 77.

54 Rule 38 UN Rules for the Protection of Juveniles Deprived of their Liberty. International instruments also require that education programmes are part of the mainstream education system of the state. The Beijing Rules insist on the need for inter-ministerial and inter-departmental co-operation on the provision of education.

55 It may be relevant in this context that the Criminal Justice Act gives responsibility for education in the Children Detention Schools to the local VEC. See new section 159A.

56 Department of Education and Science, *Care Inspection Report: St Joseph's*, p. 22.

57 *Ibid.*, p. 18.

58 *Ibid.*, p. 20.

59 See further Kilkelly et al., *In Our Care,* p. 115.

60 Rule 49 of the UN Rule for the Protection of Juveniles Deprived of their Liberty.

61 Department of Education and Science, *Care Inspection Report: St Joseph's*, p. 23.

62 According to Rule 35 of the UN Rules, the possession of personal effects is a basic element of the right to privacy and essential to the psychological well-being of the juvenile in detention.

63 Department of Education and Science, *Care Inspection Report: St Joseph's*, p. 25.

64 Kilkelly, U., *The Right to Respect for Private and Family Life: A Guide to the implementation of Article 8 of the European Convention on Human Rights* (Strasbourg: Council of Europe, 2001).

65 Department of Education and Science, *Care Inspection Report: St Joseph's*, p. 26.

66 *Ibid.*, p. 27.

67 *Ibid.*, p. 28.

68 Special Residential Services Board, *Annual Report 2004*, (Dublin: SRSB, 2005), p. 19, accessed at www.srsb.ie (17 January 2006).

69 *Residential Provision for Children,* p. 43.

70 Department of Education and Science, *Care Inspection Report: Oberstown Girls School,* p. 8.

71 *Ibid.*, p. 9.

72 *Ibid.*, p. 13.

73 See Section V of the UN Rules for the Protection of Juveniles deprived of their Liberty.

74 Department of Education and Science, *Care Inspection Report: Oberstown Girls School*, p. 18.

75 *Ibid.*, p 18.

76 Rule 39 of the UN Rules.

77 Department of Education and Science, *Care Inspection Report: Oberstown Girls School*, pp. 9–10.

78 *Ibid.*, p 21.
79 *Ibid.*
80 *Ibid.*, p 22.
81 Rule 59 of the UN Rules. See further above.
82 Department of Education and Science, *Care Inspection Report: Oberstown Girls School*, p. 23.
83 *Ibid.*, p. 26.
84 *Ibid.*, p. 10.
85 *Ibid.*, p. 14.
86 *Ibid.*, p. 15.
87 *Ibid.*
88 *Ibid.*
89 *Child Protection and Welfare Procedures and Guidelines for the Children Detention Schools 2002.*
90 Department of Education and Science, *Care Inspection Report: Oberstown Girls School*, pp. 12-13.
91 *Ibid.*, p. 20.
92 *Ibid.*, p. 7.
93 *Ibid.*, p. 24.
94 Special Residential Services Board, *Annual Report 2004*, p. 19.
95 Department of Education and Science, Care *Inspection Report: Finglas Child and Adolescent Centre,* July 2002 available at www.education.ie (18 January 2006).
96 *Ibid.*, pp. 12–13.
97 *Ibid.*, p. 14.
98 *Ibid.*
99 *Ibid.*, p. 15.
100 *Ibid.*, pp. 16–17.
101 *Ibid.*, p. 33.
102 *Ibid.*, p. 35.
103 *Ibid.*, pp. 37–8.
104 *Ibid.*, p. 44.
105 *Ibid.*, pp. 47–8.
106 *Ibid.*, p. 50.
107 *Ibid.*, p. 57.
108 *Ibid.*, p. 58.
109 *Ibid.*, p. 60.
110 *Ibid.*
111 *A Review of Finglas Child and Adolescent Centre* by Michael Donnellan, 29 April 2004.
112 Press Release 19 May, 2004 – Minister of State at the Department of Education and Science, Brian Lenihan T.D., releases review of the operation of Finglas Child and Adolescent Centre. The 2002 Inspection Report had recommended that capacity be reduced from 25 beds to 18 through the amalgamation of the two Units.
113 Department of Education and Science, *Care Inspection Report: Finglas Child and Adolescent Centre* (Dublin: Department of Education and Science, 2006) p. 4.

114 *Ibid.*, pp. 8–9.
115 Special Residential Services Board, *Annual Report 2004*, p. 19.
116 See Oberstown.com (accessed 5 January 2006).
117 See O'Connor, M.E., 'What works with Juvenile Offenders?' Paper delivered to a conference on *Children, Young People and Crime in Britain and Ireland From Exclusion to Inclusion – 1998, Scotland* available at www.scotland.gov.uk (accessed 5 January 2006).
118 *Ibid.*
119 Department of Education and Science, *Care Inspection Report: Oberstown Boys School*, pp. 17–18.
120 *Ibid.*, pp. 27–8.
121 Oberstown Boys School, *Young Person's Guide to OBS*, 2002, available at oberstown.com (accessed 3 January 2006). See also the comments of the Inspection Team, Department of Education and Science: *Core Inspection Report: Oberstown Boys School*, p. 17.
122 Rule 67, UN Rules for the Protection of Juveniles Deprived of their Liberty.
123 *Ibid.*, Rule 47.
124 Department of Education and Science, *Care Inspection Report: Oberstown Boys School*, p. 10.
125 Ibid., pp. 27–8.
126 *Outcomes 2002 Trinity House Step-Down Unit* available at www.trinityhouseschool.ie (accessed 6 January 2006). p. 3.
127 Special Residential Service Board, *Annual Report 2004*, p. 19.
128 See further Trinity House School *Annual Report 2004*, p. 5, available at www.trinityhouseschool.ie (accessed 6 January 2006).
129 CPT/Inf (2003) 36 *Report to the Government of Ireland on the visit to Ireland carried out by the European Committee for the Prevention of Torture and Inhuman or Degrading Treatment or Punishment (CPT) from 20 to 28 May 2002.*
130 Further details of the regime which operates in Trinity House and its policies, procedures and other documentation can be found on its website at www.trinityhouseschool.ie.
131 CPT *Report to the Government of Ireland*, p. 42, and Department of Education and Science, *Care Inspection Report*, *Trinity House School*, pp. 22–4.
132 Trinity House School *Annual Report 2004*, p. 4, available at www.trinityhouseschool.ie (accessed 16 January 2006).
133 CPT *Report to the Government of Ireland.*
134 Trinity House School, *Outcomes 2003*, available at www.trinityhouseschool.ie (accessed 16 January 2006) where the majority of those interviewed on release rated the school's buildings, etc. 'good' or 'excellent', p. 6.
135 See Trinity House School, *Outcomes 2004*, available at www.trinityhouseschool.ie (accessed 16 January 2006), p. 16.
136 Three young people were reported to be in residential care, two were reported as homeless and one had returned to Trinity House. *Ibid.*

137 Trinity House School *Outcomes 2002*, p. 5. This highlights rates from 2001 when the step-down unit was first established.
138 Thirteen out of the sixteen young people had re-offended by the time of the second exit interview (after six months) and that rose to fifteen out of sixteen young people involved in the third exit interviews (after 12 months). *Ibid.*
139 Trinity House School, *Outcomes 2003*, p. 10.
140 Trinity House School, *Outcomes 2002,* p. 4 (available at www.trinityhouseschool.ie (accessed 16 January 2006).
141 *Ibid.,* pp. 11–13.
142 See further Chapter Six above.
143 Young people interviewed as part of the outreach work at Trinity House recorded very low levels of involvement with the Probation and Welfare Service on release. See Trinity House School, *Outcomes 2002*, p. 5. Most young people reported relying on family and friends for support. See also the recommendation of the Inspection Team that the practice of releasing young people on licence under the Children Act 1908 be considered, p. 20.
144 See further Chapter Six.
145 Trinity House School, *Annual Report 2004*, p. 6.
146 Department of Education and Science, *Care Inspection Report*, *Trinity House School*, p. 25.
147 *Ibid.*
148 *Ibid.,* p. 4.
149 CPT *Report to the Government of Ireland,* p. 43.
150 Department of Education and Science, *Care Inspection Report: Trinity House School*, pp. 12–4.
151 The school itself reported in 2004 that a comprehensive induction booklet was being drawn up. Trinity House School, *Annual Report 2004,* p. 6.
152 CPT *Report to the Government of Ireland,* p. 44.
153 Trinity House School, *Outcomes 2003*, p. 7.
154 Trinity House School, *Outcomes 2002*, p. 4.
155 Department of Education and Science, *Care Inspection Report: Trinity House School*, p.17.
156 CPT *Report to the Government of Ireland*, p. 43.
157 CPT/Inf (2003) 37 *Response of the Government of Ireland to the Report of the CPT on its visit to Ireland from 20 to 28 May 2002*, p. 45.
158 CPT *Report to the Government*, p. 43.
159 *Residential Provision for Children*, 2002, p. 31.
160 The Board was established by Mary Hanafin, TD, Minister for Education and Science, on an interim basis on 7 April 2000.
161 Special Residential Services Board *Annual Report 2004*, pp. 6 and 17.
162 *Review of Admission Criteria and Processes for Special Care*, (Special Residential Services Board, September 2005) available at www.srsb.ie (last accessed 4 January 2006).

163 *The impact of placement in special care unit settings on the wellbeing of young people and their families* (Special Residential Services Board, 2004) available at www.srsb.ie (accessed 4 January 2006).

164 *Definition and Usage of High Support in Ireland* (Special Residential Services Board, 2003) available at www.srsb.ie (accessed 4 January 2006).

165 *Youth Justice Review*, 2005, p. 39. The Review acknowledged that 'in the context of the team's proposals some of the current responsibilities of the SRSB which would overlap with the role of the Youth Justice Service would require to be addressed. The proposed advances in the delivery of services in both youth justice and special care should warrant an examination of the future role of the SRSB', p.44.

166 When inspected in 2003, over one-quarter of the population was under 18 years. See Inspector of Prisons and Places of Detention, *Report on Inspection of Fort Mitchel Prison commencing the 15th September 2003 to 19th September 2003* (Department of Justice, Equality and Law Reform, 2004), p.8 available at www.justice.ie (accessed 5 January 2006).

167 Probation Officers in St. Patrick's told the Inspector that 'the closure of other places of detention has resulted in many inmates being subjected to the added pressure of being incarcerated far from home'. Inspector of Prisons, *St. Patrick's Institution 2004-2005*, p. 50.

168 See Kilkelly, U., *The Children's Court: A Children's Rights Audit* (Cork, 2005), p. 67

169 Inspector of Prisons, *Report on Inspection of Fort Mitchel Prison*, pp. 32–3.

170 Irish Prison Service *Annual Report 2003* (Dublin: Stationery Office, 2004) p. 48.

171 See further below.

172 See Press Release of the Minister for Justice, Equality and Law Reform, Mr Michael McDowell, TD, 2 January 2004 on www.justice.ie (accessed 2 January 2006).

173 St. Patrick's Visiting Committee, *Annual Report 2003*, p. 7.

174 For an excellent legal analysis of this category of young person see Walsh, D. *Juvenile Justice*, paras 7-07-7-14, pp 119-122.

175 According to an inspection of the prison in 2004, the building was complete but unstaffed due to industrial relations. Irish Prisons Inspectorate, *Cloverhill Prison: Revisit Inspection of Cloverhill 20 and 21 January 2004*, p.12. See also Clover Hill Visiting Committee Annual Reports 2003 and 2004. Irish Prisons Inspectorate, *Cloverhill Prison: Cloverhill Inspection 5, 6, 7 November and 17 December 2002*, p. 7.

176 Kilkelly, U., *Children's Court: A Children's Rights Audit*, p. 67.

177 See the Annual Reports of the Irish Prison Service 1999–2000 and 2004.

178 Inspector of Prisons and Places of Detention, *Report of the Inspection of St. Patrick's Institution 2004–2005*, p.27.

179 In November 2004, 78 of a possible 199 persons detained were under 18 years. Parliamentary Question 24525/05 to the Minister for Education and Science, 28 September 2005.

180 Correspondence from Irish Prison Service, 11 January 2006.
181 *Ibid.*
182 Walsh, D., *Juvenile Justice*, p. 256.
183 See, for example, the positive comments of the Visiting Committee in 2003 and 2004.
184 *The Report of the Committee of Inquiry into the Penal System* (Dublin: Stationery Office, 1985) in Walsh, D. *Juvenile Justice*, p. 483.
185 For example, football is restricted in the yards to certain nominated days to allow all prisoners whether playing football or not to have access to the yard. St. Patrick's Visiting Committee Annual Report 2004, p. 3
186 Irish Prison Service *Annual Report 1999-2000*, (Dublin: the Stationery Office, 2002) p. 38.
187 St. Patrick's Visiting Committee Annual Report 2003, pp. 2–3.
188 Irish Prison Service *Annual Report 2004*, (Dublin: the Stationery Office, 2005) p. 62.
189 Inspector of Prisons, *St. Patrick's Institution 2004–2005,* p. 42
190 *Ibid.,* pp. 4–5.
191 *Ibid.,* pp. 12–25.
192 *Ibid.,* pp. 48–50.
193 Irish Prison Service, *Annual Report 2004*, p. 62.
194 The significance of this number was downplayed by the Head Teachers interviewed by the Inspector of Prisons in 2004. *Ibid.,* p. 55.
195 The rate was 63 per cent in 2002, 47 per cent in 2003 and 49 per cent in 2004. See Annual Reports p. 58, p. 26 and p. 23 respectively.
196 Inspector of Prisons, *St. Patrick's Institution 2004-2005,* p. 21.
197 *Ibid.,* p. 71.
198 *Ibid.,* p. 5 and St. Patrick's Visiting Committee Annual Report 2003, p. 5.
199 According to the Head Teachers at St. Patrick's. See Inspector of Prisons, *St. Patrick's Institution 2004–2005,* p. 55.
200 *Ibid.,* pp. 55–6.
201 *Ibid.,* p. 72.
202 *Report on the Youth Justice Review,* p. 7.
203 St. Patrick's Visiting Committee Annual Report 2004, p. 5. See also Inspector of Prisons, *St. Patrick's Institution 2004–2005,* p. 22 where the failure to implement the project was listed as an unimplemented element of the Business Plan. According to the Inspector, demarcation between psychologists, probation and welfare service and other services had been blamed for the partial collapse of the CONNECT programme. *Ibid.,* p. 57.
204 In 2004, young people participated in accredited courses on Food Hygiene (18) and unaccredited ones on Guitar (41), Cookery (63), Introduction to Computers (56) and Modular Art (44). Correspondence from the Irish Prisons Service, 11 January 2006.
205 Hanlon, N., and Riley, L., *The Impact of Placement in Special Care Unit Settings on the Wellbeing of Young People and their Families* p. 79.
206 Lennon, S., *St. Patrick's Institution*, paper delivered to the UCC Law Society Annual Conference, Cork, November 2004.

207 See further Kilkelly, U., *The Right to Respect for Private and Family Life: A Guide to the implementation of Article 8 of the European Convention on Human Rights*. See also Kilkelly, U., et al., *In Our Care*, pp. 129–40.

208 Inspector of Prisons, *St. Patrick's Institution 2004–2005,* p. 38

209 Inspector of Prisons, *St. Patrick's Institution 2004–2005,* p. 9. See also *The Observer*, 12 September 2004.

210 Assaults between the young people were reported in both 2003 and 2004 by the Visiting Committee. See, for example, St. Patrick's Visiting Committee Annual Report 2003, pp. 6-7. Young people spoken to by the Inspector of Prisons also informed him of the bullying that takes place over drugs. Inspector of Prisons, *St. Patrick's Institution 2004–2005,* p. 65.

211 *Ibid.,* pp. 9–10.

212 The Governor's response to these allegations when they were raised by the Inspector of Prisons was to promise to investigate them if he were provided with the names of those allegedly involved. Inspector of Prisons, *St. Patrick's Institution 2004–2005*, p. 11.

213 This was raised by two solicitors who met with the Inspector of Prisons and the Human Rights Commission in 2005 to discuss this problem. *Ibid.,* pp. 52–5. See also, Kilkelly, U., *The Children's Court: A Children's Rights Audit*, p. 67.

214 Lally, C., 'Rape-gang members segregated after jail attack' *Irish Times,* 18 December 2004.

215 The 'C' wing is a self-sufficient wing of St. Patrick's with its own recreation area, exercise yard, classrooms and strip cell. Inspector of Prisons, *St. Patrick's Institution 2004–2005*, p. 37.

216 Inspector of Prisons, *St. Patrick's Institution 2004–2005*, pp. 12–13.

217 *Ibid.,* p. 18.

218 Irish Prison Service *Annual Report 2004*, p. 63.

219 Irish Prison Service *Annual Report* 2003, (Dublin: Stationery Office, 2004) p. 61. In this regard, Ireland has not had the alarming number of suspicious deaths in detention experienced in the United Kingdom. See Goldson, B., and Coles, D., *In the care of the state? Child deaths in penal custody in England and Wales* (London: Inquest, 2005).

220 *Ibid.,* p. 76.

221 *Ibid.*

222 Irish Prison Service *Annual Report*, 1999–2000, p. 16.

223 *Ibid.,* p. 7. See also St. Patrick's Visiting Committee Annual Report 2004, p. 1. A total of 376 prisoners were accommodated on the Drug Free Unit in 2004. Correspondence from Irish Prison Service, 11 January 2006

224 210 young people participated in this programme in 2004. Irish Prison Service *Annual Report,* 2004, p. 63.

225 Inspector of Prisons, *St. Patrick's Institution 2004–2005,* p. 34.

226 Probation Officers in St. Patrick's told the Inspector that 'the closure of other places of detention has resulted in many inmates being subjected to the added pressure of being incarcerated far from home'. Inspector of

Prisons, *St. Patrick's Institution 2004-2005*, p. 50.

227 The CPT had criticised the Government's decision to use this facility for such young children. The Government's responded by deciding not to use the unit afterall. See CPT, *Report on Ireland*, p. 47 and the Government's Response, p. 44. See also the comments of the Inspector of Prisons, *ibid.*, p. 73.

228 Inspector of Prisons, *First Annual Report*, p. 79.

229 Irish Prisons Service, *Annual Report 2003*, (Dublin: Stationery Office, 2004), p. 5.

230 Article 10 of the International Covenant on Civil and Political Rights and Article 37 of the Convention on the Rights of the Child. While the government entered a reservation to the former provision, it made no reservation when ratifying the latter.

231 Irish Prisons Inspectorate, *Cloverhill Prison: Cloverhill Inspection 5, 6, 7 November and 17 December 2002*, p. 5. A revisit inspection in 2004 noted that this did not take place unless requested by brothers. See Irish Prisons Inspectorate, *Cloverhill Prison: Revisit Inspection of Cloverhill 20 and 21 January 2004*, p. 11.

232 O'Brien, C. '147 juveniles placed in adult prisons' *Irish Times*, October 18, 2005.

233 Section 227(1)(b). In any event, the SRSB is to lose this role in light of recent reform. See also above.

234 Retired High Court Judge Dermot Kinlen was appointed to the position for a five year period by order of the Minister for Justice, Equality and Law Reform on 21 February 2002. The terms of reference of the office is to inspect and report to the Minister on places of detention under the aegis of the Department of Justice, Equality and Law Reform, report in particular on conditions in those institutions and the regimes in place for prisoners, investigate and report on any specific issue referred to the Inspectorate by the Minister and submit an annual report on the activities of the Inspectorate. See *First Annual Report of the Inspector of Prisons and Places of Detention for the Year 2002–2003*, p. 12 available at www.justice.ie (accessed 4 January 2006).

235 Martin, F., 'The Ombudsman For Children: An Analysis of the Strengths And Weaknesses of the Irish Model' 52(1) *Administration* (Spring 2004) 46–68, pp. 57–70.

236 Court of Criminal Appeal, 13 July 1998.

237 See McDermott, P.A., *Prison Law* (Dublin: Round Hall, 2000), p. 427.

238 Importantly inspections of the schools under the Children Act 1908 have been carried out within the framework of the *Standards and Criteria* and 'in the spirit' of the relevant provisions of the 2001 Act. See, for example, Department of Education and Science, *Care Inspection Report: Oberstown Girls School*, p. 5.

239 Regulation 9, St. Patrick's Institution Regulations, 1960.

240 First Annual Report of the Inspector of Prisons and Places of Detention for the Year 2002–2003, p. 61.

241 St. Patrick's Institution Visiting Committee Annual Report, 2004, p. 2.

242 Committee on the Rights of the Child, *General Measures of Implementation of the Convention on the Rights of the Child*, CRC/GC/2004/5, available at www.ohchr.org (accessed 17 January 2006).

243 See, for example, Department of Education and Science, *Care Inspection Report: Finglas Child and Adolescent Centre*, p. 15.

244 St. Patrick's Institution, *Information for Persons in Custody,* no date. This was also the view expressed by Mary Hanafin, T.D. who, in defence of this exclusion in the Ombudsman for Children Act 2002, highlighted children's right to apply to the courts, the European Court of Human Rights and the Committee for the Prevention of Torture for a remedy. *Seanad Debates*, Minister Hanafin, Col 710 (7 March 2002). Also, *Dáil Debates* Cols 1047–59.

245 This exclusion does not currently apply to children in Children Detention Schools but will, under the Children Act 2001 when Part 10 is commenced. See further Martin, F. 'The Ombudsman for Children: An Analysis of the Strengths and Weaknesses of the Irish Model', p. 58.

246 Concluding Observations of the Committee on the Rights of the Child: Ireland, CRC/C/15/. 85, paras. 9 and 29. See also Rule 57 of the Riyadh Guidelines, which requires consideration to be given to setting up an independent body with a remit to protect the rights of children including their referral to appropriate services. Rule 57 also recommends that this body be responsible for overseeing the implementation of international standards in this area. The UN Guidelines for the Prevention of Juvenile Delinquency (the Riyadh Guidelines) were adopted by General Assembly Resolution 45/112 14 December 1990 available at www.ohchr.org (accessed 12 January 2006).

247 See also Ombudsman for Children *Annual Report 2005* (Dublin: OCO, 2005), pp. 22–3.

248 See further Kilkelly, U., 'Children in Detention Schools: Learning from International Best Practice'.

Conclusion

Reform of Youth Justice in line with International Standards

This monograph undertook the challenging task of considering the extent to which the Irish youth justice system operates in line with international standards. As the Introduction explains, the benchmarks against which the Irish youth justice system was measured here consist of a variety of instruments from international law which represent consensus on issues of children's rights and youth justice. In general, it is accepted that all children in conflict with the law must be treated in an age-appropriate manner and with due respect for their rights and welfare. Where possible, and without undermining their rights, children should be diverted from the criminal justice system in recognition of the fact that offending among the young is a passing phase and any intervention should avoid labelling or causing other harm to the child. When diversion is not possible or appropriate, and children are sent before a court, they have the right to understand and participate in the criminal process and to receive a sentence proportionate to their circumstances and to their offence. A wide range of non-custodial measures must be available to ensure that detention is used as a last resort. Where it is the only appropriate sanction, children have the right to have their health and educational needs met, to maintain contact with family and to work on offending behaviour in preparation for successful reintegration into society on release. The international standards also require a multi-agency and holistic response to problems of offending, and emphasise the need for adequate systems of data collection and on-going monitoring and review to be put in place to ensure the system is up to date. All those working with children must receive appropriate training, including on children's rights, and children themselves must be provided with appropriate information and access to independent and effective complaints mechanisms in all areas of the system.

In applying these standards, the book first considered the crucial issue of what we know about young people who break the law in Ireland, and why we know so little, and Chapter Two then undertook a critical analysis of the legal framework of the youth justice system. The approach taken then was to deal separately with the different elements of the youth justice system: diversion; treatment by An Garda Síochána, the trial of young people, sentencing by the courts, and detention. Each chapter considered the relevant international standards and questioned how Ireland performs in meeting those commitments. While each chapter contains its own conclusions and makes recommendations as to how Irish law and practice can become more closely aligned with international standards and best practice in other jurisdictions, a number of points fall to be made in conclusion.

One of the advantages of analysing the different elements of the system in this way is that it is possible to view, in isolation, which elements of it are compatible or incompatible with international standards. This is certainly the case with the Garda Diversion Programme, which, in principle at least, meets many of the objectives set by the international standards. In particular, its high rate of success, even if it were exaggerated, makes it clear that for many young people the only contact they have with the criminal justice system is with a Juvenile Liaison Officer. They are being effectively diverted from the courts and prosecution in large numbers, if not from the entire criminal justice system itself. Questions remain about the criteria used for admission purposes, the extent to which the rights of young people in the Programme are fully protected, and the degree to which it is subjected to external scrutiny, but these elements should not take away from the overall conclusion that as a diversionary scheme it works in the interests of the young people who are engaged in it.

The gap between theory and practice is apparent with respect to the treatment of children by An Garda Síochána. Part 6 of the Children Act contains many laudable provisions, but concerns exist as to their implementation in practice. Relations between An Garda Síochána and young people have not been subjected to any rigorous analysis. What data exist are not particularly positive, although much depends on the individual experience. According to international standards, training on children's rights and youth justice, and the development of a special youth division within An Garda Síochána, would help address these issues.

Another positive element of the youth justice system lies at the other extreme. Children Detention Schools (CDS) are far less celebrated in their success than the Garda Programme. This may or may not be due to the lack of data supporting the 'success' of their work, although any attempt to apply a simplistic model such as re-offending rates to those released from CDS will fail to do justice to the extremely challenging nature of their work. The rights of children detained in CDS are, for the most part, well protected in a secure care environment with an educational focus while they are looked after by care staff who are highly trained and motivated. Clearly there is room for improvement here too, with regard to improving children's involvement in their case conferences, access to effective complaints mechanisms and advocacy within the schools, and integrating educational and health services to ensure that young people's rights are guaranteed in these areas. Dedicated and individualised work on offending behaviour must also become a priority. Overall, however, CDS stand out as an area where comparison with international standards has many positive conclusions, despite the law and policy vacuum in which they operate.

It is the arbitrary factor of age at the time of conviction that determines whether young people spend time in the relatively positive environment of a Children Detention School, where they have the opportunity to address their welfare needs, their educational difficulties and their offending behaviour, or alternatively, are sent to the punitive environment of St Patrick's Institution. Apart from the lack of educational and vocational provision, the institutional nature of St Patrick's is its most disturbing feature. Requiring sixteen year-olds to eat meals in their cells, shower just twice a week and wear prison-allocated clothing must frustrate any rehabilitative effect not to mention their damaging impact on the morale and rights of the young people themselves. The absence of a care or an educational ethos, prevalence of drugs and bullying, and other worrying elements about the regime mean that serious questions must be asked about the capacity of St. Patrick's to operate in a manner that protects and promotes the rights of young people in line with our international obligations. Comparison with the international standards thus serves to fuel rather than quell this anxiety and the fact that this situation has been allowed to continue and effectively deteriorate over the last two decades at least makes the decision to transfer responsibility for the CDS to the Department of Justice, Equality and Law Reform very worrying indeed.

The Children Court, too, acts as a bit of a lottery. Application of international standards to both the court process and the possible ways in which individual cases can be resolved does not produce a particularly positive result. To a large extent, the Children Court reflects the difficulties elsewhere in the system – failure to engage young people, problems of delay and poor organisation/management and inadequate services, which are poorly co-ordinated. But, in the case of the Court, the stakes are very high: lack of meaningful sanctions means that the behaviour of young people is not addressed in a structured way. Impunity results for some other young people, who pick up a few charges too many or get involved in more serious crime, reach the last resort of detention more quickly than international standards allow. By then, many of them are over 16 years of age and St. Patrick's is the only option. The cycle continues, and the impact of failure to implement the range of community sanctions set out in the Children Act is devastatingly clear.

These problems notwithstanding, it is clear that concern for the rights and welfare of young people is evident among many individuals – those working as judges, solicitors, Gardaí, Probation Officers, care workers and others. But, within the current system, they can only use this to help individual young people. An approach which helps many requires effective administrative and management structures to implement the commitment to the principles of youth justice; the lack of these in the current system is what appears to frustrate its operation in line with international standards.

In addition to a lack of top-down approaches, there is an almost complete absence of a bottom-up approach in terms of involving young people in the process. The marginalisation of young people from the process appears endemic despite some modest initiatives at different points in the system. It is reflected in the failure to provide young people with complete and age-appropriate information at every stage and the lack of appropriate and effective complaints mechanisms throughout. This is mandated at a political level by the exclusion of these children from the complaints mandate of the Ombudsman for Children, notwithstanding that no mechanism acts as a meaningful or effective alternative. The lack of joined-up thinking is evident here also. The National Children's Strategy made a commitment in 2000 to listen to children but that appears to only apply to those who are not in conflict with the law. The failure to consult children and young people in a structured way in the recent review of the youth justice system is illustrative of that.

The book aims to draw together many existing sources for the first time and to subject them to an original analysis based on international guidance. Despite its novel approach, its conclusions are not new. The Irish youth justice system, to the extent that one exists, is fragmented and at times chaotic. The absence of individual departmental responsibility has resulted in a serious lack of accountability for the area of youth justice as a whole and individual parts of the system are in crisis making a joined-up approach virtually impossible to implement. The system has operated in the almost total absence of policy for several decades. The system lacks leadership in strategic and operational terms and its lack of stated objectives allows the agencies involved to take different directions. Despite the best efforts of many individuals, young people who come into conflict with the law drift through the system with little or no check on their offending. There is little the Children Court, the Probation and Welfare Service or the Detention Schools can do for them by the time they reach their door. What information is available suggests clearly that the current system is failing many young people insofar as it is ineffective at addressing their offending behaviour and its causes. On this macro level – as on the micro-level referred to throughout – it is wholly out of line with international standards.

The Children Act 2001 was intended as a blueprint for children in conflict with the law. It places the Garda Diversion Programme on a statutory basis and the scope and success of this Programme continue to be documented. The novel contribution of the Act to the youth justice system is to introduce the family conference into the statutory framework of the youth justice system. Implementation of these provisions has only just begun and, while their potential to support families to prevent young people from re-offending is clear, outcomes are undocumented as yet. There is a need for continuing monitoring and research in this area to ensure that the experiences and best practice of all the agencies involved is shared throughout the system. Real opportunities are presented too by the numerous non-custodial and community sanctions in the Act, although these provisions have yet to be fully implemented. The Government's decision to undertake substantial amendment of the Act before it is fully in force is unwise, and in some respects represents a significant rolling back on commitments made to the Committee on the Rights of the Child in 1998 on the age of criminal responsibility in particular. The introduction of Anti-Social Behaviour Orders, mirroring developments in the UK, is a worrying trend that risks bringing more young people into the damaging arena of the criminal justice system. Bringing responsibility for detention together under the remit of the Department of Justice, Equality and Law Reform, while sensible, will work to reduce offending only if the good work of the Children Detention Schools, and not the containment policies of St Patrick's Institution, is the standard replicated throughout.

The Youth Justice Review, published in December 2005, if implemented, has the potential to radically change the landscape of youth justice in Ireland. While many of its conclusions are similar to the reports of its predecessors, the pragmatic nature of some of its recommendations means that it may finally succeed where others have failed in putting structure on the administration of youth justice in Ireland. The willingness of the Review team to engage with all those with a stake in the interests of young offenders and the administration of youth justice was welcome and must continue through the implementation of its recommendations.

The key recommendation of the Review is the establishment of a Youth Justice Service within the Department of Justice, Equality and Law Reform. Leaving aside objections to the home of the Service, which is to be reviewed after five years – an independent statutory office would have been preferable – the Service can play a considerable role in ensuring the development of leadership, infrastructure and management to reshape, re-organise and refocus the youth justice system. Much will depend on what standards the Service applies to underpin this work. As this book makes clear, a persuasive case can be made for the application of international standards on youth justice in this context. In practical terms, these standards, many of which constitute legal obligations, offer considerable guidance. In terms of leadership, they represent well-established consensus on the values of youth justice that should inform common and strategic decision-making within the system. In particular, it is submitted, the following principles should form the basis for the Service in the fulfilment of all of its functions. In particular, they must inform the youth justice strategy being drafted by the Service, as well as its functions in the area of policy development and the co-ordination of services:

- the best interests of young people must be a primary concern for all agencies of the youth justice system;
- children in conflict with the law must be treated in an age-appropriate manner and be involved in decisions made about their care and treatment;
- children in conflict with the law have the same rights as other children including the right to protection, to education, to health care and to development;
- detention, including on remand, must be used only as a measure of last resort, when there are no suitable alternatives to custody, and for the shortest appropriate period of time.

Apart from the opportunity to undertake an explicit commitment to these fundamental principles of youth justice, which should represent the core values of the youth justice system, the youth justice strategy should also attempt to incorporate these values into a common statement of aims. Drawing on international standards for this purpose will encourage consensus among all those working in the area. In terms of a core aim, the prevention of offending by young people is too simplistic, it is submitted. Instead, a more ambitious statement with a rights-focus is required to fully articulate the values of a progressive youth justice system in line with a commitment to the principles set out above.

In terms of process, the drafting of the youth justice strategy is an important opportunity to engage those working in all areas of the youth justice system at central but especially at local level. Those working on the ground, particularly in local communities, must be involved. The views of young people both within and having left the system must be taken into account, in line with the National Children's Strategy to which it is to be linked. The expertise and the experience of non-governmental and academic sectors must also play a role. Importantly, it is submitted, the Service must draft a strategy for the Irish youth justice system and this is where the international standards, which are capable of adaptation to the Irish context, can provide important neutral guidance. The implementation of the youth justice strategy will provide further opportunity for the guidance of international standards to be put into practice, and also to engage with young people, and those working in all areas of the system. Research of this process should be encouraged and facilitated and on-going proofing of the extent to which the strategy is fulfilling international standards of youth justice is vital.

Nothing short of a radical root and branch overhaul of the system is required to put in place a modern system capable of delivering justice to young people in Ireland in a fair and expeditious manner. In this regard it is disappointing that there are areas of the system that the Review did not address, including the necessary overhaul of the courts. This must be undertaken as a matter of urgency. The enormity of the task ahead for the Youth Justice Service is thus not to be underestimated. Reliance on the international standards to guide its work, especially in the development of the core values around which consensus will be generated and the standards used to implement those values, should ease the process. Throughout, those appointed to the

Service and charged with its functions must be mindful that the missed opportunities of recent years do not just represent policy failure; they represent a continued failure to address the offending of many young people, who, as a result, are now adults in the criminal justice system with problem children of their own. The opportunity for radical reform has presented itself once again: the problems have been identified, the solutions proposed, the administrative structures are being put in place and the resources are available to implement them. A commitment to the values of youth justice in theory as well as in practice is the only other ingredient required to ensure that another generation of young offenders will not be lost to themselves, to their families and to their communities. Rough lives, tough justice indeed.

Bibliography

Allen, C., Crowe, I., & Cavadino, M., *Evaluation of the Youth Court Demonstration Project*, Home Office Research Study 214 (London: Stationery Office, 2000).

Arthur, R., 'Preventing Youth Crime – The Role of the Child Care Act 1991 – Part 1, 9 *Irish Law Times* (2003), pp. 134–55.

Arthur, R., 'Punishing Parents for the Crimes of their Children', 44(3) *The Howard Journal of Criminal Justice* (July 2005), pp. 233–53.

Arteaga, J. A., 'Juvenile (in)Justice: Congressional Attempts to abrogate the procedural rights of juvenile defendants', 102(4) *Columbia Law Review* (May 2002), pp. 1051–88.

Bala, N., 'The Youth Criminal Justice Act: Diversion, Conferencing, and Extrajudicial Measures for Adolescent Offenders', 40 *Alberta Law Review* (2003), p. 991.

Bala, N. et al, (eds) *Juvenile Justice Systems An International Comparison of Problems and Solutions* (Toronto: Thompson Educational Publishing, 2002).

Bateman, T., 'Reducing Child Imprisonment: A Systematic Challenge', *Youth Justice* 5(2) (October 2005), 91–105.

Bateman, T. and Pitts, J. (eds), *The RHB Companion to Youth Justice* (Lyme Regis: Russell House Publishing, 2005).

Bowden, M., and Higgins, L., *The Impact and Effectiveness of the Garda Special Projects* (Dublin: Department of Justice, Equality and Law Reform, 2000).

Bowe, J., *Literature Review & System Review* (Dublin: IASD, July 2005).

Brogan, D., *Anti-Social Behaviour Orders An assessment of*

current management information systems and the scale of Anti-Social Behaviour Order breaches resulting in custody (London: Youth Justice Board, 2005).

Breaking Through, *Submission to the Department of Justice, Equality and Law Reform* (November 2004).

Brayne, 'Are we demonising or protecting children?' *New Law Journal* (9 August 2002), p. 1253.

Browne, V., 'The Making of Another Cover-up', *Village Magazine (*17 September, 2005).

Browne, V., 'Letter from McDowell to Rossiters' Solicitor', *Village Magazine* (1 July 2005).

Browne, V., 'Too Little Very Late', *Village Magazine* (1 July 2005).

Browne, V., 'Tracing the Steps of Brian Rossiter's last Day' *Village Magazine* (1 July 2005).

Burney, E., 'Still the wrong approach', 23(1) *Howard League Magazine* (February 2005) p. 5.

Centre for Social and Educational Research DIT *Study of Participants in Garda Special Projects* (Dublin: Department of Justice, Equality and Law Reform, October 2001).

Children's Rights Alliance for England, *Rethinking Child Imprisonment: A Report on Young Offender Institutions*, (London: CRAE, 2002).

Commission on Crime Prevention and Social Justice, *Restorative Justice Report of the Secretary General* (7 January 2002), E/CN.15/1002/5.

Comptroller and Auditor General, *Report on Value for Money Examination, The Department of Justice, Equality and Law Reform: The Probation and Welfare Service* (Dublin: the Stationery Office, 2004).

Courts Service, *The Criminal Jurisdiction of the Courts* (Dublin: The Stationery Office, 2003).

Cunneen, C., and White, R., *Juvenile Justice: Youth and Crime in Australia* (Melbourne: OUP, 2002).

The Children Bill, 1999 Papers from a seminar organised by the Children's Legal Centre (Dublin: Children's Legal Centre, 2000).

Dáil Select Committee on Crime, *Juvenile Crime – its Causes and its Remedies* (Dublin: Stationery Office, 1992).

Department of Education and Science, *Residential Provision for*

Children under the Auspices of the Department of Education and Science: A Preliminary Review (Department of Education and Science, 2002).

Department of Education and Science *Care Inspection Report: Oberstown Boys School* (Department of Education and Science, 2005).

Department of Education and Science, *Care Inspection Report: Trinity House School* (Dublin: Department of Education and Science, 2006).

Department of Education and Science, *Care Inspection Report Oberstown Girls School* (Department of Education and Science, 2004).

Department of Education and Science, *Care Inspection Report Finglas Child and Adolescent Centre* (Dublin: Department of Education and Science, 2006).

Department of Education and Science,*Care Inspection Report: St Joseph's, Ferryhouse, Clonmel* (Department of Education and Science, April 2004).

Department of Education and Science,*Care Inspection Report: Finglas Child and Adolescent Centre,* (Department of Education and Science, July 2002).

Donnellan, M., *A Review of Finglas Child and Adolescent Centre* (29 April 2004).

Doob, A.N. and Tonry, M. 'Varieties of Youth Justice', 31 *Crime and Justice* (2004) p. 120.

Dooley, R. and Corbett, M., 'Child Care, Juvenile Justice and the Children Act 2001', *Irish Youthwork Scene: A Journal for Youth Workers*, Issue 36 (Dublin: National Youth Federation, 2002) 4–6.

Ellison, G., 'Young People and the Royal Ulster Constabulary: A Survey of Inter-Communal Attitudes', 11(3/4), *Policing and Society* (2001) p. 321–6.

Farrington, D., *Understanding and Preventing Youth Crime* (York: Joseph Rowntree Foundation, 1996).

Feld, B., 'Will the Juvenile Court System Survive?: The Honest Politician's Guide to Juvenile Justice in the Twenty-first Century' 564, *The Annals of the American Academy of Social Science* (July 1999) pp. 10–25,

Fletcher, H., 'An analysis of the first six years of the use of ASBOs' (April 2005) at www.napo.org.

Goldson, B. (ed.), *The New Youth Justice* (Dorset: Russell House Publishing, 2000).

Goldson B., *Vulnerable Inside Children in secure and penal settings* (London: The Children's Society, 2002).

Goldson, B., 'Child Imprisonment: A Case for Abolition' 5(2) *Youth Justice* (October 2005) pp. 77–90.

Goldson, B., and Coles, D., *In the Care of the State? Child Deaths in Penal Custody in England and Wales* (London: Inquest, 2005).

Graham, J. and Bowling, B., *Young People and Crime: Research Study 145* (London: HMSO, 1995).

Green, S., 'Prosecutorial Waiver into Adult Criminal Court: A Conflict of Interests Violation Amounting to the States' Legislative Abrogation of Juveniles' Due Process Rights' 110 *Penn State Law Review* (2005) 233–81.

Guinchard, A., 'Fixing the Boundaries of the Concept of Crime: A Challenge for Human Rights' 54(3), *International and Comparative Law Quarterly* (2005) 719–34.

Hamilton, C., 'Anti-Social Behaviour Orders and the Presumption of Innocence' 23 *Irish Law Times* (2005) 215–21.

Hamilton, J., Radford, K., and Jarman, N., *Policing, Accountability and Young People* (Belfast: Institute for Conflict Research, 2004).

Hanafin, S., and Brooks, A.M., *Report on the Development of a National Set of Child Well-being Indicators in Ireland* (Dublin: National Children's Office, 2005).

Hanlon, N., and Riley, L., *The Impact of Placement in Special Care Unit Settings on the Wellbeing of Young People and their Families A Summary Report 2004* (Dublin: Special Residential Services Board, 2004).

Heffernan, L., (ed.) *Human Rights: A European Perspective* (Dublin: Round Hall, 1994).

Hodgson, P., and Webb, D., 'Young People, Crime and Social Exclusion: A Case of Some Surprises' 44(1), *Howard Journal of Criminal Justice* (2005), 12–28.

Hopkins Burke, R., and Morrill, R., 'Anti-Social Behaviour Orders: An Infringement of the Human Rights Act 1998?' 11(2), *Nottingham Law Journal* (2002) pp. 1–16.

Howard, N., 'Children Detention Schools: the impact of s 158'

Special Residential Services Board Bulletin (Summer 2005), p. 3.

Home Office, *No More Excuses: a new approach to tackling youth crime in England and Wales* (London: Stationery Office, 1997).

Horowitz, M.A., 'Kids who kill: a critique of the American Legal System deals with Juveniles who commit Homicide' 63(3) *Law and Contemporary Problems* (Summer 2000), 133–77.

'Include Youth', Paper submitted to the UN Committee on the Rights of the Child for its General Day of Discussion on 'Children without Parental Care' (2005).

Ionann Management Consultants, *Human Rights Audit of the Garda Síochána* (June 2004).

Irish Association for the Study of Delinquency, *Children Act 2001 Effective Family Conferencing: The Challenges and Implications for Ireland in the New Legal Environment*, Sixth Annual Conference, Dublin, 9 October 2003 (IASD: Dublin, 2004).

Inspector of Prisons and Places of Detention, *St Patrick's Institution Inspection: 15th–19th November 2004.*

Inspector of Prisons and Places of Detention, *Report on Inspection of Fort Mitchel Prison commencing the 15th September 2003 to 19th September 2003* (Department of Justice, Equality and Law Reform, 2004).

Irish Prisons Inspectorate, *Cloverhill Prison: Revisit Inspection of Cloverhill 20 and 21 January 2004.*

Irish Prison Service *Annual Report 2003* (Dublin: Stationery Office, 2004).

Junger-Tas, J., 'Youth Justice in the Netherlands' 31 *Crime and Justice* (2004) 293–347.

Kilkelly, U., *The Child and the ECHR* (Aldershot: Ashgate, 1999).

Kilkelly, U., 'The Human Rights Act: Implications for the Trial and Detention of Young People' 51(3) *Northern Ireland Legal Quarterly* (2000) 466–80.

Kilkelly, U., *The Right to Respect for Private and Family Life: A Guide to the implementation of Article 8 of the European Convention on Human Rights*: Human Rights Handbooks, No. 1 (Strasbourg: Council of Europe, 2001).

Kilkelly, U., et al., *In Our Care, Promoting the Rights of*

Children in Custody (Belfast: Northern Ireland Human Rights Commission, 2002).
Kilkelly, U., '*DG* v *Ireland*: Protecting the rights of children at risk – lazy government and unruly courts', 22 *Dublin University Law Journal* (2002) pp. 268–91.
Kilkelly, U., 'Children in Detention Schools: Learning from International Best Practice' 13(2), *Irish Journal of Criminal Law* (2003), pp. 15–19.
Kilkelly, U., (ed.) *ECHR and Irish Law* (Bristol: Jordans, 2004).
Kilkelly, U., *The Children's Court: A Children's Rights Audit* (Cork, 2005).
Kilkelly, U., et al., *The Rights of Children in Northern Ireland* (Belfast: NICCY, 2005).
Law Reform Committee, *Rights-based Child Law: The Case for Reform – Part 1* (Dublin: Law Society, 2005).
Law Society, *Submissions on the Children Bill 1999* (Dublin: Law Society, 1999).
McDermott, P.A., *Prison Law* (Dublin: Round Hall, 2000).
McDermott, P.A., and Robinson, T., *The Children Act 2001* (Dublin: Thomson Round Hall, 2003).
McDiarmid, 'Age of Criminal Responsibility: Raise it or Remove it? 5 *Juridical Review* (2001) pp. 243–58.
McPhillips, S., *Dublin Children Court A Pilot Research Project* (Dublin: IASD, 2005).
Manfredi, C.P., *The Supreme Court and Juvenile Justice* (Lawrence, University of Kansas, 1988).
Martin, F., 'The Ombudsman for Children: An Analysis of the Strengths and Weaknesses of the Irish Model', 52(1) *Administration* (Spring 2004) pp. 46–68.
Mehlbye, J. and Walgrave, L. (eds), *Confronting Youth in Europe – Juvenile Crime and Juvenile Justice* (Copenhagen: AKF, 1998).
Millie, A., et al., *Anti-social Behaviour Strategies: Finding a Balance* (London: Policy Press, 2005).
Mitchell, D., *A Report on the Law and Procedures Regarding the Prosecution and Disposal of Young Offenders* (Dublin: DPP, 1977).
Morris, A., 'Youth Justice in New Zealand' 31, *Crime and Justice* (2004) pp. 243–92.
Morgan, R., 'Anti-social behaviour: getting to the root of the

problem', 23(1) *The Howard League Magazine* (February 2005) pp. 13–14.

Mullan, S., and O'Mahony, D., *A Review of recent youth justice Reforms in England and Wales*, NIO Research and Statistical Series: Report no 8 (Belfast: NIO, 2003).

National Children's Office, *The National Children's Strategy Our Children their Lives* (Dublin: Stationery Office: 2000)

National Crime Council, *Tackling the Underlying causes of Crime: A Partnership Approach* (Dublin: Stationery Office, 2002).

National Crime Council, A *Crime Prevention Strategy for Ireland – Tackling the Concerns of Local Communities* (Dublin: The Stationery Office, 2003).

Ombudsman for Children, *Annual Report 2005* (Dublin: OCO, 2005).

O'Connor, M.E., 'What works with Juvenile Offenders?' Paper delivered to a conference on Children, Young People and Crime in Britain and Ireland From Exclusion to Inclusion – 1998, Scotland.

O'Donnell, T., 'The Children Act 2001: A practical analysis from a judicial perspective', Law Society Criminal Law Committee Seminar for Judges of the District Court, 3 December 2004.

O'Dwyer, K., *Restorative Justice Initiatives in the Garda Síochána Evaluation of the Pilot Programme*, Garda Research Unit, Research Report No 4/01(Templemore: Garda Research Unit, 2001).

O'Dwyer, K., 'Garda Restorative Justice Programme – Highlights and Insights' Paper delivered at a Conference on Youth Justice, Croke Park Dublin, 12–13 September 2005.

O'Dwyer, K., Kennedy, P., and Ryan, W., *Garda Public Attitudes Survey 2005* (Templemore Garda Research Unit, 2005).

O'Mahony, P., 'Punishing Poverty and Personal Adversity', 7 *Irish Criminal Law Journal* (1997), pp. 152–70.

O'Mahony, P., *Prison Policy in Ireland: Criminal Justice versus Social Justice* (Cork: Cork University Press, 2000).

O'Mahony, P., 'Contextualising the Children Bill as a response to youth crime', paper delivered at the National Conference of Youthreach Co-ordinators, Monaghan 12 February 2001.

O'Mahony, P. (ed.), *Criminal Justice in Ireland* (Dublin: IPA, 2002).

O'Mahony, D., and Doak, J., 'Restorative Justice – Is More Better? The Experience of Police-led Restorative Cautioning Pilots in Northern Ireland' 43(5), *Howard Journal of Criminal Justice* (December 2004), pp. 484–505.

O'Sullivan, E., 'Juvenile Justice in the Republic of Ireland: Future Priorities', 14 (3/4) *Irish Social Worker*, Autumn/Winter 1996.

Quinn, K., and Jackson, J., *The Detention and Questioning of Young Persons by the Police in Northern Ireland* NIO Research and Statistical Series: Report No 9 (Belfast: NIO, 2003).

Ramsay, P., 'What is Anti-social Behaviour?, *Criminal Law Review* (2004), pp. 908–25.

Report of the Committee on Reformatory and Industrial Schools Systems (The Kennedy Report) (Dublin: Stationery Office, 1970) Prl 1342.

Report of the Committee of Inquiry into the Penal System (Dublin: Stationery Office, 1985).

Report on the Youth Justice Review (Dublin: Department of Justice, Equality and Law Reform, 2005).

First Interim Report of the Interdepartmental Committee on Mentally Ill and Maladjusted Persons (Dublin: Stationery Office, 1974) Prl 4688.

Second Interim Report of the Interdepartmental Committee on Mentally Ill and Maladjusted Persons, The Provision of Treatment for Juvenile Offenders and Potential Juvenile Offenders (Dublin: Stationery Office, 1974).

Report of the Committee on Children and Young Persons in Scotland, 1964 (The Kilbrandon Report) Cmnd 2306.

Report to the Government of Ireland on the Visit to Ireland Carried out by the European Committee for the Prevention of Torture and Inhuman or Degrading Treatment or Punishment (CPT) from 20 to 28 May 2002 (Strasbourg: Council of Europe, 2003).

Report of the Committee Appointed to Monitor the Effectiveness of the Diversion Programme, 2003.

Report of the Committee Appointed to Monitor the Effectiveness of the Diversion Programme, 2004.

Rowlands, M., 'The state of ASBO Britain – the rise of

intolerance', *European Civil Liberties Network Essays* no 9 available at www.ecln.org.

Scottish Law Commission, *Report on the Age of Criminal Responsibility* (Edinburgh: Stationery Office, 2002).

Scraton, P. (ed.), *'Childhood' in 'Crisis'* (London: Routledge, 1997).

Scraton, P., 'The denial of the liberties and rights of children in the UK and the North of Ireland', *European Civil Liberties Network Essays* no 14 (2005), available at www.ecln.org.

Scraton, P., 'Disrespecting Children's Rights', 23 *Safer Society,* forthcoming Winter 2005/06.

Sentlinger, E.D., Comment, 'V. v. United Kingdom: is it a "new deal" for prosecuting children as adults', 16, *Connecticut Journal of International Law* (2000) 117–48.

Seymour, M., 'Juvenile Justice in the Republic of Ireland', prepared for the Thematic Working Group on Juvenile Justice, European Society of Criminology (2004).

Shannon, G., *Child Law* (Dublin: Thomson Round Hall, 2004).

Smith, R., 'Welfare versus Justice – Again!' 5(1) Youth Justice (June 2005) pp. 3–16.

Special Residential Services Board, *Review of Admission Criteria and Processes for Special Care* (Special Residential Services Board, September 2005).

Special Residential Services Board, *Definition and Usage of High Support in Ireland* (Special Residential Services Board, 2003).

Squires, P., and Stephen, D.E., *Rougher Justice: Anti-social Behaviour and Young People* (Devon: Willan Publishing, 2005).

Sutherland, E., 'Parenting Orders: A Culturally Alien Response of Questionable Efficacy', 49 *Judicial Review* (2004) pp. 105–32.

Tanenhaus, D.S., *Juvenile Justice in the Making* (New York: Oxford University Press, 2004).

Task Force on Child Care Services, *Final Report* (Dublin: Stationery Office, 1980) Prl 9345.

Thornberry, T.P., et al., 'Family Disruption and Delinquency' *Juvenile Justice Bulletin* (Office of Juvenile Justice and Delinquency Prevention, US Department of Justice, September 1999) pp. 1–5.

Tisdall, K., et al,, 'Listening to the views of children? Principles and mechanisms within the Children (Scotland) Act 1995

24(4), *Journal of Social Welfare and Family Law* (2002) pp. 385–99

Utting, D., *What works with young offenders in the community?* (Essex: Barnardos, 2000).

Van Dijk, C., Nuytiens, N., and Eliaerts, C., 'The Referral of Juvenile Offenders to the Adult Court in Belgium: Theory and Practice' 44(2) *Howard Journal of Criminal Justice* (2005), pp. 151–66.

Vaughan, B., 'Breaking out of Jail: Generating Non-Custodial Penalties for Juveniles', 10(3), *Irish Criminal Law Journal* (2000) pp. 14–18.

Walsh, D., *Juvenile Justice* (Dublin: Thomson Round Hall, 2005).

Warren, A., *Study of Participants in Garda Special Projects* by the Centre for Social and Educational Research, DIT on behalf of the Department of Justice, Equality and Law Reform (October 2001).

Weijers, I., and Duff, A. (eds), *Punishing Juveniles Principle and Critique* (Oxford: Hart, 2002).

Weijers, I., 'Requirements for Communication in the Courtroom: A comparative perspective on the Youth Court in England/Wales and the Netherlands' 4(1), *Youth Justice* (July 2004) pp. 22–31.

Wells, E., and Rankin, J., 'Families and Delinquency: A meta-analysis of the impact of broken homes' 38(1), *Social Problems* (1991), pp. 71–83.

Whyte, B., 'Effectiveness, Research and Youth Justice', 4(1) *Youth Justice* (July 2004), pp. 3–21.

Young, P., O'Donnell, I., and Clare, E., *Crime In Ireland: Trends and Patterns, 1950 to 1998*, A Report by the Institute of Criminology, Faculty of Law, University College Dublin for the National Crime Council (Dublin: Stationery Office, 2001).

Zilli, L., 'Children's Rights to a Fair Trial under International Law' 5, *Trinity College Law Review* (2002) pp. 224–50.

Index

YOUTH JUSTICE IN IRELAND

JUSTICE IN CONTROVERSY SERIES

Editors: Mike Milotte and Donncha O'Connell

This series of monographs addresses a range of controversial legal topics in a format that will appeal to audiences beyond the purely professional and academic legal worlds. It is written by a combination of established and emerging authors with legal, academic, journalistic and other backgrounds. By virtue of their subject matter on the interaction between law and society, the books will inform academic debate; but, given the profound and enduring effect of the law on the lives of all citizens, it is also envisaged that the books will have a much wider appeal and impact. The series aims to provide a distinctive contribution to public discourse by providing a publishing platform for authors who wish to transcend the rather exclusive borders that separate public and academic debate.

Already published in the Justice in Controversy series:

An Ambition for Equality, by Niall Crowley

Forthcoming in the Justice in Controversy series:

The Blame Game: Rethinking Ireland's Sustainable Development and Environmental Performance, by Brendan Flynn

The Presumption of Innocence and Irish Criminal Law, Whittling the 'Golden Thread' by Claire Hamilton

Roadmaps to Reunification, by Richard Humphreys

Exploitation or Employment? Prostitution and the Law, by Ivana Bacik

The Future of Irish Nationality and Immigration Law, by Bernard Ryan